To Wendy

Love, Wing

CareyOn

The true story of a young love that tore a family apart

Cindy Graves

FriesenPress

Suite 300 - 990 Fort St
Victoria, BC, Canada, V8V 3K2
www.friesenpress.com

Copyright © 2015 by Cindy Graves
First Edition — 2015

CareyOn is based on the author's memories, conversations with the real-life characters
represented in the story, and existing written documentation. While the story is
based on true events, poetic license has been applied to the narrative. Some names
and identifying details have been changed to protect the privacy of individuals.

ISBN
978-1-4602-6712-7 (Hardcover)
978-1-4602-6713-4 (Paperback)
978-1-4602-6714-1 (eBook)

1. Biography & Autobiography, Personal Memoirs

Distributed to the trade by The Ingram Book Company

TABLE OF CONTENTS

For my family, then and now.

And forgive us our trespasses,
as we forgive them that trespass against us.

The Lord's Prayer

CareyOn

CareyOn'78

Cindy

I could hear the notes of my mother's high-soprano laugh rise above the noise of the guests. She always did love a good party. When I finally found her amongst the crowd in the barn, I watched her coax a reluctant Daddy Bill from his lawn chair onto the starkly lit dance floor determined to work her charm on him. He was cold and stiff from sitting in the drafty shadows of the old barn, but when my mother flashed one of her dazzling smiles at him, the kind that instantaneously transforms her face from worry and fret to carefree abandonment, her father-in-law relaxed and resigned himself to the role of dance partner. My mother laughed again and her high cheekbones pushed big, round glasses back into their rightful place on the bridge of her up-turned nose. When I was a child, I used to say she had a "ski jump nose" as it gently swept up at the tip like a long ski jump at the Winter Olympics. Behind the oversized frames, her eyes, small and sloping down at the outside corners so that they were often accused of harbouring sadness, folded into thin dancing slits on her suddenly youthful face. It didn't take long before my grandfather conceded to her will and let himself be guided by her movements on the dance floor.

I elbowed my way between couples dancing and stomping to the twangy country music until I stood under the hay loft where the three-piece country band played. I could feel the worn wooden floorboards beneath me strain and tremble with the dancers' pounding feet. Tired beams supporting the loft groaned and complained against the deafening music like gently scolding parents, while the gaping walls, normally accustomed to the sound of nothing more than the soft flapping of bats' wings, could not be counted on to contain the noise of the party.

Warily, the sagging barn had been roused from its long retirement and the large, main floor transformed so that it managed to appear fresh and rejuvenated. The floor had been reinforced, cleared and swept of any garbage or debris that may have been left from the last farmer who worked the farm several decades ago. Bales of hay placed strategically around the circumference provided cozy makeshift seating for the many guests. Perched lopsided on the bales of hay were "hay folk," country people that Christine had made from hay that morning - farmers wearing overalls, work boots and cowboy hats, women with ample hay bosoms, aprons tied at their waists and straw hats. They wore exaggerated lipstick-drawn smiles on their stuffed-pantyhose faces. A string of light bulbs and spot lights harshly lit the bar and dance floor so that people entering the barn from the dark night had to blink to get used to the artificial light. The end result was that, under the cover of night, the barn's gaping holes and rotten walls were soon forgotten, and the barn seemed solid and strong. Meanwhile, the stalls underneath the main barn, which once housed cattle and horses, had long since succumbed to the passage of time and neglect and their stone walls lay crumbled and broken.

On the dance floor, Daddy Bill had now fully succumbed to his daughter-in-law's magic and warmed up to her groove. He was still quick and spry for his age and, surprisingly, even added a few moves of his own. The barn dance was in full swing. I noticed family and friends up from the city, some of whom I hadn't seen in several years. I spotted the bobbing of my father's cowboy hat, black with a white trim, into which he'd stuck a white feather, in the throng of dancers. His shoulders, hips and knees moved fluidly under him, as loose-jointed as a scarecrow come to life. Like my mother, my father shared my mother's love for parties. He devoted himself to this one. The barn dance was his inspiration and a project he gladly took on that September, welcoming the distraction that came with weeks of planning and preparation.

Looking at my father now, you'd never guess how hard he'd worked behind the scenes. He was the life of the party, cracking jokes and laughing the loudest at their punch lines, vigorously shaking men's hands and hugging women to his chest. He moved easily amongst his peers, enjoying himself, working the room, like a politician running for office. Wherever he went, either on the dance floor, or to the bar, or outside to the fire pit, the party moved where he moved. He left people feeling welcome and excited to be in his wake, and for this, they genuinely liked him. He was the central hub for friends and family and had their support as a loyal friend, a good husband and father. He was a respectable business owner, a dedicated member of the Rotary Club and, most recently, President of the Orangeville Curling Club. All in all, my father was an upstanding member of the community and genuinely respected and admired. That night he was having too good a time for anyone to stop for more than a brief second and question his enthusiasm.

I was distracted when I saw Paul, dash from behind someone in line at the bar and grab a dripping beer from one of the ice-filled tubs. Michael, home for the party, saw him too and yelled, "Hey!" with enough authority to briefly halt the eleven-year-old in the midst of his illegal retreat. But when Paul looked back and saw the playful indulgence on his brother's face, he knew it was a harmless threat, and was willing to gamble on his big brother's leniency. He tucked the confiscated bottle under his jacket and sped into the crowd, past the oblivious eyes of Nana Darwen and Grampa Russ, toward his friends who were waiting to experience their first beer.

The band began the prelude to a polka. Geoff grabbed me around the waist and whisked me onto the middle of the dance floor underneath the spotlight. He held me close pressing one hand firmly into the centre of my back and clasping the other in my own expectant grip. Our hips melted together while I looked up into his smiling green eyes. His full red moustache stretched across a grinning upper lip. I leaned my face into the shoulder of his flannel shirt. He smelled clean and crisp like the fresh fall night tinted with sweet hay and a hint of smoke. Then the polka started and Geoff scooped me away. We spun and swung around the floor feverishly, nearly colliding with other couples, including my father who was now dancing with Christine.

The frenzied polka finally came to an end and I was catching my breath when I saw my father still holding my sister in his arms. Taking her hands, he tenderly moved her to arms' length so he could study her face. Christine looked embarrassingly away from this public show of affection, but as he continued to gaze at her fondly, his head tilted to one side, a small, proud smile playing at the corners of his mouth, she began to lose her self-consciousness and allowed herself to enjoy his rare attention. She bloomed under his warmth like an exotic flower under a heat lamp. It was unusual for my sister to look so happy. Despite myself, I felt an old childhood twinge of jealousy by my father's uncharacteristic outward demonstration of love for my sibling.

A swarm of dancers surrounded my father and sister, temporarily blocking them from my view. Over the sea of bouncing heads, floated the white painted sign on the beam of the loft, proclaiming: "CareyOn Fest '77, 78". This was our second annual barn party and, judging by the ample space left deliberately on the sign after "78", we planned many more to come. Why shouldn't our future hold more parties? Nothing could stop us Careys from having a good time. Not even the obvious absence of one of us. But we didn't talk about that. Look how we could howl with laughter! Look how well we could kick up our heels! We wanted the world to know how happy we were when we were together.

The crowd moved away and I saw my father give Christine a peck on the cheek before he released her and walked away. How could he seem so at ease after all that had happened? Everyone at the party must know. It had been all over the news. My father was facing a charge of attempted murder. And my sister, Natalie, was gone, perhaps forever.

I grabbed Geoff's hand like a life rope and he pulled me close to his chest. I felt how perfectly we fit together. For the moment I felt safe and loved and everything was as it should be.

CHAPTER ONE

Witness

 Cindy

For a second time that night the car woke me up. I heard it roar back into our driveway from the highway, headlights slashing through the darkness into my bedroom. I got up and opened my door. Moonlight filtered through the sheers in the window at the end of the hall. I heard no stirring behind Paul's door, or from the attic. Could it be that no one else in the house had heard?

I crossed the hall to my parents' bedroom and found their bed empty, the covers flung back. The fluorescent arms of the alarm clock on their night table read 12:45 a.m. The car's engine growled angrily below their bedroom window and its headlights careened wildly around me, illuminating with a flash the family photographs on my mother's dressing table. For a brief moment, I recognized myself in cap and gown - my high school grad photo taken the previous year. I went to the window to look out.

The light above the side porch was on highlighting thinly falling rain and throwing everything beyond its narrow reach into heightened darkness. Our property line, marked by a low cedar-rail fence separating us from the farmer's cornfield, lay in shadow under the row of maple trees. The car now left the gravel driveway and cut across our lawn. It fishtailed in the slippery grass and then spun completely around spewing up grass and mud in its wake. The dogs were barking furiously below me, trying to escape their confinement. Thank God, this time they were locked up safe in the mudroom.

I watched the car run right over a couple of lawn chairs pulled out of storage that afternoon to welcome the first sunbathing rays of the year. At the driveway into our garage, it wheeled around full circle again, hitting the garage door with its bumper. It sped back across the lawn, shot into reverse and ran backward up the two cement steps onto the porch. Thinking it would run right into the living room window, I braced myself for the impact and sound of broken glass, but at the last second, it stopped. The car's rear end lay jacked up on the porch, its headlights shooting into the drizzle and the dark field ahead.

Suddenly, a crack split the air. Reeling, I watched a figure in white run from the house. It was my father. I pressed my forehead into the cold windowpane, straining to see. How ludicrous he looked as he hopped barefoot across the wet lawn in the dark in his stark white pajamas. What on earth was he doing? The car crashed down the porch and slid across the lawn toward the driveway. My father chased it for a few feet and then stopped. He shifted his weight and lifted his arms up to his chest. It was then I saw he was carrying a shotgun.

He raised the gun to his shoulder, aimed, and fired a second shot. The car screeched to a halt. Silence descended on the house. Even the dogs stopped their barking. I remained rigid at the window unwilling to breathe or move peering into the dark. My breath made a circle of fog on the glass. Finally, the driver floored the gas pedal, hit the highway and sped out of sight.

It was quiet. The whole event had happened in only a few minutes, but it seemed like time had stood still. I turned my gaze away from where the car had exited onto the highway to the dark outline of the old barn behind our house. The barn had long since lost its purpose of sheltering anything more significant than field mice or cats, but it still loomed authoritatively over our property. I pulled slowly back from the window.

I could hear no movement, no note of unrest. It was as though the house refused to be disturbed from its usual snug night sleep. I thought for a moment I might be sleepwalking down the stairs, compelled by some dream to find my parents. The only sound was that of my heart pounding in my ears.

As I reached the living room, I found them standing in the semi-darkness, their silhouettes lit from the porch light outside. Without a word, they watched me enter the room. My mother was standing in front of the large front window and turned away from me to resume her vigil. I later discovered that she had seen everything from her post at the living room window. Apparently, my siblings remained fast asleep in their bedrooms upstairs.

My father bounced about the room in adrenalin-induced agitation. "For cryin' out loud!" he cried as he popped outside to the porch, leaving the heavy oak door wide open. The cool night breeze blew in stirring the door's gauzy window dressing that hung like an ill-fitting bandage.

Satisfied the car was nowhere in sight, my father came back into the house. "We won't have to worry about those guys again," he said with certitude. Locking the screen door, he then shouldered the solid door shut and locked it tight. My mother reached over and turned on the lamp.

"Well, I sure as heck scared the life out of them," he said, breathing quickly. His thick peppered hair was standing straight up and pieces of wet grass clung to his damp feet; the bottoms of his pajama pants were wet with rain. "This time I think I put a stop to them once and for all." He chuckled nervously under his breath.

He walked quickly down the hall to the front door and pulled on the handle. "Damn sticky door. It damn near cost me." He turned and noticed us watching him, waiting for him to explain. "I wanted to go out this door," he said, frustrated. "It's jammed solid from being shut all winter." We were eager for him to reassure us that everything was fine again. He came back into the living room. "I wanted to shoot their radiator," he said in explanation. "That was the plan."

He looked at Mom to gauge her reaction. He wanted her support and seemed surprised and disappointed to find a worried frown puckering her forehead. "But I had to use the side door," he said, her increasing distress fueling his own anxiety. "I couldn't believe it when I opened the door and found the car sitting on the porch. It ran up two concrete steps for Christ sake! I shot at their tires then instead."

I was staring at the shotgun hanging from his right hand. The rancid smell of gunpowder emanated from the barrel. It screamed danger and was both repugnant and intoxicating. I wanted to warn him to put it down before someone got hurt. I had never seen Dad with a gun before. I had no idea he owned a gun or knew how to use one. A strange feeling of detachment came over me, as if I was watching a scene in a play unfold from the last row of a theatre. I wasn't sure at that point who my father was. He noticed my stare and sheepishly leaned the shotgun against the wall.

"Did you hit their tire, Dad?" I asked.

"Oh, yeah. When they started getting away, I shot at the tires again. They won't be going too far on those tires," he said. "We need to call the police so they can pick them up."

"Did you see who they were?" I asked. Until this time, my mother had remained peering out the window, vigilant in case the intruders should return. But my question pulled her away and she glanced anxiously at my father for his response.

"No, it was too dark. But there were three of them again," my father said.

"It was the same car, wasn't it?"

Preoccupied with his thoughts, my father took a minute to answer. "Yes, Cindy. It was that old Plymouth again." Then he turned to my mother, "You better call the police again, eh, Dee."

My mother tiptoed into the hall and quietly dialed the Ontario Provincial Police. She didn't want to wake her other children sleeping upstairs. My father and I huddled behind her. In a faltering voice she said she was phoning to report an act of vandalism. Another one. She asked if Corporal Bryant was available. She sighed as she waited to be transferred to him and then described as best she could what had happened. When the questions became too much for her to answer, she handed the phone over to my father.

Reciting his story to the policeman clearly and confidently, he told him he had fired two shots at the car's tires in an attempt to stop it from driving off so that he could find out once and for all who the occupants were. He also explained that the car must have a flat tire by now and couldn't have driven far. My father insisted they conduct a search for the car and then suddenly he hung up.

He paced the hallway, his blue-white bare feet slapping along pine floorboards worn to a dull path by feet we never knew. He was still in his white pajamas. The "Ice Cream Man", I thought numbly. That's what we had called him, laughing, when he put them on that Christmas morning several years before.

He climbed the stairs without further explanation. We waited to see what he was going to do. I trusted my father to protect us.

When he came down, he had pulled on a pair of pants and socks. "I'm going into town," he announced, heading for the back door. We followed him through the kitchen and into the chilly mudroom where he was grabbing his coat and keys.

"Harry, I wish you wouldn't. Let the police handle this," my mother pleaded.

"I can't just sit here. Who knows when or if the police will even get around to looking for them? You called them the first time two hours ago. Where the hell are they?"

"But what are you going to do?" she asked, her face knotted with worry.

"I'm just going to go see if I can find the car."

"And what if you do? Who knows what those maniacs are capable of?"

"It'll be fine. Don't worry. You two go to bed."

As we watched him drive away, the car's headlights disappearing through the window, my mother muttered, "Stubborn fool!" and locked the back door.

Duke, our young German Shepherd, was curled up asleep on the old couch in the mudroom, but Toby, our terrier/beagle cross was watching us. She followed us into the kitchen and I picked her up. Toby was our first family dog. I always considered her my dog since I was the one who initiated bringing her into our family. The day we got her I lay with her under the kitchen table for hours patting her I loved her so. We got Toby when I was in grade six from a teacher at my school who couldn't keep her and was looking for a home for her. The teacher wrote a letter all about Toby describing what a wonderful dog she was and that she was fully housetrained. My parents read the letter and decided they could at least take a look at the dog. The teacher and her husband brought Toby to our house so we could meet her. Toby had black short hair with a white stripe down her nose and brown stocking feet (that was the beagle part). Despite the fact the first thing she did when she arrived at our house was run into the living room and pee on the new Persian rug, my parents said we could keep her.

I joined Mom in the living room where she eased herself onto the rocking chair and began to rock absent-mindedly back and forth. My mother's anxiety and doubt began to penetrate my unfailing belief in my father's abilities to fix everything. I began to suspect that I was naïve and decided I couldn't go to bed until Dad returned home safely.

My mother seemed not to notice when I turned on the television and settled in the wingback chair with Toby on my lap. Her fervent rocking and vacant staring at the television distracted me. Normally, watching my mother watch television was more entertaining than any program. She did not watch much TV, preferring to spend her time sewing in the evenings, but when she did sit down with us, she got such a kick out of seeing the commercials for the first time, the ones we had all viewed numerous times already and which no longer registered with us, that we sat up and observed with renewed interest. She took it all in with fascination and glee, stimulated by the new messages. Her explosive laughter and squeals amused us, but also made us wonder if we were missing something. She saw things we didn't.

But tonight Mom wasn't finding anything funny about the commercials or Johnny Carson. I got up and switched the channel to the news. The program headlined a newly released report on teenage pregnancies. "It is estimated that more than one million American teenagers will become pregnant by the end of 1978," the announcer declared. Mom abruptly stopped rocking. I glanced over at her profile, illuminated by the light of the television, and saw her face freeze. Normally, I would have pressed her to tell me what was wrong, but after everything that had happened tonight, it didn't feel right to try to draw it out of her. Besides, I already knew the answer. I turned back to Johnny Carson.

I took in very little of the show; I was too busy listening for my father's car. An hour passed and it had stopped raining by the time he finally returned home. We met him at the back door and waited for him to hang up his coat. His movements were deliberate and strained - we knew best to keep silent. Any questions asked now would only irritate him further and, not wanting to risk a longer silence, we impatiently waited for him to begin. If I understood one thing about my father it was that it paid to wait until he was ready to talk.

He entered the kitchen and sat down at the table, humming a little tune under his breath as was his custom when he was lost in thought. We pulled up chairs and he finally looked at us and recounted how he had driven up and down the main street of town and searched the side streets, but hadn't spotted the car. Relieved he was home safely, my mother put the kettle on and made some tea. After, with nothing more to be done, we filed upstairs to bed.

Alone in my bed I grew increasingly tense and uneasy. I kept hearing the blast of the shotgun in my head. In the living room my father had done his best to regain his composure and restore calm, but I couldn't shake the strange image of him shooting a gun in the middle of the night. It was a frightening, alien picture. I lay awake tossing under my covers until I was disturbed for a third time that night.

CHAPTER TWO

Caught

 Cindy

This time I heard voices coming from downstairs. I checked my bedside alarm clock. It was almost 3:30 a.m. Pulling on my housecoat, I headed downstairs and into the living room once more.

My mother and father were talking to someone at the door. Toby and Duke were growling and barking at the intruders from the mudroom where they were shut in. The living room lamp was on and, as I entered the room, I saw my parents were talking in muffled voices to two uniformed Ontario Provincial Police officers.

My father was politely and gravely answering their questions. I thought, naively, they must need my father's help very badly to bother us at this hour of the night.

"Do you know someone by the name of Daniel Cocker?" the young officer with the moustache asked my father.

"No, constable."

"Grant Hewlett?"

My father shook his head. The officers glanced at each other. Something was wrong. It dawned on me I may have made a mistake. The police were here because of something my father had done.

"Do you know a John Ranberg?"

My father jolted, like his spine had snapped. My mother gasped. They were as shocked as I was to hear John's name. It was the first time we realized John was involved. My father threw a quick, intense look at his wife before he answered. "Yes, sir," he said quietly as to be almost inaudible.

The second officer, middle-aged and grey, looked uncomfortable, like he was sorry to disturb us. The young constable continued, his speech clipped and officious, "Cocker and Ranberg checked themselves into the hospital earlier tonight. They have shotgun wounds. They have accused you of shooting them."

A small moan escaped from my mother. The older officer took a step closer to my father.

"I'm afraid you'll have to come with us, Harry," he said, looking uncomfortable.

My father couldn't move; he just stood there with his mouth hanging slack. The officer who seemed to know my father said gently, "You'll need to come down to the station with us now and make a statement, Harry." My father turned uncomprehending eyes toward him.

"Do you have a lawyer you can call, Mr. Carey?" asked the young officer.

My father shook his head to clear his thoughts. "Uh? A lawyer? No, what use would I have with a lawyer?"

"Harry, what about Doug Maund?" prompted my mother, surprising me with uncharacteristically thinking clearly under pressure.

"Maund? Oh, yes, I suppose I could call him," said my father slowly as he forced himself to gather his thoughts.

"Are the boys going to be all right, officer?" asked my mother.

"I believe they have head injuries," said the young constable.

This couldn't be happening. "Dad?" I said. I needed him to say something. He looked at me and opened his mouth but no words came out. In the end, all he did was ask my mother to get his coat. His hands were shaking as he did up the zipper. My mother and I watched as my father was led away by the policemen into the back seat of their cruiser. He was still wearing his pajamas under his coat.

I turned to my mother. "Did you know John was in the car?"

"Of course not," she said.

We didn't say what we both were thinking. That Natalie must have known.

CHAPTER THREE

First love

 Cindy

The first time my mother met my father she fell off her bike. At thirteen, Diane was already well-developed and looked older than she was. She was self-conscious about her new, full breasts and hips, which only increased her natural shyness. She was sitting on her bike seat leaning the handle bar against the brick wall of her house watching him come up the driveway. He was delivering the *Toronto Star*. She'd seen him on her driveway before and she'd been waiting, hoping to see him again.

He looked directly at her and held out the paper for her to take. This caused her foot to suddenly slip off the pedal and she lost her balance. The handlebars wobbled and she tumbled ungracefully to the ground, landing on her bottom on the gravel driveway.

The boy picked her up under the armpits, dragging her to her feet. "You can't pick a girl up like that," she huffed, red in the face.

Now it was his turn to be embarrassed. He didn't know. He had never picked up a girl before. She brushed off her pedal pushers while he reached down and picked up the rolled newspaper where he'd dropped it in his haste to help her. "Here's your paper," he said, holding it out to appease her.

She noticed the mask of childish freckles across his nose and cheeks that gave him a little boy look. She saw he was also nervous and this relaxed her. "My name's Diane," she said, reaching for the paper.

The boy stared at her. She felt her confusion growing. He continued to hold onto the paper. "I live here," she said, taking the newspaper from him and smoothing back her pony tail.

The boy picked up her bicycle and leaned it back against the wall. He was so skinny his belt was cinched as tight as possible to keep his pants from falling off. The free end of the belt flapped loosely at his waist. He was getting ready to leave.

His ears stick out too wide, Diane thought, but he's cute. "What's your name?" she asked.

"Harold. Harry. Carey."

"Well, Harry Carey, would you like some lemonade? It's fresh this morning."

"That would be nice." She disappeared into the house and soon returned with a glass of lemonade. He thanked her and finished it without stopping. "Not bad," he said. Then he asked, "You don't go to Danforth Tech, do you?"

"No," she said glancing away demurely, flattered at the possibility she could be mistaken for a high school girl already.

He couldn't take his eyes off the dimple in her left cheek that flashed at him when she smiled. "I didn't think so. I would have noticed you there." Her smile intensified.

"I'm in my senior year." He saw her surprise. He knew he didn't look old enough. "I have a late birthday. I'll be seventeen in October," he said, standing up taller and pushing his shoulders back. Who was he kidding? He could never hope to impress her with his scrawny physique. "I skipped a year in public school," he added, feeling the need to explain himself. "Well, I've got to be going. People are waiting for their papers."

He waited for her to say something. "There's a dance at St. John's Norway Church this Friday," she said.

"Will you be there?"

"Do you like to dance?"

He searched her face longing for the dimple to reappear. "I don't know. I think I might."

"I'll see you there," she said, and there it was. She turned and walked back into the house.

Diane was awoken by a sharp rattling sound. She got out of bed and crept over to her bedroom window in the dark. Pellets bounced against the window pane. She pulled back the curtain and peered out into the night. In the shadow of the tall oak tree on the front lawn she spotted a figure throwing stones up at her second floor window with one hand while clutching something big to his chest with the other.

"Dee!" he grinned widely.

"Crazy fool," she muttered to herself. She pushed the window open and leaned out. "Harry, what are you doing? It's the middle of the night," she said, scolding him but excited despite herself.

He lifted his bundle with both arms straight out in front of him and did a little jig.

"You're nuts," she cried with delight. "What have you got there?"

"Only the most coveted trophy of the Toronto Hockey League Juveniles. Come on down and kiss the MVP."

"That's wonderful. But I can't. My father will kill me."

"He'll never know. Come with me to Cherry Beach. I want to celebrate with you."

"I can't. It's way past my curfew."

"Marry me."

"What?"

"Then marry me and we can do whatever we want."

"Have you been drinking?"

"You'll see, one day you will. I promise."

A porch light went on across the street. "Go home, Harry. Goodnight." She shut the window and twirled around on one foot. Her heart beat excitedly in her chest. She flopped down on her bed, her arms flung out wide. She hugged her pillow to her chest, closed her eyes and murmured a little sigh.

By the time my mother started high school at Danforth Tech in Toronto in 1945, my father was working at his first full-time job as a supply clerk for Ontario Hydro. He took the job on a recommendation from a friend so they could play hockey together on the Industrial League team. He was paid thirty five dollars a week, out of which he managed to save enough to buy his first car, a hand-painted, two-tone blue 1939 Plymouth.

When I was a teenager I learned that the car was the perfect place for making out. I realized that my generation was not the first one to make that discovery. According to my father, his Plymouth provided a ready-made private facility for their sexual activities. Contrary to my innocent ideas of couples in the 1950's waiting until marriage to "go all the way," my parents had sex for several years before they were married.

My mother pointed out to her children on several occasions that when she met my father, "he didn't even wear any underwear". She liked to remind us of this fact whenever she felt it necessary to portray her husband as the poor motherless boy he was when she first met him, and herself as his saviour. According to her, Harry was a lost, underwear-deprived soul in need of mothering. As a little girl, I wondered how my mother could have known my father didn't wear anything under his pants. I knew they were too shy to undress in the bedroom together on the eve of their wedding because I asked her once out of curiosity. Turning her back to me (was that the hint of a smile I saw?) my mother said she went into the bathroom on that first night together to change into her nightie. I believed her. But many years later my father told me the truth.

Not only did I discover that my parents weren't virgins when they married, but I learned they often had unprotected sex. There was one time, my father confided, that my mother was "late". They were parked in the Plymouth in the lot of the Woodbine Racetrack when she told him. She was very upset. The next day, my father left the Hydro office and picked my mother up after school. Together they went to see the family doctor, who told them it was too early to tell. All they could do was wait and see. A couple of weeks later, to their great relief, my mother's period resumed. Even after their scare, my parents continued to have sex without using any method of birth control. They just didn't think it could happen to them.

CHAPTER FOUR

Kids

───────────────── Cindy ─────────────────

As luck would have it, they were married over a year when their first baby was born. That was Michael, born on the last day of 1956. Almost two years later, I was born, followed by Christine eighteen months later and Natalie eighteen months after Christine. My parents moved from their 1930's Brookside Drive house in the working class Beach neighbourhood of eastern Toronto to a new four bedroom house on Whitman Street, a cul-de-sac in the suburbs of Willowdale in North York, at the far northern reaches of the boundary of Toronto.

Natalie was daughter number three. Both parents were convinced their fourth baby was going to be a boy. My father liked to joke about his reaction when he found out he had another girl, he told the nurse, "Hells bells! Take her back and trade her in for a male model." It was one of the family stories my father liked to tell. Natalie always laughed along with us; it never occurred to us that it might be hurtful.

As a child, Natalie grew into her story and developed into a true tomboy. She loved to play outdoors, and in the summer her skin turned a beautiful shade of light brown, causing my father to dub her his "Little Brown Berry". She was the perky daughter with the big dimples, turned-up nose, pixie cut and dark mischievous eyes. A little imp of a girl who my father, fond of nicknames, also called Pepperpot, or Pepper for short.

For all her natural spunk, Natalie was also the most fearful sibling. She was afraid of things like trying new foods (she absolutely refused to eat any vegetables no matter how long my parents made her sit alone at the kitchen table after dinner and the dishes had been washed and dried and put away) and heights and bridges. When we were children, this knowledge had been ammunition for Michael, who lived to taunt his sisters. Once, on a family hike, he coaxed Natalie onto the middle of a swinging bridge and then deliberately jumped up and down on it, causing it to sway from side to side. She screamed for her life and clung to the rope railing immobilized by fear. Even after Michael had run past her and off the other side and the bridge had long since stopped moving, Natalie couldn't be persuaded it was safe to move. Finally, our father had to descend the bridge, pry her fingers from the rope and lead her patiently off the bridge onto firm ground. She has been afraid of bridges since.

My mother had four children in six years. After Natalie was born in 1961, my parents didn't want any more kids. My mother went to her doctor to get a prescription for the birth control pill which was new to Canadian women. She took the pill without complications for five years, but began to get worried when she heard stories about side effects from women who had used the pill for a few years. Convinced her ankles were swelling more, and afraid of growing a beard like the woman in California she read about in the supermarket tabloid, my mother went to her doctor to voice her concerns. Her doctor wrote her a new prescription for a birth control pill with less estrogen. Within a month, my mother was pregnant again.

She was distraught. Harry was angry. He went with her to the doctor for the first time to demand an explanation. He accused the doctor of giving his wife the wrong medication and wanted to know what she was going to do about it. When the doctor said there was nothing she could do, my parents' anxiety rose. They worried that perhaps there were complications with the fetus. This worry was magnified when the doctor refused to treat my mother after that visit.

My mother grew increasingly suspicious that something was wrong with the baby. She became depressed and her eczema flared up. My father was irate. He threatened to sue the doctor. There was nothing to be done but wait and pray the baby would be healthy.

I was seven years old when my mother confided in me that she thought she was going to have a baby. I was thrilled, but she told me she couldn't be sure until she saw the doctor. I understood it to be our secret. I hugged it to me and kept it to myself. I felt grown up and special. The next day, while I was at school, she went to the doctor. I was too excited to concentrate. I desperately wanted my mother to be pregnant with a new baby sister or brother. I hurried home from school to find her pinning wet clothes to the metal clotheshorse outside our back door. I was just about to run up to her and throw my arms around her when I caught myself. Something about her expression held me back. I hesitated at the side of the house and watched her. I knew there was something different and wonderful about her. She didn't need to tell me new life was growing inside her. However, as she lifted the soaking heavy sheets to the line I saw her weariness and frustration and, for a moment, what it was like for her to have this child. Then she noticed me and instantly wiped away her tired and troubled self with a smile. I had witnessed what she didn't want me to see and this alarmed me, but I needed her to feel good about this baby as I did. She answered the unspoken question between us with a simple "Yes!" and I ran into her outstretched arms. I pressed my ear to her tummy, determined to hear the baby and be happy enough for all of us.

As the country celebrated its hundredth birthday, the Careys celebrated the arrival of our little brother. We were jumping up and down on my parents' disheveled bed. My father was under the covers trying to dodge our flying limbs and avoid being trampled. He was lying in late; it felt like a holiday. My mother had been six nights in the hospital with our new baby brother. We hadn't seen him yet. We screamed as my father grabbed Natalie around the waist with both hands and sailed her high above his head. She squealed with pleasure. We jumped higher and yelled, "Can I be an airplane too?"

The phone beside my parents' bed rang and my father told us to keep it down. "Birthdate? February 15, 1967," we heard my father say. "His name?" He paused.

"Oh, we don't have a name picked out yet. Call him... call him... 'Centennial Sam'. Another pause. "Yeah, you heard me right." He put down the telephone and grinned at us. "Don't tell your mother," he said.

We cheered and resumed bouncing on the bed. With each landing, we sang out in rhythm: "Cen-ten-ni-al Sam!"

The next day, under the birth announcements in the *Toronto Star*, we read, "Centennial Sam little brother to Michael, Cindy, Christine and Natalie." A few days later, my parents decided on the name Paul Douglas, but by this time my father had another nickname for my baby brother - Pillroy Paul, in honour of him beating the birth control pill.

1967 was also the year we got a built-in swimming pool. For my father it was a matter of logistics - he said he would rather have a pool in his backyard than drive three hours to a cottage every weekend. The pool was the best thing he could ever have given us. We spent all summer in that pool. It was concrete with a twelve-foot deep end and a diving board. The slide came later. In my father's typical handyman style, he had the slide custom-made from blue fiberglass and attached it to a regular steel ladder. (He could never be accused of being a spendthrift.) We never tired of finding new ways to slide down the slide. Dad liked to play the clown, and sometimes would don costume pieces, like a World War II army helmet, while sliding head first down the slide on his tummy.

The skin on our fingers and toes would be white and wrinkled from hours spent in the water by the time our father arrived home. He would either be hot and bothered from a day at the office, or dripping wet with perspiration from a scorching day on the golf course. He'd head straight for the little change house he'd built, and quickly pull on his bathing suit and dive into the pool. He'd come up with a smile on his face and we'd start our chorus, "Do your Periwinkle Dive, Dad!"

"Oh, not right now," he'd say.

"Come on, Dad, just one!"

And our father would climb onto the diving board while we jumped up and down in the shallow end, yelling with anticipation, "Just one Periwinkle Dive, Dad!"

My father would dive, and just before he broke the surface he would tuck his feet together under him, bringing his knees into his chest, and give a little "tee hee!" before quickly releasing his legs and diving neatly into the water.

"One more!" we'd scream. One was never enough.

CHAPTER FIVE

Bessie

 Cindy

Bessie, our 1963 American Motors red Rambler Classic station wagon, was home to many favourite childhood memories. No food has ever tasted quite as good as the greasy hamburgers and fries I ate packed in tight in the back seat with Natalie, Christine and Michael while we sat in the parking lot in front of the Red Barn. We didn't eat out often as a family, and going out for a meal of any kind was treat enough, but the fact we got to eat in the car made the outing even more exciting. My father always ordered for us (we always got the same thing - as far as we knew, there were no other choices) and we'd wait with mouths watering for him to carefully dole out the food. We savoured every bite, trying not to get any on the seats so that Dad would be pleased with us. He said if we were old enough to eat in the car we were old enough to keep it in our mouths.

I loved going to the drive-in movies in Bessie. It was like sneaking along on a date with my parents. We got to stay up really late, and could see adult movies if we could keep our eyes open through the cartoons, the feature film, and the intermission. Once we found the ideal viewing spot, my father hooked up our sound speaker. The speaker was attached to a cord which ran from a post in the ground and hooked over the driver's window. With Bessie's headset in place, we waited until the sun set low enough on the horizon for the show to start. We wore our pajamas in the car and we each settled into our staked-out territories in the station wagon - Michael in the back, girls in the middle, Paul up front with Mom and Dad, when, right on schedule, darkness fell like a silky blanket tucking us in for the night. The car windows were down and a soothing mid-summer night balm caressed our car and whispered in our ears.

Eventually, we'd start in about treats from the concession (it was an unwritten rule that we were to hold out until the main film if we were to have any luck at all). My father said, as he always did, "We didn't come here to eat," but my mother produced a steel thermos of cold Kool-aid and one gigantic bag of stove-popped popcorn with real melted butter. We took turns plunging our fists into the popcorn, and when it was all gone, we snuggled back against the warm seats and paid close attention to the movie, the reason we had come.

Bessie carried us regularly between our home in Willowdale and my grandparents' home in Orangeville. I was two years old when my grandparents moved from the Beaches in Toronto to Orangeville. As long as I can remember, we made the almost two hour drive every other weekend for Sunday supper. I shared the back seat with my oldest brother and two sisters until we were too big to all fit comfortably and then we took turns lying in the back trunk of the wagon. Sometimes one of us (usually Christine) would start to feel sick lying in the back, "from the fumes" Mom said, and we'd swap seats.

Upon arriving in Orangeville after the long drive our first stop was often my grandparents' store. They owned an office supply store on Mill Street. Much to their grand-children's delight, the store also sold a wonderful assort-ment of school supplies. Entering via the back door into the warehouse, we were treated to a whole tempting smorgas-bord of school supplies at our fingertips - boxes and boxes of pencils, pens, pencil crayons, crayons, markers, tape, scissors, staplers, writing pads, notebooks, binders, duo-tangs and erasers. Oh, the erasers! They were like candy! Jiggly green or pink jelly rubbers that squished between your fingers and smelled good enough to eat. We each got to choose one item. I inevitably chose a jelly rubber.

The warehouse also stored my grandmother's office desk and adding machine. The machine was as much a curiosity to us children as was the fact my grandmother was in charge of it. She was the bookkeeper. We were used to women being responsible for the cooking, cleaning and laundry in our family, not sophisticated mechanical devices. Sometimes if we were good she'd let us punch the keys.

After the visit to the store, we'd drive a short distance through town to my grandparents' small, brick bungalow on Zina Street. When I was little I pictured Orangeville a place full of oranges. Row upon row of orange trees like in the Anita Bryant television commercials for freshly squeezed orange juice from Florida ("A day without orange juice is like a day without sunshine!"). When I was older I discovered Orangeville was named after Orange Lawrence, an early settler and businessman, and part of the Order of the Orange, a protestant association dating back to eigh-teenth century England and Ireland. Orangemen didn't like Catholics and originally banned them from worshipping in their town. By the time we moved to Orangeville in 1975, the town had relaxed its rules and allowed a Catholic church to be built inside its boundaries.

I never saw one orange tree in Orangeville, but there was a plum tree. Right in my grandparents' backyard. It grew sweet purple plums in the summer. Their backyard was large and level, more than big enough to throw a ball, or bat a birdie, or wack a mallet, or even play capture the flag, but we never did any of these things back there. It was not a place for children to be children. There was no place to hide, no tree to climb, nothing to explore. Except the basement.

The basement of my grandparents' home was the one room in the house where as children we were free to run around without restraint or raised eyebrows. The basement was one large, long cavernous room in which our voices echoed off the bare walls and cold, concrete floor. The only piece of furniture was an old abandoned side table. Tucked inside the sticky drawer of the side table was my grandfather's Playboy collection! After the first time we'd happened upon this discovery, it became a magnet drawing us into the basement every time we visited. We knew we weren't supposed to be in there, and so it was the first place we went. We'd pull open the little drawer carefully to avoid the squeaking that caused us to look over our shoulder every time to see if someone had heard. We'd sneak peeks at the photos and cartoons of naked women, working up the courage to open the full-page colour centerfold. Soon, however, we'd grow tired of looking at nudity, and tossing the magazine back in its drawer, we'd play tag or take turns holding onto the concrete pole in the middle of the basement and spinning round and round until we were dizzy and our arms were sore.

The freedom of the basement came with an element of risk and danger. In one lonely corner stood the scary silhouette of my grandmother's wicked wringer washing machine. My grandmother was one of the last of a dying breed of customers who preferred a wringer washer to a modern top loading machine, but I didn't trust that contraption. It looked to me like it belonged in the ancient collection of terrible torture chambers I had once seen in a wax museum. I preferred to stay well away from it. Fearfully, and from a safe distance, I would watch her feed the laundry into the wringer, afraid she was going to get her fingers crushed.

Natalie was afraid of the basement. She always joined us last after she tentatively crept down the slippery stairwell gripping the handrail. She was easily frightened and the sibling we derived the most pleasure out of tormenting with spooky stories and scary episodes. For years, all we had to do was mention the striped leggings of the wicked witch sticking out from under the house in the *The Wizard of Oz*, and Natalie would burst into tears. She was most afraid of the cold little antechamber at the far end of the basement, which was a work room or cold pantry, with a dark hole in the floor. Natalie was deathly afraid to go near the hole, never mind peer down into it like the rest of us did. She was afraid she would fall in. We saw her fear and mercilessly heightened it telling her it was a perfect home for monsters to hide in, vicious things with yellow eyes and sharp claws that grabbed at little girls' feet as they scampered by and dragged them down never to escape. We giggled as she ran away from us. For years Natalie suffered nightmares about being sucked down that hole.

One of my favourite things was falling asleep on the way home in the back seat propped up between the car door and a sibling. Sleeping in the car offered one of those rare quiet times that seldom happens in a large family. The soft click-clack of the indicator light and the drowsy "shshsh" of the brakes lulled us to sleep. As our sleeping bodies nestled against each other in the dark, we forgot for a while our daylight squabbles and rivalries. If the car came to a stop, forcing my head to wave on my neck, I would waken for a brief instant afraid that we'd reached our destination and the ride was over, but wishing for it to continue. I wanted to lie snug and safe inside the car all night.

But the best was yet to come - being carried up to bed when we got home. As we drove into our driveway and my father turned off the engine, we always made certain to appear dead asleep, if we weren't already. We would wait our turn to be carried out, worming further down in our seats, trying our hardest not to let the cool night air coming through the open car door wake us up. Sometimes we couldn't help ourselves and we had to break the silence.

"Cindy, are you asleep?" Michael whispered to me when we were alone. Being the oldest, we were always last to be carried in.

"Yeah. Shhh! Here comes Dad," I said, squeezing my eyes closed. My father carefully scooped me up in his arms and carried me into the house and all the way up the stairs, gently laying me on top of my bed. I dared not stir; the last thing I wanted to do then was brush my teeth. I would lie on my bedspread for what seemed a very long time without moving before my mother finally came to take off my shoes, tuck me under the covers, and kiss me goodnight. Then I'd fall immediately into a deep, delicious sleep.

The drive home from Nana and Grampa's was not always tranquil, however. One time, my father really lost it. Michael was ten years old and loved to torment me. He always got a big rise out of me by telling me I was adopted.

"Am not!"

"Are too!"

"Prove it!"

My father lashed out at us suddenly between clenched teeth, "Do I have to give you kids a clip on the ear? Now sit still and be quiet!"

We settled down. When our father yelled at us, we knew he meant business.

It was summer and the car windows were down to the catch the evening air. The secret damp smells of the encroaching darkness drafted around us. I was wedged warmly between the door and Christine. My eyes were heavy, hushed by the soft sounds of my father singing along with the car radio.

Suddenly, Bessie swerved sharply into the oncoming lane throwing Christine into my right shoulder. The tires screeched and slid on the highway and my mother yelled, "Harry!" My father swore and yanked the car around until we were in the other lane heading back the way we had come. With a jolt that sent me flying forward into the front seat, he swerved to the shoulder of the road, slammed into park, and tore out of the car.

He left his door open. We watched nervously as my father strode angrily to a car idling on the shoulder of the highway a few feet in front of us.

"What the hell do you think you're doing?" he yelled at the man in the driver's seat. I had never seen my father so angry. The driver's window was down and my father pushed his face through it. "You almost killed us! Can't you look where you are going? Didn't you see us?" Now my father had his hands wrapped around the driver's neck. "You didn't even look when you pulled out of your driveway, Goddamn it!"

A woman screamed. My father became even more upset when he noticed the woman in the passenger seat and the two children behind. He began to tremble with fury. "What kind of idiot are you? You risked the lives of my children. And yours."

The man just sat there, immobile. My father shook him by the neck and shoulders. The woman started yelling at my father to leave him alone. But he was too far into his rage to listen to her or to stop. He stuck his red face further into the driver's and hissed, "Get out of your car, you coward."

I heard someone crying. I looked around and saw it was Natalie. She was pressing her hands tight between her little legs.

My eyes turned back to my father when I heard the slow creak of a car door. The man opened it just enough to slide out, and my father was forced to briefly let go of the man's neck. He quickly grasped it tight again as the man slowly stood up to his full height. My father's arms kept going up and up until they were high above his head. The man was a full head taller than my father.

A moment of panic spread across my father's face, but he quickly resumed his threatening stance. By this time, the man's wife had run around to the driver's side and cried, "Stop, he's sorry! Leave him alone." Meanwhile, the big man made no motion to resist.

Once my father finally realized the man was not going to argue or fight with him, he released his grip. With a final curse and shake of his head, my father returned to our car. He got in, turned the car around and drove away. No one dared utter a word. I stared straight ahead until I heard Natalie whimpering again. There was a dark, wet stain on her shorts.

CHAPTER SIX

CareyOn'78

 Cindy

Geoff and I left the warmth of the party inside the barn and were heading toward the house when I heard a car from the highway rev its engine. I stopped and held my breath trying to see in the dark. The car screeched and sped down the highway and I felt a chill creep along my skin. The sound reminded me of the car that had too many times trespassed on our property and caused havoc and fear. But the metallic taste in the back of my throat was intensified by an earlier fear dating back to my childhood. A dark pit formed in my stomach from a time when another car had unleashed panic on me.

I was nine years old and walking to ballet class the first time the car crept up behind me. My regular walk took me six residential blocks from our house to the corner of Yonge and Steeles in Willowdale, North York, where the Eunice Frost School of Dance resided in the basement of the Royal Bank. I'd been taking dance lessons at the school twice a week since I was seven and been riding my bike or walking there on my own from the age of eight. (When I was twelve, Ms. Frost relocated to a new studio too far for me to get to on my own, and then my parents had to drive me.) This particular Saturday afternoon, however, I became aware of a car following slowly behind me.

I moved over to the farthest edge of the shoulder next to the ditch, and quickened my pace, keeping my head down. The car pulled up beside me and, stealing a glance, I saw it was a red sports car. The driver was a young man with dark hair. He drove silently beside me turning his face to stare at me out his window. I ignored him and prayed he'd leave me alone. After a long stretch of following me for two or three blocks, he drove away. That evening, I told my parents about the car. They exchanged uneasy looks with each other.

The next Saturday, I was on my way back home after dance class and several blocks from home, when the same red car drove up behind me again. I started walking faster, but again the driver idled up beside me. This time the dark stranger rolled down his window and said, "Hey, baby, want'a fuck?" I bolted. I ran and ran not looking back until I turned into our cul-de-sac. The car was nowhere to be seen.

I ran in the house and found my father. I told him the red car had followed me again. I also told him what the stranger said. It was the first time I had heard an adult use the "f"-word and the first time I had ever repeated it. My father tore out the front door and into his car to find the guy.

When he arrived back home later he said he had searched all the streets in the neighourhood, but didn't see the car. He was worked up. He asked me again what the driver looked like and what he'd said to me. This was my second time saying the really bad word.

For months I looked over my shoulder for the stranger in the red car. Luckily, I never saw him again. I had however seen a glimpse of the ugly underside of the world, and I would never shake off the fear of that car following me.

My father's reaction stayed with me. I had known him to be quick to anger before, but had never seen him so propelled into action by something I said. At the time, I did not have either the words or the knowledge to express what I found so loathsome - I just knew in a vague sense it was dirty. His reaction made it seem even worse than I imagined and increased my fear. I also knew that my father would do anything for me if he felt I was in danger.

I heard the car again approaching the farmhouse from the opposite direction. It looked familiar. I saw Dad on the verandah and hoped he hadn't seen it too.

Natalie

I heard about CareyOn '78. I knew my family was planning another barn party. I told John and he said, "What do you care?" I shrugged my shoulders and told him I didn't. Still, on the night of the party, I made him drive by the farmhouse. I just had to take a look at what I was missing.

I heard the band as soon as we rounded the sweeping curve in the highway. It was a cool September night but I rolled down my window to let the sound in. The sweet smell of grass and cornstalks heavy with the damp night air flew in from the fields as we approached the house. I asked John to slow down. There were long lines of cars parked along the gravel shoulder of the highway in both directions. It was a dark night, but the house glowed with lights inside and out welcoming the guests. Behind the house, the ragged frame of the barn was lit up from the inside like an x-ray exposing its broken ribs.

I could make out silhouettes of people clustered in the broken light outside the barn and along the driveway, but it was too dark and we were too far to clearly identify anyone. The noise of the partiers mingled with the music of the band while above the buzz the odd shout or burst of laughter reached inside the car. One recognizable voice rose clearly above the others. I looked over at John to see if he had heard it too. Immediately, he slammed his foot on the gas. We sped past the farmhouse and the barn until John suddenly changed his mind and cranked the car around. As we headed back toward town and past the house again I thought I saw Cindy and Geoff walking toward the house. I also saw my father standing on the front verandah looking toward the car. I thought he was straining to see me.

CHAPTER SEVEN

Questions

 — Cindy —

The barn party was one of many parties my parents hosted. They loved throwing parties. Parties marked the events of our life and no cause for celebration was overlooked. While I was growing up, my parents held extravagant Grey Cup and Stanley Cup parties, birthday and anniversary parties, New Year's Eve and New Year's Day parties, high school and graduation parties, pool parties and theme parties, Christmas parties and confirmation parties, and going away and welcome home parties. From the time I was eight years old, New Year's Day parties, or REBOS, as we called them, became an annual tradition in our house. REBOS is "sober" backwards and for many years we held a REBOS breakfast party every New Year's morning that began at 7:00 am. Sometimes our guests stayed up all night going from one party to another; as one neighbour said, "Why go to bed for a few hours when you can party?" REBOS usually lasted late into the afternoon until the last guest was sent home satiated and, oftentimes, freshly inebriated from the REBOS party alcohol.

My father was head chef. He lorded over his large electric frying pan purchased especially for the occasion and saved exclusively for that day, cooking ham and eggs (sunny side up or lightly over only, no scrambled or custom orders). He stood sentry at his skillet wearing an enormous chef's hat, a mutant marshmallow stuffed on his head, a long apron wrapped around his skinny torso, and a red tartan vest. He wielded his spatula and called out greetings to his friends as they arrived, all the time cracking and sizzling, flipping and frying with finesse.

One year while we still lived in the city, my father set the theme for a REBOS party with a live hen which he set up in a large wire cage on our kitchen table. The hen came with eggs in her cage and I spent the entire morning watching and waiting hoping she would lay another one right in front of me. Finally, Michael, fed up with waiting for me to leave my post so he could beat me at crocinole again, told me that I could wait forever but I was never going to see that bird lay an egg.

"Why?" I asked him.

"Cause, stupid, Dad put the eggs in the cage."

When I persisted that that didn't mean the chicken couldn't lay one today, he said with exasperation, "That chicken is a rooster!"

I was embarrassed and confused. I couldn't wait to grow up so I would understand these things like my brother did.

I was frustrated with being a dumb kid. I believed once I became a grown-up I would simultaneously and miraculously comprehend things that until then had remained muddled and mysterious. I had a vague notion reaching adulthood would gain me automatic membership into an exclusive club that would answer all my questions like:

How come grandmothers always carried mints in their purses?

Why did my arm turn to pins and needles if I slept on it?

Who named the Big Dipper and what is a dipper anyway?

Why was there a Sunday but not a daughter day?

And, by the way, who *was* Jack Benny?

I was certain the answers would be revealed to me when I grew up. In the meantime, until I reached that magic age of enlightenment, I was forced to resign myself to living in a world of childhood bafflement, biding my time until I too became a member of the adult world. What I didn't know then was that there would always be things I would never fully understand. Like how it happened that Natalie left home when she was still a child and became estranged from us for several years.

My father had a deep, rich voice good for telling jokes and stories. During mealtime he seldom spoke as he listened intently to the news on the little transistor radio beside him on the kitchen window sill. And unless we wanted to risk a "clip behind the ear" we knew better than to interrupt the serious 6:00 o'clock news. After he finished eating, Dad would make his inevitable "Not bad, Dee" comment in reference to her cooking before reaching for a toothpick from the lazy Susan in the middle of the table. If he then pushed back his chair and focused on a spot in the corner of the ceiling it was a sure sign a story, or better yet a joke, was coming.

He'd clear his throat, which meant if we weren't already paying attention we better now, and then he'd say, "Did you hear the one about the O'Malley brothers?" in his best Irish accent.

"Oh, tell the one where they're sitting at the bar with the corpse!" one or more of his children would shout with excitement. Just before he got to the punch line we all knew off by heart, we would start giggling hysterically, even my mother who always laughed loudest at my father's jokes. At times like these, it seemed we could be happy to sit and listen to my father telling jokes forever. We tried forestalling the end of mealtime by manipulating our parents' good mood to grant us seconds of dessert. Sometimes Dad's jokes became personal attacks and the meal would end abruptly with Mom ordering us to clear the table.

My mother was scraping the bowl of lemon snow when my father said, "Better take that spoon away from your mother, kids, before she eats that too."

My mother didn't say anything but her eyes turned to metal slugs aimed at her husband.

He pretended not to notice. It was no secret that my father thought his wife was fat. The way he talked, my mother should have been the size of a house, not a size fourteen.

My mother tried to lose the additional weight she had accumulated with each pregnancy. She joined Weight Watchers and for several weeks meticulously weighed her individual portions on a little scale that quickly claimed a place beside the bread box. The diet worked, and she lost weight, so much so that I noticed and commented on how great she looked. I thought she'd be pleased, and was confused when she complained bitterly, "You think so? I don't think I look good at all."

The next day I noticed the little scale was no longer on the counter. My father had also mentioned his wife's diet, except his barbed comments made her feel all her sacrifices and efforts were for nothing. She put the scale away in the cupboard above the fridge. It never resurfaced again and my mother swore off diets forever.

Dad could draw out a story for as long as we were able to "sit still and be quiet." He was especially fond of any story that offered an educational or moral lesson. At heart he was a frustrated teacher. As a young man, he had done well at school and wanted to go on to university and become a teacher. His dream wasn't realized because his father wanted his oldest son to work with him in construction. At that time, my grandfather, Daddy Bill, had purchased a bulldozer and was in the business of supplying well tiles. My father drove the bulldozer for a couple of years before he exchanged his overalls for a business suit and got a job at Bell Canada.

Bell offered to put my father through university and, for several years while he was newly married, he attended night school at the University of Toronto. A black and white framed photograph of Dad and his graduating class in cap and gown stood proudly on our living room shelf for years. By the time he graduated with a degree in business, Dad had four children and a promotion at Bell that made it too difficult for him to leave and start a new career in teaching. My father stayed with the phone company for seventeen years. He never lost his inclination to teach, however, and when his children were born, he discovered a wonderful ready-made audience.

Quite often, and most naturally, my father slipped into the role of teacher, especially at the supper table where he had a captive classroom. Like a strict schoolteacher, my father was happiest when his students sat politely and listened attentively to him. Rarely was he curious to discover his students' opinions of his anecdotes and lessons. It never occurred to him to find out what his children were thinking. I wished that just once he would finish his tale and then turn to us and say: "Now, children, what do you think of that?"

My father also shared personal stories treating us to boyhood tales from when he lived with his father and brother in remote Northern Ontario in Kirkland Lake, or with his grandparents on their farm in Georgetown, Ontario. One evening after supper Paul asked Dad if it was true Daddy Bill had been a hobo.

"Yes, son, it's true," he said, as he pushed back his chair from the table.

"Whath' a hobo?" asked eight year old Paul in his slight lisp.

Dad removed the perpetual after-dinner toothpick from his mouth and said, "A hobo is someone who traveled by train to find work during the Depression. You see, Son, when I was a boy, there were no jobs in Georgetown and your Daddy Bill had to leave us, me and your Uncle Bill, to find work."

He examined the toothpick, rolling it between his fingers. "I never knew my mother," he continued. "She died of tuberculosis when I was four. When I think of my mother I see me as a little boy standing at the side of her bed. She must have been very sick and I think I knew she was dying. My little brother, your Uncle Bill, was not yet two years old when our mother died. He had TB for the first few years of his life and was in the hospital until he was three or four. Our father struggled to look after us and make ends meet, but there just weren't any jobs to be had. After his wife died, he travelled across Canada by train in search of work."

"Ith thith the part where he wath a hobo?" Paul asked. He was still young enough to get away with cutting into my father's story without much risk of the inevitable "no one ever learned anything with their mouth open" scolding. (I often wondered about the validity of that statement, as I sat there dying to ask a question, but afraid to interject or contradict him.)

My father answered with uncharacteristic tolerance for being interrupted, "Yes, Paul, Daddy Bill hopped on and off the trains across Canada. He went from one city or town to another, wherever there was work. In fact, your grandfather lived like a hobo on the trains for quite some time."

"Who looked after you?" asked Paul.

"I was sent to live with my grandparents, your great grandparents."

"But how could your father have left you like that?" I said in disbelief, throwing caution aside.

My father paused and looked gravely down at his hands lying flat on the table. When he looked up at me I could see he was grappling with his answer. "He had to. He didn't want to, but he didn't have a choice."

"Nana Carey ithn't our real nana, right, Dad?" Paul asked.

"She is your step grandmother. May lived next door and used to cook and clean for my dad after Mom died. I was living with my grandparents by then and Bill was sent to live with Daddy Bill's brother, Oliver, and his wife, Suzie. Your Great Uncle Oliver and Aunt Suzie loved Bill like he was one of their own. As a matter of fact, Uncle Bill grew up believing Uncle Oliver and Aunt Suzie were his parents."

I found this revelation hard to bear. I understood my relatives believed they had acted in Uncle Bill's best interest by protecting him from the truth, but I was angry with them. They were adults, they should have known better than to lie.

I needed to speak my mind. "That was so mean. How could they have lied like that?"

"They thought they were doing the right thing, Cindy," said my father growing impatient with me.

"Then what happened, Dad?" asked Paul.

"Eventually Dad settled in Kirkland Lake where he had a stable job in the goldmines. He sent for us then to join him. I remember taking the train from Toronto all by myself when I was eight years old, your age."

"Wow!" said Paul. "Weren't you scared?"

"No. I remember a nice lady on the train with a little boy of her own. She saw me reading my book, *Jack the Giant Killer*, and she asked me if I wanted her to read it to me. I'll never forget. When she came to the part where the page was ripped out, she just carried on reading without missing a beat like the words were right there in front of her. I was amazed! The train trip took all day and finally pulled up to the last station where Dad was waiting for me. At least I remembered him. Poor Bill, when he arrived later, he not only didn't know him but found out this stranger was his father."

I wasn't convinced. I knew I would be very upset and resentful if my father left me. But Dad made it sound like it wasn't a big deal. Like it was just the way it was.

He tried to explain. "Listen, I was just happy to have my dad back. He was my father. Some things you need to accept for the way they are and carry on."

CHAPTER EIGHT

Fathers

 Cindy

My mother once said that she didn't know how she ever learned to be a nurturing mother since she could never remember a time when her own mother, Helen, had shown her any love or tenderness. Mom was four years old when her mother married Russell Darwen. They lived together in the upstairs apartment of a house in Kew Beach in Toronto. During the war, Russell joined the Navy and was stationed in Halifax. Helen worked full-time at the Harvey Woods factory sewing seams along lyle stockings. She left Diane alone while she went to work on the understanding that the young mother living on the first floor flat would "keep an eye on her." Mom was seven years old.

Mom never forgave her mother for not telling her who her father was. My grandmother could not bring herself to speak about the father, or that time in her life, to anyone. My mother grew up prohibited from mentioning her father. She was never even sure of his real name.

By the time my mother was an adult, she had pieced together, from comments she heard from relatives, that her mother had been married for a short period to a Robert Dagliesh who died of Tuberculosis in a sanitarium. She was

44

led to believe this was her father. She was in her forties when she learned of a different version of the truth from her mother's last surviving sibling who lay dying in a hospital bed.

I was twelve years old when I visited my Great Aunt Eva with my mother at St. Michael's Hospital in downtown Toronto. We found my aunt in a large dimly lit ward with several beds feebly separated by bleak curtains hanging limply on metal rods. The antiseptic hospital smell made me feel sick and nauseous. Aunt Eva was lying in bed, her frail fingers wrapped around white bed sheets pulled taught under her chin. The sleeves of her white dressing gown hung loosely revealing bone thin, blue veined arms. Her thin pure white hair was pinned in tight little curls on the top of her translucent scalp like a halo. She looked like she had already begun the physical transformation into an angel.

As we walked into her room she looked at my mother and exclaimed in a high creaking voice: "Oh, you look just like Bill!"

"Bill?" my mother asked smiling indulgently at her Aunt. Eva had always been the most spirited of the four sisters and my favourite Aunt.

"Your father," Aunt Eva croaked.

"I thought Robert Dagliesh was my father," my mother said, the corners of her mouth puckering into a frown.

"He wasn't your father." Aunt Eva's voice was weakening and we leaned into her bed to hear her. "Your mother married him when you were a baby."

"Well, who's my father then? Who's Bill?" demanded my mother, her anxiety growing.

"William Fretwell. He was your father. You have his dimples."

"Why didn't anyone tell me before?" Mom cried.

"We all made a pact. The three sisters, Grace, Laura and I were sworn to secrecy. It was to protect Helen. She would kill me if she knew I told you."

Helen was the youngest of four daughters. When she was born, her mother, Lottie Mae Marcroft, suffered postpartum depression. Her father, Thomas Marcroft, had his wife committed to an asylum for the mentally insane in Hamilton, Ontario. My mother told me that her grandfather had Lottie Mae committed because she played with her young daughters in public in the park. He maintained this behaviour demonstrated she was not of sound mind and an unfit parent. My great grandmother lived to be ninety six years old and never left the institution. The family always believed there was nothing wrong with her.

Helen was raised by an aunt. She never visited her mother. The closest she came to acknowledging that her mother was alive was at Christmas when she used to wrap a box of chocolates up and give them to her sister to take to their mother in Hamilton. Lottie died without ever knowing her youngest child who had been taken away as an infant.

"All these years I've thought my father was Robert Dagliesh," my mother said close to tears.

Eva inched her body up further from under her covers and shakily reached for the water glass on the table beside her. My mother handed it to her and Eva took a sip before continuing,

"Your Aunt Grace and her husband, Uncle Edward, arranged the marriage between Robert and your mom. It was a disgrace for Helen to have a child and be unwed."

I watched the stone wall face replace my mother's face. Her dry eyes scared me more than anything.

"What happened to William Fretwell?" she asked coldly.

"I don't know. The last time I saw him you were six months old. He came to the house wanting to see you but the family turned him away. They never let him see you."

My mother sunk down on the foot of the bed in a daze. I cleared off a space on the little bedside table for the vase of red and white carnations I was still holding in my hands. I asked my Aunt if she needed anything. She asked me to adjust her pillow. Eva lay back and closed her eyes, clearly spent from exertion. We stayed with her a little longer. No mention of my grandparents was made again. This was the last time I saw my Aunt Eva.

On the way back to the car I asked Mom what she was going to say to Nana.

"It doesn't matter what I say," she said walking briskly. "She refuses to speak to me about it. When I was a child I used to ask her who my father was, I knew it wasn't Russell, and she just told me to keep my mouth shut."

"I'm sorry, Mom."

She slowed her pace and took my hand.

Despite Mom's reluctance to broach the subject with her mother, a few weeks later she resolved to try again. We were up from the city visiting my grandparents. I was in the den with Nana keeping her company while she watched the hockey game. My mother stood in the doorway with her legs firmly planted, hands on her hips, and demanded, "Mom, who's William Fretwell?"

Nana froze staring at the television. Mom repeated the question. Her mother raised a cigarette to her lips and continued to stare at the hockey game.

"Well?" asked Diane.

Nana glared at her through her cigarette smoke. She didn't say a word. Her daughter waited, turned on her heels and walked out of the room.

Aunt Eva died a few weeks later. For as long as she lived, Helen never said a word to her daughter about her biological father.

We moved to the farm late August of 1975. My father quit his sales job in Toronto where he worked for the Yellow Pages. He'd had success selling ads for the previous five years for the company that "Let Your Fingers Do The Walking," making salesman of the year. He had become tired of the rat race. He said it wasn't a job you could do for more than five years - too much pressure, impossible to stay on top - and bought into his in-laws' office supply business in Orangeville. He claimed he wanted out of the city, that he was ready to return to his roots in the country. It was no secret my father had always had a soft spot for the country, but it wasn't until many years after we moved that I discovered the real reason my parents moved from the city.

The move was my parents' attempt to get a fresh start on their marriage. I had no idea their marriage needed fixing. They never argued or fought in front of us. It came as a shock when my mother confided several years later that it had been in trouble for a long time and their move to a new life in the country was a last effort to get it back on track.

Before we moved to the country, my mother liked to crow that, contrary to public opinion, raising teenagers was "a joy". She was testament to the fact, having at the time four of them living at home ranging in age from eighteen to thirteen. She said this to incredulous neighbours and friends who, with open-mouthed wonder, would turn to her with renewed respect and envy wanting to know her secret. She would laugh and say it was just how it was. She didn't know why it worked. If she could attribute anything to her success, she would acknowledge it took a lot of love, and luck, that she had been blessed with wonderful children. Her audience wanted to believe this, but it sounded too good to be true. It would take a move to the country to completely topple my mother's naïve sentiments about raising teenagers.

CHAPTER NINE

Uprooted

 Cindy

As far as anyone knew, we moved to the country because my parents wanted to live there and my father wanted to return to his roots. Dad had spent most of his childhood growing up on his grandparents' farm near Georgetown, Ontario, and had many times shared memories with us of that time in his life. My father fancied he had farming in his blood. Well, as it turned out, my father may have had the country in his veins, but he had a lot to learn about animal husbandry.

During our second year in the country, he bought two young cows. His plan was to get them nice and fat and slaughter them in the spring to fill our freezer. He made sure they were well fed all winter and was proud when they grew fat and healthy, especially one that grew particularly plump.

One early spring day Paul came running excitedly into the house yelling, "Mom, Dad, come quick. The cow is having a baby!"

Our parents followed Paul out to the field in bewilderment just in time to see the cow deliver a healthy calf.

Unknown to us, and completely undetected by our father, the young heifer was not only fat but pregnant.

Another time, Dad decided the crop of hay behind the old barn would improve in the spring if he burned off the old crop and weeds in the fall. Unfortunately, his field burning technique went awry and before he knew it the fire got out of control and threatened to burn down the old barn. The fire department had to come to put it out.

The move to Orangeville impacted the females in our family more than the males. My oldest brother, Michael, started at the University of Waterloo a few weeks after we moved and was only ever a temporary resident at home after that. (This was just as well as there was no bedroom for him anyway. Besides, he was severely allergic to cat hair and the farmhouse was covered in it.) Paul was eight years old, too young to be upset for long by the move. For my teenage sisters and me, the move to the country was the worst thing that could ever happen to us. Yanked from the home and friends we loved in the suburbs of North York, a large urban centre north of Toronto, and plunked down on the outskirts of Orangeville, population 12,507, became our worst teenage nightmare.

My sisters and I had a lot of reasons to hate the farm. Following our initial visit to our new house, we were so against moving to the country at the ages of thirteen, fifteen and sixteen, that we compiled a long list of all the things we hated about the farmhouse and addressed it to my father. Dad tried to appease us by promising we could get a horse when we moved. This worked until our second visit, which only rekindled our disappointment and fired our zealousness in completing our list. We continued to add to it even after the move, even though by that time we knew it was futile to try to change our father's mind.

Uprooted and vulnerable, we took our frustration out on our surroundings. Nothing was good enough. How we complained and carried on! To us, the farmhouse was an ugly, square, red brick box that had neither charm nor character to compensate for its loss of modern amenities. What we would give to have a furnished rec room again. And two bathrooms. Our new place had only one bathroom for the seven of us; its two doors were constantly revolving. "Oh, well, a family who bathes together stays together," my mother exclaimed when we complained. There weren't enough trees, there weren't enough bedrooms, there weren't enough windows. There were too many flies, it was too windy, it was too close to town, yet too far to walk. And, the highway was too close to enjoy the peace and tranquility of country living.

My sisters and I shared the same contempt for the farmhouse, but I was the one who led the way in hating the town. Being the oldest girl, I had enjoyed more freedom to experience the delights of city life and was just beginning to taste the urban possibilities when I was unfairly transported to the boonies. Orangeville offered the entertainment options of a main-street cinema, where the "new releases" had already finished their runs in the city; one strip mall at the end of town that featured a Zellers department store ("You call this shopping?!"); a bowling alley, pool hall, sports complex, and curling club. After growing up in an affluent urban setting where we were accustomed to a wide variety of leisure-time activities, restaurants and shopping with easy access by choice of bus, subway or streetcar, I found the small town facilities insulting. I was never so bored in my life and didn't know how I was going to stand it. I couldn't relate to a place where the front page news of the week was the announcement of a ribbon won by the 4H Club ("What the heck was 4H?"). I felt stifled, thwarted, and robbed.

It was toward the end of August; we'd lived in our new house for a week. Flies were everywhere; buzzing on the windowsills, the kitchen rug, the insides of our shoes, the bathroom sink. One morning I was washing my face and didn't notice the dead fly stuck to the bar of soap until I lathered it onto my cheek. I screamed and ran downstairs into the kitchen where I found my father sitting at the table.

"There's a fly in the soap," I said to the newspaper blocking my father's face. I waited for a reaction. "It's gross," I whined. The paper rustled. "The fly died in the soap and I washed my face with it." A broad shiny forehead and receding hairline appeared above the paper. The page was turned and neatly creased again while I waited impatiently for him to say something.

"Well, at least it was clean," he said.

I stormed out the house and stomped angrily to the end of the driveway. I cast a bitter glance toward the miserable town. My eyes traveled down the paved road that stretched out flat and straight before it curved into a wide arc just before the town line. I resented its length and dullness, there was no physical landmark, no dip or twist to break the monotony, which seemed unfair in this land of rolling hills and hairpin turns. We lived far enough away that I couldn't see the houses in town, but I knew if I followed the highway around the bend I would soon reach Beckers on the left-hand side, the convenience store that marked the town's border.

I turned and saw someone walking toward me on the other side of the highway. She was old, but held her back straight and walked purposefully. I watched her cross the highway, greeting me at our driveway.

"Hello. I'm Celia Rose. I live in the farmhouse across the way," she said pointing to the farm down and across the highway, our nearest neighbour.

Mrs. Celia Rose had dyed blue-white hair in tight curls that framed heavily blushed pink cheeks, and bright painted lips. She smelled like Lilly of the Valley and mothballs. She had come over to welcome us to our new home. She was a widow and had first come to live in her farmhouse as a new bride over fifty years ago. She had seen many families come and go from our house and remembered when it had been part of a real working farm.

"But that was a while ago," she said in the peculiar local accent, a slow drawl combined with clipped vowels and short endings. "There've been several young families like yers in here since. Have you hear told about the quarter mile line in front of yer place?" she asked.

When I told her I hadn't, she said: "Didn't yous realize yous were livin' right in front of whar the quarter mile races took place?" looking at me like she couldn't believe how ignorant us folks from the city could be.

She was pointing to something on the highway. I feigned indifference and shrugged my shoulders as if to suggest it didn't matter one way or the other to me about any race. But when she told me that a young man had been killed in a quarter mile race here two years ago she got my full attention. She told me that before the accident, the quarter mile was a favourite summertime hangout, a place of entertainment, for the kids.

"Gangs placed bets on thar favourite souped-up cars. Lots-a times fights broke out by the highway. You see that white line thar? That's the starting line."

Sure enough there was a white line painted across the highway. I hadn't noticed it before. I imagined a scene from the movie "Grease!" with tough-looking guys wearing slicked back hair, leather bomber jackets, and cigarettes hanging out the corners of their mouths as they sat behind the wheels of their loud, fast muscle cars while girlfriends with rolled-up jeans and red lipstick cheered from the side of the road.

"The police knew about these road races; don't think they didn't," Mrs. Rose said. "But they didn't do much to stop 'em. They looked t' other way. Until Brian was killed."

"Killed?"

She pointed down the highway toward her house. "He lost control just beyond my driveway. Hit the ditch and turned over. Hung onto life fer a few days but never gained consciousness. He died soon aftar."

I looked across the highway to where she was pointing and felt a shiver run along the tops of my shoulders. "What happened to the other driver?" I asked.

"He was charged. Criminal negligence causing death. He got two years. After Brian's death the town and police decided they needed to pay more attention. They started clampin' down hard, tried to put a stop to any more races. Of course, if truth be known, they had the townsfolk on thar side. Even the young folks didn't feel much like racin' anymore." She paused, shaking her head in pity, "Brian was such a nice kid."

"Cindy?" called my mother from the back door.

I turned away from the highway. "Come in and meet my family, Mrs. Rose," I said leading the way.

CHAPTER TEN

O.D.S.S.

 Cindy

It was Labour Day weekend; the last day of the summer holidays and the day before I was to start my new high school. I was visiting my grandparents and was crouched in their little den on the floor pouring over the *Toronto Star*. We didn't get the newspaper delivered to the farmhouse and I was excited when I saw they had a copy. My breath caught in my throat when I found what I was looking for. There I was on the back page beside a cute boy in a full-page ad for Levis.

It had been Mom's idea for me to become a model. When I turned sixteen, she said modeling would pay for my dance lessons, suggesting my parents were finding it hard to pay for them. But to become a model I had to go to modeling school. I had my sights set on a course at the Eleanor Fulcher School of Modeling on Bloor Street. But modeling school was expensive -$900.00! - too much for my parents to afford. Mom said I should ask Nana to pay for it.

"She always wished she'd been on stage," she said, as if that was good enough reason as any for her to want to support my dancing ambitions. "She won't give it to me, but if you ask her for the money she might give it to you," she said.

I was pretty sure I was Nana's favourite, I had spent many overnights with her and Grampa as a child since I was three years old. I'd also spent a week with them during the summer holidays for a couple of summers. The overnight visits were saved for me, my siblings were not extended the same invitation, yet despite this I was uncomfortable in asking my grandmother for money. She wasn't an easy person to talk to and, although Mom was convinced she was interested in my dancing career, I wasn't so sure. She had never shown excitement or interest in anything I did.

However, I really wanted to go to modeling school and the next time we went to see my grandparents for Sunday dinner, I got up the courage to ask her. We were in her little foyer standing in front of the large console when I told her about my plans.

"Nana, I was wondering if you'd like to pay for my modeling school." Nana frowned. Mom hung back in the kitchen listening.

"It's $900.00." Nana's eyes grew smaller and colder. "But I'll pay you back."

She ground her teeth until I heard her dentures click. She never said a word, just turned and left the room. I didn't know what to expect but later that night when we were leaving to go back home after dinner, Mom showed me a cheque. Nana had given me the money.

I went to the Eleanor Fulcher School of Modeling in downtown Toronto every Saturday for six months where I joined a group of teenaged girls hoping to be the next Cheryl Tiegs. We learned makeup application, consulted with hair stylists, explored new wardrobe options, worked with photographers, and practiced our catwalk on a small runway for hours until we got it down pat.

I graduated in the spring and was asked to join their agency. They arranged for a photographer to do my comp card (another cost, this time my parents paid) and I dutifully trudged my collection of headshots and full-body shots around the city dropping them off at tony photography studios in Yorkville and out-of-the-way industrial warehouses. Sometimes, if I was lucky, someone was available to meet with me. Once, at a remote warehouse, I was asked by the owner to come to his back room office. The place seemed deserted, there was no one else around. Flipping through my binder he stopped at a photo of me in a two piece bathing suit. "This is you?" he said surprised, taking a second look at me. I was wearing a coat and for a moment I thought he was going to ask me to remove it. I was grateful when he turned his attention back to the photos. In the end I left without incident, but his preying eyes stayed with me and reinforced the sense of panic I felt to be alone with him. Meanwhile, my parents never asked where I was when I was gone for hours pounding the pavement in the city in hopes of a modeling job, and I never thought to tell them.

When I got the job for the Levis ad, I remembered the client's disappointment when I arrived for the photo shoot. I was meeting the client for the first time. She was expecting someone 5'6" as stated on my comp card, when in fact I was just shy of 5'4". My agent had recommended we list my height as 5'6" to make me more marketable. "Besides," she said, "you're that tall with your shoes on".

"I hate when they do that," the client said as she jabbed pins into the bottom of the pants making a quick hemline before the shoot.

Now, sitting on the floor of my grandparent's den, I tore out the ad for my scrapbook. Despite my height, I was thrilled to be a model in the newspaper. It helped make the move to the country and starting a new high school a little more bearable.

***

I hated everything about my new high school. Orangeville District Secondary School, O.D.S.S., was a sprawling concrete structure that sprouted wings as the town and neighbouring population grew. It was the only high school for several miles in all directions and students were bussed in from remote farms and outlying towns and villages with names like Grand Valley, Shelburne, Mono Mills and Alton. It was an eclectic mix of town and farm children, children of wealthy estate owners, lawyers, pilots, and businessmen who made their money in the city but chose to raise their families in the rolling country hills. All I saw however was the backwardness of a small town school full of "hicks".

My school spirit for my old high school, Newtonbrook, was never higher than after I left. At Orangeville High they didn't cancel classes for the Jewish holidays as they did at Newtonbrook, which was half Jewish. My best friend at Newtonbrook, Judy, was Jewish. I never met a Jewish student at O.D.S.S. There was one girl who had olive skin and dark hair and could have been of Italian or Portuguese descent. There was a Chinese girl at school, but there weren't any Japanese, or east Indians, or blacks at school. Once, as a child I had been walking along Broadway, the main street in town, with my grandmother when she stopped and pointed out the "chocolate coloured family" across the street. "They've just moved to town," she told me, taking my hand, as though she needed to protect me. Nana Darwen had lived in Orangeville for many years by that time, but this was the first time she had seen a black person in her town. She was afraid what it might mean for her community.

Her daughter, Diane, wasn't like that. The more foreign the person she met, the more she considered them exotic and likely to strike up a conversation with them. She embarrassed her teenage daughters with her boldness, asking questions of strangers like, "Where they were from?" and "What did they think of Canada?" Mom had a particular affection for eastern Europeans. Once, when I was thirteen, I was shopping with her at Eatons department store in downtown Toronto when we stopped for lunch at the cafeteria. I followed her with my plastic tray carrying my grilled cheese sandwich and pickle on-the-side, and was mortified when she stopped at a little round table where an old man wearing a dusty, battered brimmed hat sat alone. There were empty seats at other tables, but my mother smiled and asked if we could join him.

He removed his hat revealing greasy hair plastered to his head in strands of grey and motioned for her to sit.

"I think maybe I have plague. Everyone," he waved his arm to include the other tables, "don't want sit with me."

In no time, my mother had charmed the stranger. It turned out this man was from Dubrovnik. My mother was ecstatic.

"Oh, did you hear that, Cindy? I have *always* wanted to go to Dubrovnik!" she cried clasping her hands together. "I was in Spain last year," she told the man, "and ever since I have wanted desperately to go to Dubrovnik. It's beautiful there, right?"

"Yes, very beautiful," he said smiling. Not like here. People friendly. Like you."

My mother found out the man had owned a jewelry store in Dubrovnik. The thought of precious gems from Yugoslavia put her over the top. The man wrote in strange slanted letters on the back of his napkin. It was the name and address of his family's store, now run by his brother, along with the name of his mother and her village.

"You must go! Better than Dubrovnik!"

My mother was as delighted as if she'd just found a missing diamond from her wedding band. She promised to look up the man's mother if she ever got to that part of the world. And, she meant it. Her vision of visiting the historic city on the Adriatic coast left her inspired for hours so that for the remainder of the afternoon she shopped with renewed vigor. My mother hung onto that napkin for years, believing it would come in handy one day.

O.D.S.S. bunched grade nines together with grade thirteens, which I didn't appreciate, having previously attended separate middle and high schools. I missed the respect of being in a high school where the students had earned the titles: "Women" and "Men" on the washroom doors, as opposed to "Girls" and "Boys" that labeled the doors at O.D.S.S. I commiserated with my sisters on the total unfairness of it all. Lonely and bored, I built a wall around my vulnerability and retreated behind a mask of snobbery.

Sometimes I felt my loneliness and boredom would swallow me whole. One suffocating boring afternoon, I vowed if I lived through this painfully long day, I would make it my life's goal never to be bored again. Restless, I went outside.

I headed past the original carriage house, now used as a car port, and Dad's red 1970 Mustang parked inside. How he loved that car! He'd bought it while he was still on the road with Yellow Pages. The day he drove it home from the dealership with its custom initialized plates, HAC, for Harold Albert Carey, was the day our father was cool.

A light breeze blew the branches of the tall cedars that bordered the pasture behind. I ambled beside the ruins of an old piggery, until I came to the wooden fence that marked the end of our property. The quiet was broken only by the swish of the long grass rustling in the breeze and the sorrowful note of a lonely bird. Beside me and up a short bank, soundless swallows darted in and out of the gaping door of the old barn. I saw Fred, our new grey and white kitten, engrossed in the birds.

This was as far as I had previously ventured. The "back forty," as my father called it lay beyond. Nothing to get excited about – just fields beyond which I could make out a border of poplar trees marking the edge of a forest. And yet I felt a slight thrill to explore the country. The fields had lain fallow for a long time, but the earth was still scarred from when it had been tamed by a tractor. Long, straight rows of ruts ran over the fields from years of being tilled. I tread cautiously, watching for sudden groundhog holes in the earth that could twist an ankle without warning.

I imagined myself the epitome of loneliness; a lovely, lonely girl lost in a field. I encouraged my own romantic isolation and distress. I urged it to envelope me in all its dramatic glory so that I could achingly experience the deep anguish that songs of longing and love had the power to stir in my soul. My loneliness engulfed me in tragic proportions until it built up inside me like a vague, painful lust.

I had walked for about half a mile in the fields behind the barn before I came upon the pond. I hadn't seen it until I almost stumbled upon it. It wasn't visible from the field as it lay hidden in a little hollow. Here the land dipped, forming a natural recession which, over the years, had filled with rainwater, creating a swampland and a pond. It lay surrounded by shoulder high grasses and shrubs, a natural wonder concealed by bulrushes, fox sedge, and horsetails. Two ducks flew over head and landed skidding across the water. Bull frogs honked and red winged black birds flitted between the bulrushes.

I was filled with unexpected awe. I felt I had discovered a strange, mysterious place, one that the rest of the world couldn't have known existed. I wanted to keep it that way, hidden from others, a secret place that belonged to me and my family only. A place where we could feel safe and free from the rest of the world.

CHAPTER ELEVEN

John

 Natalie

The first time I saw John he was smoking a cigarette with his buddies on the tarmac behind the school. It was the beginning of the fall term and the second week of classes at my new high school. I was fourteen, in grade nine. John was sixteen and in grade eleven. I was aware he was watching me, sneaking peeks from over his shoulder as I stood in a circle with my new girlfriends. He stole shy looks at me from under a lock of dark hair that swept across his eyes. With his hands jammed in his pockets and his hunched shoulders, he gave the impression of being at odds with the world, and despite his sullenness, or maybe because of it, there was an undeniable sexiness about him.

His friends noticed him staring at me and elbowed him in the side, and jeered, taunting him into action. He sauntered over, hands thrust deep in his jean pockets, to where I stood with my giggling group of friends.

John bummed a cigarette off my friend, Bev Simpson, glancing at me as he did this. His presence sparked a current of electricity amongst our group; we couldn't believe that this good looking older guy was speaking to us. Our nervous giggles intensified and he grew uncertain and

64

embarrassed. He was too adorable. He continued to peek at me from under his bangs. I resisted the urge to brush the hair across his forehead with my fingers. I sensed that underneath his tough boy stance lay a sweetness he tried to hide. I wanted to draw it out of him. In that moment I knew for the first time I was capable of doing just that.

I boldly reached up and took the lit cigarette out of his mouth and put it in my own. John couldn't pull his eyes away from me. A slow smile spread across his face. I took a deep inhale and immediately started gagging and sputtering.

"Are you ok?" he asked with a teasing smile.

Now I was really coughing. I had no idea how foul cigarettes were. I nodded my head. "Sorry," I said, when I could talk. My girlfriends were laughing. "I don't really smoke."

"You don't say," he said taking back his cigarette and drawing on it.

I studied his face behind the cloud of smoke. "What's your name?" I asked him.

"John."

I gasped. His name started with a "J". Just like the old Indian said it would.

"What's the matter?"

"Nothing. I like your name, that's all. I'm Natalie."

"I know." I was astonished. "You just moved into the farmhouse by the quarter mile right?"

More astonishment. "Yeah."

"Well, good. Maybe I'll see you around some time, Natalie." And he left to join his friends.

I let out my breath.

"He likes you," said Bev. I heard the new respect and approval in her voice. I smiled, and as John walked away, I remembered what the fortune teller had told me, and knew it was my fate to be with John.

It was during our last REBOS New Year's party in our old house in the city, and Father thought it would be a good idea to not only help sober up his friends from the previous night's celebration, but offer them a chance to start the New Year by having their fortunes told. He drove an old Indian Chief from a boarding house he found somewhere in the dregs of downtown Toronto to our house in the suburbs to read his family's and friends' fortunes.

Mom had always let it be known that she felt sorry for the North American Indians, but I had never seen a real Indian before. The Chief had a thick-lined bronze face, no front teeth, wore a plaid shirt and a flimsy felt cowboy hat stuck with a single black feather. He also had a fake leg that stuck out straight when he sat down until he pressed a button on his hip and then the leg swung down at a ninety degree angle to the floor. I thought this must be a trick or some kind of black magic, and kept my eye on him. My parents set him upstairs in Paul's bedroom with our card table and two chairs facing each other. Those who wanted to know what their future looked like according to the Chief (and who didn't mind paying) took turns going up to have their readings done.

Toward the end of the day I got my turn. He read my cards and told me I was determined and destined to follow my heart. He also said that a male with the initial "J" would play a significant role in my future.

John was waiting by my locker after school the next day. I was excited and nervous to see him there. I opened my locker and grabbed my gym bag.

"I have a volleyball practice now," I said. He looked disappointed. "But I don't think I'm going to go," I said.

"Are you sure? Cause it doesn't matter. I mean, you should go."

"Do you want me to go?" I said, grinning at him.

He smiled back at me. I melted. "Come on. Let's go get somethin' to eat," he said. He held out his hand, and I took it, and we walked outside.

We walked to the *Coffee Corner* and ordered fries and cokes. We didn't say much at first, but I was happy to be sitting at the little table with John sharing fries with him. The disco beat of *Macho Man* echoed from the transistor radio behind the counter. When there were only a few fries left, John lit up a cigarette. Remembering my coughing fit earlier, I blushed.

"That was your first time smokin', eh?" he asked.

I nodded. "It's awful at first," he admitted. "You have to keep tryin' fer a while and then you'll be hooked."

"That's what I'm afraid of," I said.

"What do you mean?"

"I think I could easily become addicted to something that I have no control over."

"Not me. I don't ever want to feel I'm bein' controlled by anythin'. Or anyone. My old man is always tryin' to control me. Wants me to hurry up and finish school so's I can start drivin' with him."

"Driving?"

"His truck. An eighteen wheeler. Real beauty. Silly bugger, he's so damn proud of that truck. He's always washin' and polishin' it like it was a bloody shrine. Mom says it's his own personal religion. My ole man said he can't wait until he teaches me to drive it."

I was learning John liked to talk. You just had to find the right topic. "You're lucky your father wants to share something he loves so much with you," I said.

"Yeah, I guess so. I don't know." He had pulled a pencil from his jacket pocket and doodled on a napkin. "The thing is I don't know if I really want to drive a truck. All those hours sittin' behind a steerin' wheel."

"What would you like to do if you could do anything?" I asked.

He looked at me deciding if he could trust me. "Do you have any paper?"

Curious, I removed a piece of paper from a binder in my backpack. Gently, he reached over the table and tilted my chin. Satisfied with the position, he began to draw, squinting at me in concentration. I watched from the corner of my eye careful not to interrupt. Several minutes later, he put the pencil down, turned the paper to face me, and sat back in his chair.

It was me. He had drawn me with my head cocked, lips parted lightly in a dimpled grin, and eyes sparkling. I felt powerful knowing this was how he saw me. For the first time, someone saw me as more than a mere child.

"That's amazing."

"I'm terrible."

"No, you're really good, John."

"Really?"

I placed the drawing carefully into my binder.

John pulled on his cigarette and I could see he was pleased. "Come on, I'll walk you back," he said.

We went back to school to catch the "late" school buses for students who stayed late for extra-curricular activities. Standing outside my bus, John slipped his arm around my shoulders and let it gently slide down my back and across my hips before he said goodbye. I thought for an agonizing moment he was going to kiss me in front of the kids on the bus and the bus driver, but at the last minute he just gently caressed my lips with his finger and walked away.

After dinner that night, John called to see if I wanted to go to the movies with him on Friday night. He asked if I had seen *Jaws*. My heart was pounding when I said I hadn't. I tried to sound blasé, as if I was used to going on dates, and asked if he was going to meet me there. While we were talking, I looked over my shoulder to see if anyone was listening. I didn't want anyone to know about John. I guess I already knew they wouldn't approve. Our phone was located in a quiet part of the house, at the bottom of the staircase near the rarely-used front door. No one was around, but I whispered anyway, and John did too. It was as if our plans would be jeopardized if we were overheard. Already we were behaving like fellow conspirators guilty of what exactly we weren't certain, but attracted and united by secrecy.

CHAPTER TWELVE

Belonging

 Cindy

I hadn't made any new friends at school. At least none I wanted to hang out with. The worst time was the period between the school bus dropping me off at school and before classes started. For over half an hour, I had no one to hang out with and nothing to do. Within two weeks of starting our new school, Christine and Natalie had made friends of their own, which left me alone.

There was one girl who wanted to be my best friend - Brenda Potts. Short, chubby and disheveled, Brenda latched onto me from the second day of classes. By the third day, she asked me to a sleepover on Friday night. I was thrilled to have made a new friend so quickly. A week later, I was seriously wondering how to get rid of her. She irritated me with her non-stop chatter about things like her mother's new French provincial mail-order living room suite. She wore cherry red tartan jumpers over frilly white long-sleeve shirts. The frills on her cuffs and all the way down her collar were constantly stained from her last meal. It's not that she got up in the morning and put on dirty clothes - I know her mother did her laundry - but within minutes, food would ultimately find its way dribbled across her clean garments. It got to the point where I could tell what she had for breakfast by reading her collar and cuffs.

Brenda was the kind of girl who, unbeknownst to her, came out of the school washroom with her skirt tucked up at the back into her pantyhose showing everyone her underpants as she walked down the hall. I now understood why she didn't seem to have any other friends. I felt sorry for her.

Brenda lived in town and didn't take a bus to school, which left me alone between 8:30 am and 9:00 am Monday through Friday. I pretended I had a destination as I roamed the halls waiting for the bell to ring. I made the circuit past the glass display case of rugby and track and field trophies (never football, long before I attended, the school had banned football after a student was killed playing on the school team). I tread quickly past the occupational wing where the "Occs" were segregated to learn trades such as auto mechanics and hairdressing; through the bright new wing dedicated to the seniors whose lockers captured the sunlight streaming in from long south-facing windows designed to keep the sleepiest students awake; past the interior courtyard of the smoke pit, the cafeteria, the gymnasium, and finally around to the library. The library was my last stop and I ducked inside, grateful to have a refuge. Here, I would dig into my books to look busy.

Before long, Brenda started to come to school earlier so she could walk with me. Now as I circled the school's interior, I had Brenda just slightly behind my right shoulder, taking two little baby steps on her short, pudgy legs to every one stride of mine. As we traipsed the halls, she fell just out of my field of vision; that way I could pretend she wasn't there if she bothered me. Most of the time I was torn, I didn't know which was worse, being lonely or having someone stuck to me who I didn't like. I ignored her a lot, but she didn't get the message. She continued to hang around me until after Christmas when she moved away to Hamilton. I told myself I didn't need to have friends in Orangeville and waited for the weekends to arrive when I could flee the lame town.

Meanwhile, Natalie had hooked up with John. As soon as she got off the bus each morning he was there waiting for her. John was tall with slender hips and rounded shoulders that remained slightly hunched over, like he had grown too fast and had never gotten used to his height. He wore a black leather jacket and had long hair that hooded his eyes. He never looked at me full on, which made it hard to trust him. But Natalie was lucky. She had a boyfriend.

Natalie

It was late September and the leaves had turned to brilliant shades of orange, red and yellow, when John and I wandered together in the school yard during lunch. Legs glued together, John's long arm stretched across my hips, we ambled to the bank of grass behind the school. It was an exceptionally warm Indian summer day and being stuck indoors seemed unbearably unfair. The summer-like weather justified our decision to cut class, and we didn't go in when the warning bell announced the end of lunch hour. We plunked down in the short dry grass together getting tangled in each other's legs and arms before we settled with me sitting cross legged in the space between his legs, my back to him.

The final bell sounded, but we ignored it. Everyone had gone inside and we were alone. Although John had already kissed me in the back seat of his friend's car after the movie,

I was still nervous being this close to him. I didn't want my uncertainty to spoil the moment. I leaned back against him and tilted my face to look up into his. I saw he was a little unsure too and this gave me confidence. I brushed his hair from his forehead and smiled at him. He bent his head to mine and I closed my eyes as our lips met. He tasted like cigarettes. I opened my eyes before he pulled his lips from mine and I quickly closed them again. We pulled away from each other. I looked down into my lap and held my breath.

"Turn around," he said. I shuffled around to sit facing him. He gently lifted my chin up and smiled at me. "I love you," he said. I was shocked. He bent his lips toward mine again and I ignored the warning going off in my head: "But you don't even know me!" This time I kissed him back. His tongue parted my lips and pressed against my tongue. I gasped but didn't pull away. We kissed hard and long. When we broke apart I wanted to wipe my wet mouth but didn't think it'd be cool.

John asked me if I liked the kiss and I told him, "What do you think?" as I sat on his lap and wrapped my legs and arms around him. There was no turning back now. I pushed my hips toward his torso inching closer to him.

My body surprised me, it seemed to know what moves to make before my mind instructed it. I was sexy, bold and wild. I was me as I had never experienced me before and I never felt more alive. I was out of control. I was also aware of one part of me observing this new behaviour.

We kissed again and this time John ran his hands up and down my back. Over my bra strap. His fingers went down the gap in my jeans where they stretched over my hips. I leaned away from him and he ran his hands over my jeans and down the zipper. I felt a deep ache in my groin I had never experienced before. I sighed and closed my eyes.

He ran his fingers inside my jeans below the waist of my underpants. My loins pulsated under his touch.

I heard the sound of voices nearby and was suddenly conscious of the time and place. I put my hand on his wrist and opened my eyes. He was smiling at me. He understood that we had gone far enough. I pushed back on my arms, unwrapped my legs from around him and stood up. We walked back into school holding hands already formulating a lie about why we were late for class.

The next day I was eating lunch in the cafeteria with my girlfriends when John walked over and tapped me on the shoulder. He crooked his finger at me for me to come with him. I grabbed my sandwich and followed him to a table in the back corner near the stage. He looked upset.

"What's wrong?" I asked, concerned, taking the seat beside him.

"Nothin'. I just don't want you eatin' with your friends."

I was confused. "Why?"

"Because I want to spend more time with you. You're my girl and I want us to be together. Just you and me."

His girl! The words exploded in my head. I reached for his hand. I thought my heart would burst.

John and I began spending all of our free time together. We didn't share any of the same classes, but hung out together after school while waiting for our separate buses to take us home. At home, we spent long evenings lingering on the phone to each other making plans for the weekend, or dreaming what it would be like when John got his license so we could be together more. John would wait for my bus to arrive in the mornings and we would walk the halls holding hands or go for a smoke in the "pit" before classes started.

At first I only watched John smoke and declined his offers to share his smokes. I was a firm anti-smoker. I hated cigarettes and I had always made a point of speaking out against anyone who smoked in our house. I nagged my grandparents, both pack-a-day smokers since they were my age. When I tried John's cigarette the day I first met him, I was more surprised than anybody. I decided to try it a second time, just to see what all the fuss was about. I told myself that I wouldn't get addicted and could stop at anytime. That I persevered beyond the initial coughing fits and nausea to become someone who actually enjoyed sucking tar and nicotine into my lungs confirmed two things that I had always suspected and feared about myself. Firstly, that I was an addictive person and lacked the will-power to beat a controlling substance; and secondly, that I could fool myself into believing just about anything, no matter what the personal cost.

I got cut from the volleyball team because I missed too many practices to spend time with John. I didn't care. Not really. I had a cute boyfriend who loved me. On our first month anniversary, he bought me a bouquet of long-stemmed roses and told me I was beautiful.

CHAPTER THIRTEEN

Forbidden

Natalie

The first time that John came to the farmhouse we'd been dating for three months. He drove his mother's white Impala down the driveway, left the engine running, and waited for me to come outside. I ran outside, climbed in his car and we drove away. The second time he came to our house to pick me up, my mother stopped me in the kitchen on my way out.

"Ask your friend in, Natalie. I'd like to meet him."

"Do you really have to Mom? We're late."

"It'll just take a minute."

"Next time, I promise."

"Now."

I went to the car and leaned in the window apologetically. "My mom wants to meet you." John groaned. "Please?" He reluctantly turned off the engine and got out of the car. My mother was in the kitchen waiting. As was my father. John stayed at the back door in the mudroom.

"Where is he?" asked my father.

I motioned to the mudroom behind me.

"Ask him in, for Pete's sake," he said.

I showed John into the kitchen. "Mom, Dad, this is John." Mom said hello-nice-to-meet-you, while my father extended his arm in greeting. John shook my father's hand and looked down at the floor.

"So, John, you're at school with Natalie?" asked my father.

"Uh- huh."

"Got to go," I said making for the door.

My parents followed us into the mudroom.

"Is that your car, John?" asked my father.

"My mom's."

"Where are you going?" my mother called as I opened the car door.

"Into town," I threw over my shoulder from the driveway.

"Don't be late."

As we pulled away, my parents watched us through the window in the mudroom. I was certain they were reading the car's bumper stickers: "Keep on Truckin'" and "Truckers go the Distance".

We drove into town turning right onto Broadway at the grand turn-of-the-century house on the corner that had been converted into a funeral parlour. We drove past the cinema, the Royal bank and turned left at the *Coffee Corner*. We took the first left onto Zina Street and drove past the old jail building that now housed the County Court and Supreme Court offices. Parked in front of the Courthouse was *Sam's Catering* truck. The truck advertised:

Sandwiches, Snacks, Hot Coffee, Donuts and More
Delivered Fresh to your Door.

John pulled up to the stop sign, did a sudden u-turn and parked right behind the truck. The driver disappeared into the Courthouse. The upper half of the truck's tailgate was left open. From where we sat, we could see the snacks and light lunches inside.

"I don't know about you, but all of a sudden I'm hungry," John said. "What if I just go grab us some snacks?"

"You're insane. What if you get caught?"

"I'll be quick. Stay here and watch out for the driver."

John got out of the car and sauntered over to the truck. He looked around and then casually leaned over the bottom tailgate and reached inside. He stuffed something under his jacket, and then, looking around to make sure no one was watching, grabbed something else. He walked back to the car and ducked inside.

"What a rush!"

"What'd ya get?"

He emptied his coat and took out a bottle of Coke, a bag of chips, and a donut. "Why don't you go get another Coke?" he asked me.

"Me?" I looked at the Courthouse and up and down the street. No one was around.

"Never mind," he said impatiently. "I'll go."

Before he had his door opened, I was out of the car. I walked over to the back of the truck, reached in and nabbed a bottle from the shelf.

"Hey! What do you think you are doing?" The driver yelled from the walkway. He started running toward me. I ran like hell back to the car and jumped inside. John put on the gas and we took off down the street.

"That was close!" he said looking in the rear view mirror.

"Oh, my God, my heart is racing."

"You're one crazy girl."

"At least I got the Coke," I said laughing.

My grandparents lived in a post-war bungalow on Zina Street near the high school. Our first January in Orangeville, they went to Florida for a month-long vacation. They asked me to collect their mail and newspapers while they were away and gave me a key to their house.

The first week they were gone, I asked John if he would like to come with me at lunchtime to my grandparents' house. We trudged a path through deep snow to the back door. The snowdrift was piled high close to the house allowing the door only a small opening. We squeezed through onto the landing stamping the snow off our boots. I was immediately struck by the suffocating stale air. It was as though the air in the house had been sanitized, deodorized and doused in bleach then rinsed with the smell of my grandmother's breath when she kissed me - mouthwash rinsed over nicotine.

The house was spotless as always. I don't remember ever seeing a dirty dish sit unwashed on the counter, or a bed remain unmade, or the laundry basket nearly full. No untidiness here; the owners were careful to rid the place of anything reminiscent of the messiness of the human condition. Any dirt was removed or swept under the carpet. Any reminders of unpleasantness were hidden away in the back of a cupboard or drawer and forgotten. I made sure to remove my boots at the door.

The kitchen linoleum was freezing under my feet. The house was eerily quiet. As children, our foreign childhood noisiness had pinged off the laminate kitchen dinette and bounced down the stairs to echo in the dark, cavernous basement. Now, with its owners absent, the silence in the house was oppressive. The roof was covered in an insulating coat of snow that dulled outside noises. The windows were shut tight, their heavy drapes drawn together, barricading the fresh outdoors. Truth was, even when my grandparents were home, it was a vacant, lifeless house, devoid of warmth and love.

There was little evidence to indicate the house was lived in at all. I collected the mail and paper from the mailbox and relocked the front door. I wiped my finger along the top of the large wooden console in the foyer enjoying the streak left behind in the light covering of dust. My grandmother wouldn't approve. I lifted the lid of the stereo. My mother had told me my grandfather loved to listen to opera music and had played it all the time when she was a little girl. I couldn't remember hearing music in this house and wondered if my grandfather still listened to it.

John had come into the kitchen and was watching me, his arms folded across his chest, head tilted to the right, brows knotted. "What are you thinkin' about?" he said.

I closed the lid carefully. "I was just thinking about my grandparents. I wonder how they ended up with each other. How they stayed together so long."

I brought the mail into the kitchen and laid it on the table. I removed my coat and hung it on the back of the kitchen chair.

"It's freezing in here. I'm going to put on the kettle," I said. As I filled the kettle from the tap I looked out the kitchen window over the sink. The backyard was a smooth block of snow and ice, unmarred by any leftover trace of a terrace or garden, unstained by any sign of human touch. Then I noticed the lone tree at the back of the yard sticking out of the snow like an oasis in the desert. It waved to me like an old friend, and I remembered an afternoon when I was a little girl and had spent a few days visiting with my grandparents on my own.

I was in their backyard and I was bored. I saw the plum tree at the back of the lawn heavy with plump purple plums. I slunk toward the tree and the sweet smell of ripe fruit was so strong it stung my nose. My grandmother's words rang in my head: "You can play out in the back yard, but don't touch the plums!" I looked back at the house, but seeing no one there, reached up on tiptoes and brushed the forbidden fruit with my fingers. If I stretched as long as I could, I could cup the lowest one in my hand. I marveled at the purple black skin. Carefully, I twisted it around to check out all sides. It spun off its stem and landed with a little plop in my hand. The crow in the tree behind the lane cawed angrily at me and I quickly checked the back door expecting to see my grandmother charging toward me.

I leaned my back against the trunk of the tree away from the house and inspected the plum. It was perfect, no wormholes. I was heady with excitement and desire. I bit into the flesh trembling with anticipation, the thin skin easily tearing away and the slimy purple-veined fruit trying to escape. The juice squirted down my chin, sticky and delicious. I ate the flesh and then clenched the pit between my teeth. I couldn't quite close my lips around the large pit and I half sucked half chewed it, saliva escaping out the corners of my mouth. I was content. Until I remembered Michael telling me inside the pit there was a poisonous nut. I spit it out and wiped my mouth with the back of my hand.

I went to the garage attached to the house. It was dark and chilly inside. Everything was in its place. I found what I was looking for and returned to the glaring sunshine. I dug a hole in the earth with my grandmother's trowel and dropped the plum pit into it. I buried my treasure, watered the dirt and said a prayer that it would grow into a plum tree. But it never did. I still felt a vague disappointment that the pit didn't grow.

The kettle whistled, loud and shrill. I turned off the stove and poured the boiling water into the teapot. I put out two mugs on the cold dinette table where my grandmother routinely ate her lonely breakfast of half a grapefruit with a startling red cherry on top. "Come on," I said to John, my voice echoing in the sterile room. "I'll show you around."

We walked down the narrow hall. "This is my grandfather's room." The room was furnished with heavy, dark mahogany headboard and footboard, matching nightstand and chest of drawers. The air was stale with the smell of cigarettes, the only clue to the room's owner.

Across from my grandfather's bedroom was the lilac bathroom, the tiled floor, walls, tub, sink, and toilet all lilac. This room still contained a hint of Nana's lavender soap. As a little girl, I had watched my grandmother put on her makeup in this room leaning over the sink toward the mirrored cabinet and spreading her lips wide as she applied deep red lipstick to her pretty face.

"And this is my Nana's room," I said as I led the way to the end of the bungalow. This room was also furnished with somber heavy pieces and smelled of tobacco. We stood in the doorway.

"Why do your grandparents have separate bedrooms?" John asked.

"Mom says Nana thinks sex is dirty. Apparently, she won't let my grandfather near her. I heard Grampa once complain to my dad about Nana cutting him off." I leaned into the doorframe and cocked my head coyly. "I think my grandmother would like sex," I said. "Only not with my Grampa."

"Too bad," he said. "And what about you?"

"Oh, I don't think I would like it with my Grampa either," I smirked.

"Funny." Then he added, "How about with me?" and he put his mouth to mine.

We kissed as John pressed his body against me. He worked his hand up under my shirt and cupped my breast. He ran his thumb over my bra tickling my nipple. A flash of fire and longing pierced my body and ran deep between my legs. Still kissing, we moved further into the room toward the bed. I peeled off his coat. John pushed me gently down before he fell on top of me. He undid the buttons on my shirt and ran his fingers down between my breasts until my belly button. I wanted him. I rolled over and sat up undoing my bra and lay back down pulling him on me. He tasted like forbidden fruit. We made love for the first time during our lunch hour on my grandmother's bed.

CHAPTER FOURTEEN

Accidents

Cindy

I had no idea what Natalie was up to. I wasn't around much. For the first several months we lived in Orangeville I went to Toronto every weekend to take dance lessons. I boarded a Greyhound bus every Friday afternoon at 3:15 from the corner of Broadway and First bound for the main bus depot at Bay and Dundas in downtown Toronto. I took the subway to the foot of Yonge Street at Front Street before climbing eight flights of stairs (our dance warm-up) to the top floor of a tired, old building which housed the Lois Smith School of Dance. Lois Smith was Canada's first prima donna ballerina and I had been taking classes at her school for more than four years. The previous year I had been invited to be part of her select performing group. I trained until 9:30 p.m. when I hopped back on the subway this time heading north to the end of the line where I spent the night with my Aunt Heather who lived in a two bedroom apartment beside the 401. On Saturday mornings, I retraced my steps, took three more dance classes, then boarded a bus back to Orangeville.

My weekends in the city prevented me from developing a social life in Orangeville, and took me away from my family. After Christmas, the O.D.S.S. music and drama departments announced the school was going to put on the musical, *The Wizard of Oz*. I auditioned and was cast as Dorothy. The rehearsal schedule conflicted with my weekend dance trips to the city. I figured that I was probably never going to be a dancer anyway, and stopped going to dance classes to be in the play.

I had also stopped going to modeling auditions in Toronto. Soon after the Levis ad was published in the *Star*, I got an audition for a televison commercial for Kotex. I had to be downtown Toronto for 11:30 am on a Wednesday. My parents couldn't drive me but Dad had a solution. "David can take you," he said. David made the deliveries for Darwen Office Supply. Dad said David was going to Toronto that morning and could take me with him in the van.

When Wednesday came, I climbed into the passenger side of the company van at 9:30 am and we pulled away. We had a full two hours to get to my downtown destination, which should have been plenty of time. I'd never met David before. He was only a couple of years older than me and didn't say a word to me the whole trip. We were on the road for about twenty minutes when he pulled off the highway to make a delivery while I waited in the van. We resumed heading south but shortly after David made another stop. Now it was 10:30 am and we were only approaching Brampton. I checked my hair and makeup in my pocket mirror. I had taken extra care with my makeup that morning applying the techniques I'd learned at modeling school. I reapplied my lipstick and wondered if I had what they were looking for.

When David climbed back into the van, I wanted to ask him how many more stops he had and remind him of my appointment, but I was too shy to speak up. I sat stiffly beside him willing him to hurry up. In the end, David made two more stops before he finally dropped me off downtown Toronto near the address of my audition. I raced out the van muttering a curt "thanks" before slamming the door. By the time I found the building and ran up the stairs my heart was beating frantically in my chest and my underarms were wet with sweat. It was noon.

"You're late," said the receptionist. "You've missed them."

I was devastated. Just then a woman popped her head outside the audition room door and saw me. "We're done here," she said. She saw my disappointment. "We were just about to break for lunch," she said uncertainly. "Oh, well, why don't you come in now that you are here."

Although they were kind enough to see me, I didn't get the job. I appreciated that the competition was fierce and I had to go on many auditions before I could expect to land something, but the next time I got a call for an audition I passed. It was just too difficult to get there. After a while, the agency stopped calling.

I met Geoff in the spring at the cast party for *Wizard of Oz*. He was on the lighting crew. I'd seen him before on the rugby team. The first thing he said to me was, "Do you know you have a run in your pantyhose?"

"How rude is he?" I thought, but I had also never met someone who paid such close attention to me before. I was flattered someone would care so much.

The next day at school, he came by my locker and asked me if I wanted to go roller skating with him on Friday night.

Friday came and my mother invited a co-worker, her boss's daughter, Wendy Harkness, over for dinner. My mother had been doing alterations from home for

Harkness Women's Clothing on Broadway. During this time, she also worked part-time in the store selling fabric. Norm Harkness had been dressing the women of the area for two generations. His store was located in one of the oldest buildings on the main street. It was a dank, musty-smelling place that slanted down toward the sidewalk in the front so that you had to walk an uphill slope to reach the change rooms at the back. The floors were the original hardwood that sagged and squeaked when you walked on them.

Wendy was in her early twenties and grew up in Orangeville. She knew just about everyone. When I announced at dinner that I was going out with Geoff Graves that night, she choked on her mouthful of steak and kidney pie. When she thought no one was listening, Wendy leaned into my ear at the table and said, "Be careful, Geoff Graves has a reputation for reckless driving. He's rolled a car!"

"I heard," I whispered back. "As a matter of fact, he rolled another one this afternoon."

"No way! You aren't still going to go out with him are you?" she exclaimed, looking afraid.

"It was an accident," I said, wondering what all the fuss was about.

It was true. Geoff had rolled his mother's car earlier that same day, on a dirt road, navigating a tight turn. Thank God for the recent seat belt legislation introduced the previous January making seat belts mandatory. Geoff and his friend had been wearing their seat belts when they ended up hanging upside down. Luckily, they weren't hurt.

When Geoff drove in to pick me up later that evening, he was the passenger of a friend's car. My mother watched from the living room window as Geoff, wearing a yellow and green striped rugby shirt and crisp white painter pants, got out of the car and knocked on the back door. Before I left, I heard my mother exclaim, "But he's got red hair!"

I climbed into the back seat with Geoff. The driver and front seat passenger were two guys I recognized from school. We pulled away and one of them lit a joint. Geoff took a toke and then offered it to me. My first reaction was to refuse, I had never tried pot before. But when it got passed to me a second time, I changed my mind and inhaled my first joint.

Soon Geoff and I were walking the halls together and, by the end of the school year in June, we were dating. Through Geoff I gained acceptance into a circle of friends that otherwise would have remained impenetrable. They were the popular kids who I had previously only envied and observed from a distance. Now, I found myself part of their group and, miraculously, before long I began to feel living in Orangeville wasn't so bad after all.

For the first time in six years my sisters and I found ourselves attending the same school together, but we never hung out (at least not since the first week when we didn't know anyone else and having lunch with our siblings was better, barely, than eating alone). Like many sisters, we ran in different social circles and only spoke to one another if we happened to pass each other in the hall. We slept, ate and did our homework in the same house, boarded the same school bus to and from school every day, but we went about our teenage lives focused on our own self-absorbed worlds.

I rarely saw Natalie at school and I barely knew her boyfriend. I was too wrapped up in my own life to spend much time thinking about my little sister's. I still thought of her as a young tomboy. At fourteen, Natalie continued to dress in the tomboy role, she wore jeans or denim overalls, little make-up, and her dark brown hair in a pixie cut. She was still cute as a button; however, if I had looked closer, I would have noticed she was no longer Daddy's little girl.

Natalie

While I was housesitting for my grandparents when they were in Florida, I had a key cut to their house. When they were back in town, they were both working and, conveniently for John and me, not home five days a week, from nine in the morning to six o'clock at night. Inadvertently, my grandparents had offered John and me the perfect place to make out. We used that key a lot.

By April I suspected I might be pregnant. My periods had never been regular so at first I wasn't concerned, but after a few weeks I felt nauseous and my breasts were tender and sore. I could no longer ignore the signs. I confided in Bev. Bev was a year and a half older than me and I trusted her advice. She said it sounded like I was pregnant for sure, but we needed to have it confirmed by the pharmacist. I didn't like the idea of going to the local pharmacy and risk being identified, so Bev offered to drive me to the city of Brampton.

Brampton was a forty five minute drive straight south along Highway 10. I felt my ears pop as we descended the Caledon hills. I placed my hand over my churning stomach to calm it, careful not to spill my urine sample which threatened to splash over the brim whenever the Pinto hit a bump or braked. I stared at the braided friendship bracelet Bev had given me. I hadn't taken it off since she made it for me last year.

By the time we reached Brampton, my stomach was in knots and my armpits were damp with sweat. Brampton was a flat, flavourless city of row after row of identical brick subdivisions, nondescript plazas and sprawling malls. Bev parked her Pinto in the mall parking lot and we dropped off my sample. The pharmacist said it would take a couple of hours. We poked around the mall killing time while I tried not to think beyond getting my results.

My heart was racing as we returned to the pharmacy.

"Positive," the pharmacist told me.

"Are you sure?" I said, feeling the colour drain from me.

"Oh, yes. This one was definitely positive."

My test was positive. I backed away from the counter in shock.

Bev led me outside to the parking lot. I felt lightheaded and she had me sit on the curb with my head between my legs. She sat down beside me and put her arm around me.

"It's going to be all right," she said. "I know a girl who had one and she is fine now".

Had one what? I thought. A baby? Or, ... I couldn't bring myself to think of the alternative. I felt numb. I asked Bev to take me home.

I didn't know what I was going to do. Bev drove me back up north, up the hills that separated our town from our southern neighbours. The closer we got to home, the more things seemed different. The world outside my window had changed. We drove by a familiar landmark, the famous Reversing Hill. Was it optical illusion or powerful magnetic force? I never knew which, but if you drive onto a one lane gravel road off the highway at the bottom of the great hill leading into Orangeville, put your car into neutral facing uphill, you will actually feel yourself being pulled uphill to the top of the road. It is a strange and eerie feeling to be pulled by an invisible presence like that.

By the time we crested the last hill and dipped down into the town, I knew my life had taken a new course. The thought of going home to my family terrified me. My parents would never understand. They would be angry, appalled and disappointed; never accepting. It was obvious they didn't really like John. If I told them, they would never trust him again. They would try to stop me from seeing him. I could no longer stop seeing John than I could prevent a powerful magnet pulling a car uphill. I didn't know what was in store for me, but I felt pulled in one direction and knew where I was headed. I needed to be with John.

Bev dropped me at home. Inside I found Cindy stretched out in a wide straddle on the living room rug, chest, arms and head lying flat on the floor. Dramatic lyrics from some Broadway musical filled the room. It was a familiar sight, my sister stretching, but this time seeing her like that somehow really irritated me. She lifted her head from the floor when I came into the room. "Hey, you don't look too good. What's wrong?" she said.

For a second I thought I would blurt it out, but decided against it. These things didn't happen to our family. Besides, she couldn't possibly know what to do. "Nothing," I said.

I went to the phone under the stairs and called John. Fred the cat appeared and wrapped herself around my ankles, purring. I picked her up and held her close.

"I'm pregnant, John."

After a long pause he said, "I think I need to smoke a joint." Once we talked it over and he'd had a chance to get over his initial shock, John said he was happy about the baby. He said he would look after me and the baby. I told him I wasn't sure. I hadn't made up my mind yet.

"What do you mean, what is there to make up your mind about? We are havin' this baby, Nat. I love you," he said.

CHAPTER FIFTEEN

Telling

 Natalie

We knew we were going to have to tell our parents. During those first few weeks, I prayed my mother would know by just looking at me so I wouldn't have to tell her. I thought maybe I would look different somehow, like the heroines in the romantic history novels I liked to read whose indiscretions were exposed early on by subtle yet profound changes in their physical appearance and demeanour. In these stories, close observers were on hand who recognized the signs and revealed the truth. I hoped my mother's intuition would not let her down now so that I wouldn't have to be the one to broach the subject. But although she had been pregnant five times, and was always telling us she was psychic, my mother never noticed anything different about me, or at least never said if she did.

I thought about telling her all the time, practicing my lines in my head, changing the setting but maintaining the script:

"Mom, Dad, John and I have something to tell you. We are pregnant. We are going to have a baby. Yes, I know we are young, but this doesn't mean we can't make it work. Mom, don't be sad. We love each other. John wants this baby as much as I do. You can either be happy for us or not, but you can't make us change our minds."

John offered to be with me when I told my father. I think he wanted to do the right thing and be up front so that my father would know he loved me and he would take care of me and the baby.

It was a grey Saturday afternoon in May. John and I stood on the driveway looking nervously toward the back fields. The heavy sky sunk low over the barn pulling it down toward the earth. Its rotten roof and crumbling walls were thrown into sharp focus highlighting the structure's decay. I realized the barn was in serious decline and at danger of falling into the ground. I shivered and linked my arm through John's, leading him toward the barn.

We found my father in the shadow behind the barn whistling a ditty and digging holes for a fence he was building around his cows' pasture. If he was surprised to see us, he didn't let on. He just sighed, "Mother, Mother McGee," then turned back to his digging and whistling. My father was fond of that expression and other inane phrases that often revealed he was lost in thought, or at least, wanted those around him to think he was. He must have known something was up though because normally we would never intentionally seek him out.

John had only been over to our house a handful of times when he had picked me up in his mother's car. He was shy and awkward around my father. A couple of times my father had asked John to come into the living room instead of standing outside at the back door waiting for me, but their conversations had been tense and stunted. I knew he didn't like my boyfriend, but I couldn't understand why. On this particular day, the fact that John and I sought out my father's attention would have been cause enough for suspicion. Still, he didn't make it any easier on us. My knees shook as I stood there watching my father and waiting for someone to say something.

When Dad saw that John and I intended to hang around, he gruffly asked John to grab a shovel and make himself useful. Each time John heaved dirt over his shoulder, I prayed for my boyfriend to speak, and each time he dug again into the earth, I was disappointed. He couldn't bring himself to tell my father and, watching him struggle, neither could I. The lines I had run over and over in my head seemed whimsical now even to me. I cursed my father for not helping us out.

Dad stopped digging and looked at the cows lying down in the adjacent pasture.

"Storm's coming," he said.

He looked at John in expectation, clearly waiting for him to say what was on his mind. But John couldn't muster up the courage to tell him. Dad sized John up and down, nodding his head slightly to himself in a "I thought so" kind of way, as if our silence confirmed what he had always suspected to be true. He shrugged his shoulders in resignation and resumed digging, now humming a little tune under his breath. My father never asked what was on our minds, and we never told him.

I lay awake in my bed in the attic deciding how to tell her, watching the lights from the cars on the highway below bounce off the sloped walls. Too many nights I had lain awake like this trying to summon the courage to tell Christine in the bed beside me.

Now, I saw myself as a little girl of eight or nine years old standing on the diving board, big toes wrapped around the edge, arms locked by my ears, thumbs hooked together over my head, trembling with fear. We had been at this for days.

"Come on, Pepper," said Dad treading water in the deep end. He was losing his patience. "Just go!"

I stood there, knees shaking, teeth chattering, frozen in place.

"If you don't go, I'm getting out. Now just point your head down and go. Come on, I'm right here."

I was petrified. I didn't want to give up. I didn't want to disappoint him. Finally, I took the plunge and dove in, head first. My first dive. When I came up for air, my father was right there to catch me.

I had decided she was the one in my family I could tell. I was also secretly hoping she would tell our parents.

"Chris," I said to her back in the dark. "Chris, I'm pregnant," I blurted.

"Oh, Nat!" she cried. She paused. "How do you know?"

"I took in a urine sample."

"Oh, my God," she said sitting up. "How... How far along are you?"

"I'm not sure. I haven't had my period for a while."

"When was the last time?"

"January. Early January."

"Oh, my God, Natalie. We need to tell Mom and Dad right away."

"I can't. I've tried but I can't."

Chris came over to my bed and sat down. She rested her hand on my shoulder. "What are you going to do, Natalie?"

"I don't know," I said and I let her hold me as I started to cry. "Chris, I'm so scared."

Chris told my parents I was pregnant, like I knew she would, and right away my mother made an appointment with her gynecologist in Toronto. She told the doctor I needed an abortion. The doctor said we would have to act fast.

CHAPTER SIXTEEN

Pain

Natalie

There was no discussion. My mother did not care to consult with me. She took control of the situation from the start and decided I was going to have an abortion. I went along with it. She seemed so sure. A part of me was glad to have someone lead me by the hand and make the decision for me. It didn't appear to be a difficult decision for my mother to make. The way she saw it, I was only fourteen, a child myself. She had no interest in raising another child.

A couple of days later, Mom drove me to Women's College Hospital in downtown Toronto. Once I was admitted, she said she would see me tomorrow and left me. I was prepped, wheeled into surgery and given a general anaesthetic.

When I came to, I was delivered into a ward with four beds two of which were occupied. I was given the bed beside a skinny pale girl who was reading a *Seventeen* magazine. She watched the nurse settle me into bed. When the nurse left she said, "Be sure to ask for more Demerol. You're going to need it when the painkiller wears off in a few hours," she said to me.

"Thanks," I said weakly. I felt nauseous and sore.

"Uh-huh. Don't worry. By this time tomorrow the cramps will die down and you'll be watching Mary Tyler Moore and eating pepperoni pizza. I'm Lizzie, by the way. And the girl over there is April," she said pointing to the bed across from me. April was staring out the window and didn't respond.

"I'm Natalie," I said.

"This your first time?" Lizzie asked.

"Yes."

"Thought so. The first time's the worst. After that it's a walk in the park."

"You've been through this more than once?" I asked in amazement.

"Yep. Twice as lucky!" she said removing a cigarette from a carton and putting it between her lips. "It's really no big deal. But April takes the cake. It's her third time right, Ape?" said Lizzie grinning at the chunky girl in the bed by the window.

"Fuck off, Elizabeth," said April.

"Don't pay any attention to her. She's just cranky 'cause her boyfriend didn't show up this afternoon."

"Are you supposed to be smoking in here?" I asked Lizzie, astonished at her gutsiness.

"Who cares. What are they going to do - kick me out?"

The tobacco smoke increased my nausea. I had quit when I read a newspaper article that said smoking could be harmful to the fetus. Now I couldn't stand the smell.

"Is your boyfriend coming?" asked Lizzie.

"What? Here?" I said, mortified. "Oh, no. I don't want any visitors."

"Uh-huh," she said in a way that told me she didn't believe me. "He knows you got rid of it, right?"

I had not been able to tell John before I left. I wasn't looking forward to breaking the news to him. I knew how much he wanted the baby. "I plan on telling him as soon as I get home," I answered.

"He'll be fine with it. Guys don't have any clue what we girls have to go through. They leave all the details up to us."

I turned over letting Lizzie know that I was done talking. I lay on my side mulling over what she had said. I hoped John would understand, but I wasn't so sure.

The next afternoon Mom arrived angry and annoyed. She said the doctor said I could leave and helped me dress and pack my things in silence, filling my overnight bag with an abrupt efficiency that reflected her irritation.

On the way home we barely said a word to each other. The tension in the car was painful. I turned the radio on. My mother finally seemed to realize I was there as she turned the music down and looked over at me.

"Natalie, I know I must seem cold and callous to you, but I hope you understand I did this for your own good. And for the child. I know what it is like to come into this world and not be wanted. I *know* what it is like to be lonely and alone. There is nothing worse."

I noticed then her hands on the steering wheel. They were red and scaly and sore. With remorse, I realized her eczema had returned.

"I couldn't wish that pain on anybody," she said.

I stared out the window. I knew her parents had never given her enough love. I thought of the time when I was little and playing tag with my sisters and brothers outside the front of our house. It was a warm summer evening. My father stepped off the covered verandah and started pulling weeds out of the lawn. I ran over and jumped on his back. He stood up and I held on tightly to his neck. He started running around the lawn and I screamed with delight. I slipped off and ran through the grass barefoot. My father chased me making big animal sounds.

I saw my mother smiling at us from the verandah. I ran up to her to catch my breath and because I wanted to include her in our fun. She watched her husband who was now chasing his children around the lawn and said, "You kids are so lucky you have a father who plays with you." Her words made me wonder about those kids whose fathers didn't play with them. If we were so lucky, why did my mother sound so sad?

Mom had never known a father's love. Russell came into her life when she was four but he never learned how to be a father to her or how to handle her when she was young. Whenever she spoke out of turn or got in the way, which was often, he beat her and sent her to her room. He was still beating her with his belt when she was twelve years old. My mother said she endured endless hours as a child alone in her little bedroom, her constant punishment. It was during these lonely hours that she discovered her love of singing. She found singing eased the pain and helped while away the time.

It was a lesson she shared with us. As young children my mother always led us in song whenever we had to walk anywhere. We did a lot of walking because we didn't have a car. With four children under the age of seven, a trip to the grocery store, or doctor, or library was no small event. Mom pushed Natalie in the stroller while encouraging the rest of us to keep going by singing to us. She said singing was often the only way she got us to our destination. She understood better than anyone the power of singing to lighten the load and pass the time. Singing had gotten her through her own difficult childhood, and she used its restorative magic to ease our journeys and take our minds off our tired marching feet.

I realized Nana Helen was a distant mother and my mother grew up feeling unwanted. I knew my mother felt unloved as a child, but I thought in my case she had made a mistake. My baby might have been wanted.

When we pulled into our driveway, my father was cutting the grass. He looked up at us, his mouth falling slack as though we had surprised him with our return, like he hadn't expected us back. But he didn't miss a step pushing the lawnmower. My mother parked and helped me out of the car. I was weak and dizzy and gratefully let her lead me inside. By the time I climbed the two flights of stairs to my room in the attic, all I wanted to do was collapse. I put on my pajamas, catching my pale reflection in the mirror over the dresser. I trembled with chills as I climbed into bed. The attic stairs groaned as my mother climbed the steep ascent to check on me. She rarely came up here. It was odd but comforting to have her in my room. She handed me a Tylenol and a hot water bottle for the cramps before she left, carefully maneuvering her way back down the complaining staircase.

The familiar whine of the gas powered lawnmower reached the open window. I listened to the comforting sounds rising with intensity as the mower drew near, receding as it fell away. A gentle breeze blew the sweet smell of new mown grass over to my bed. I closed my eyes and took a deep breath. I felt a heavy pulling sensation in my groin. I lay my hands over my empty tummy and the tears that I had held back managed to now squeeze from the corners of my eyes. I ran my hands along my inner thighs and between my legs. My body felt almost back to normal, but I wondered if I would ever be the same again. What had I done?

Finally, the droning of the lawnmower stopped and from below my window I heard my father mutter to himself: "Ho Hum and a bottle of rum!" I pictured him tidying up outside, putting the lawnmower away, and finishing his chores before he came upstairs to talk to me. I waited for the sound of his footsteps on the attic stairs.

It was not cold in the room, but I was shivering and couldn't get warm in my bed. My feet were icy cold. I thought about that first winter we had our pool when my father left the water in to freeze over so we could skate on it. I was so excited to have our very own skating rink in our backyard. Dad always tied my skates. He did them up so tight my feet hurt before I even went outside. But there was no point complaining. He said firmly, "Natalie, they have to be tight". He brought a kitchen chair onto the ice and showed me how to skate behind it and push it along so I could get my skating legs. Michael joined me on the ice with his hockey skates on and slapped his hockey stick around making me nervous. He zigzagged around me for a while, but soon grew bored with the limited ice surface and said he was going to the schoolyard rink to play. I pushed the chair up and down the length of the pool over and over again until Dad said I didn't need it any more and took it away. Soon I was sailing across our pool from end to end on my own. By the time I came back inside and removed my skates I could no longer feel my toes. My father wrapped his big, warm hands around my frozen feet and held them there. They began to prickle and burn. He gently massaged my toes until the pain went away.

I opened my eyes and the room was now grey with the evening shadow. The only sound coming through the window was the passing of a vehicle on the highway below. I had fallen asleep and been in bed for several hours. I had expected my father to want to see me. But he never came.

CHAPTER SEVENTEEN

Loss

 Cindy

My mother said she had something to tell me. Tears were already welling up behind her glasses, but I could never have guessed what she had to say. I was stunned when she told me that Natalie had an abortion a few days ago. I thought she'd been in bed with the flu. I felt foolish for not seeing what was going on around me. I was hurt knowing I had been deliberately excluded, and jealous of Christine who, I discovered, had known for a while and had been the one Natalie had chosen to confide in.

I was ashamed by these selfish thoughts, for making it about me, when I needed to think of Natalie's ordeal. My mother told me she and Natalie had made two trips to the city; the first time to confirm the pregnancy, the second to have the abortion. I wanted to know everything, all the facts, but my mother could barely bring herself to talk about it. She spit out the words quickly from tight lips. I asked her if Dad knew.

"Of course," she said.

"Does Paul?"

"No. He's too young. He doesn't need to know."

"What about Nana?"

"No," she said, her irritability growing. "This is not something we need to discuss with other people, Cindy." She lumped her own mother in this category. She got up from the kitchen table and went to the sink turning her back to me. The conversation was over. I had one more question.

"Mom, how far along was she?"

She started scrubbing the dirty pot in the sink. My question hung in the air. Finally, she said in a whimper, "It was almost too late."

I sat outside reading in the sunshine on our backdoor stoop. Heavy, purple blooms of the adjacent lilac tree spilled onto me bursting with perfume. The back door opened and my mother yelled, "Don't run or you'll hemorrhage!" Her words exploded into the bright outdoors. I put my book down and watched.

Natalie was chasing Paul toward the barn. They were laughing and running, one dark head and one sandy head tilted up toward the sky. A couple of children burning off energy, enjoying the fresh air. As Mom's words reached Natalie, I saw her look over her shoulder at her mother and continue running a few paces. Then, as the words registered, she reluctantly slowed down and stopped.

Paul called to her while he ran ahead, oblivious to why she was no longer in the chase. Natalie took a couple of hesitant jogging steps forward again before she looked back once more toward her mother who shook her head. She gave a couple of kicks at the earth, then turned and walked back to the house, hanging her head. As she reached for the door she caught me looking at her from the porch. Her face flushed red and she scrunched her mouth into an uneasy smile. "Who cares?" she said and went inside.

My father avoided me for several days after I was home from the hospital. I think he was under the impression it was best to leave me alone while my body mended. His silence felt like a punishment. He withdrew from me; not an about turn, but one degree at a time, ever so slightly turning away. He never got angry or upset. He just didn't speak to me directly. Eventually, however, he could no longer avoid me.

One evening after I had been back at school for a couple of days, he waited until the dinner dishes were cleaned and put away and everyone had left the kitchen before he told me he wanted to speak with me.

"I've been thinking about you a lot, Natalie," he said, carefully picking his words. "I want you to know that regardless of your um... problem, well, I'm glad your mother and you dealt with it. I'm just glad you're OK. What I'm saying is, I'm glad you are back to normal."

OK? Normal? His words leapt down my throat, choking me. Is that how I seemed to him? I thought of my day at school, how my teacher sympathetically asked me about the bad flu bug I must have had last week and how I had turned beet red and mumbled that I had been sick but was fine now thank you. I thought I heard everyone talking about me behind my back as I walked down the halls. I felt certain everyone knew but no one said anything.

"Nat," he was saying, "I love you. I don't believe a person can stop loving someone."

I loved him too, but now I was scared. What if he hadn't been able to continue to love me? I hadn't previously considered his love like a commodity he could weigh and withdraw if he found it came at too great a cost. What would I do if he stopped loving me? I felt his disappointment as heavy as his love. How tenuous was his love after all? If I continued to fail him, would his love grow weaker until it surrendered to his increasing dissatisfaction with me?

He asked me if I was still seeing John. I was tempted to lie. But I wanted my father to know that my relationship with John was bigger than what we had just been through and stronger for it. We would last because our love for each other was undying. So I told him the truth.

"Yeah, I'm still seeing him."

Dad digested this information with a slight nodding of his head while he weighed the consequences. "You can see John on Friday and Saturday nights only. Not on school nights," he announced.

"What?" I asked incredulously.

"You heard me."

I couldn't believe it. "Why?"

"It's for your own good. Natalie, you know I have always encouraged you and your sisters and brothers to think for yourselves, to stand up for yourselves. I hope you will remember that now," he lectured.

I understood he was warning me against following John's lead when I knew better. I knew he didn't trust John. I couldn't believe that my father knew better than me what was good for me. I needed to trust myself.

Later that night, when Dad had left to go into town, I crept downstairs and quietly dialed John's number.

"Harry, said I can only see you on weekends," I said.

"That's fucked up."

"Yeah, I know." I watched a house fly land and spin drunkenly on top of the piano near the phone.

"Well, he can't stop us from seein' each other durin' the week. I've seen the way yer ole man looks at me. It makes me so mad. Yer folks tell you all kinds of shit about me when the're the ones who are screwed up." The fly buzzed round and round on its back, trying to right itself. "I don't know what I'd do if I lost you. You're the best thing that has ever happened to me, Natalie."

"I love you."

"I love you too. Listen, will you do me a favour?"

"Anything."

"Whenever yer parents say anythin' about me or us, anythin' at all, you make sure you tell me. OK? It's important."

"OK but why?"

"I need to know what they're sayin' that's why."

"Oh." The fly stopped buzzing.

"I'm afraid they are tryin' to brainwash you against me."

In my mind's eye I can see the two of us walking down the street holding hands. I see us from behind, in silhouette. I am three years old. On my feet are brand new red rain boots. I am skipping along beside my father. He has just taken me shopping for the first time. Just the two of us together. Another first. I look up into my father's face and smile. He melts when he sees my dimples. He squeezes my hand and whistles a little tune.

John said, "I'm just...I...I can't stop thinkin' about it."

I touched the fly with the tip of my finger. It didn't move. "I know. Either can I."

"It's just always there you know?"

I couldn't talk about it. Biting my lip to keep from crying, I turned my hand over and focused on the new blue sapphire ring on my finger. "I love the ring. Thank you again, John." I took a deep breath. "And, don't worry about my parents. We can still meet in town. Now that you've got your own car everything will be great."

CHAPTER EIGHTEEN

Sex

———————————— Cindy ————————————

It would be several years before my mother and I ever discussed Natalie's "situation" again. No one spoke about it in our house. Not that I expected my parents to discuss much of it with me. They belonged to the generation of parents who weren't encouraged to spend a lot of time finding out how their children felt. Dad was raised by his grandparents. His grandfather was a quiet man whose parenting was founded on the 1-2-3 rule of doling out punishment. For example, his Grandad would say it was OK to leave the pasture gate open once.

He'd say, "Harold, that's once."

If Dad did it again, he'd say, "That's twice."

If he did it a third time, he'd look Dad in the eye and say, "Too bad, Son, that's three." Then he would wait until Dad was not expecting it and kick him in the behind hard enough to make sure he wouldn't make the same mistake again.

My parents' style was in line with the "because-I-said-so" school of parenting. Not that pulling rank didn't serve a greater purpose; it certainly enabled my parents to get a lot more stuff done around the house. If there had been an authority on parenting who might have suggested my parents offer their children a reason why they enforced a rule or handed out a punishment, chances are they would have been open to the suggestion; however, first my mother would have to finish the laundry and my father would have to finish the grass.

Debates with their children were something my parents rarely entered into. Sometimes discussions about important issues were overlooked. Like the time I quit dancing in the city. It wasn't until months later when I received my progress report from Lois Smith that the matter came up for discussion.

My mother saw the opened envelope in my hand. "What does it say?" she asked.

"It says she's disappointed I quit. That I had improved and had potential." I was beginning to think I had made a mistake. "Maybe I shouldn't have quit," I said.

"I don't know why you quit in the first place. I never wanted you to."

I felt miserable. We had never discussed it. I hadn't known she cared one way or the other.

A discussion on an issue like birth control was off my parents' radar screen. Not only were they ill-equipped to discuss such matters, there were no expectations on them to do so. It was easiest and accepted to simply avoid communication.

I never spoke to Natalie about either her pregnancy or her abortion during this time. It was as if it didn't happen. I was shocked about Natalie's abortion, but equally surprised that she had slept with her boyfriend. She was fourteen. I was seventeen and still a virgin.

Geoff and I had not gone any further than heavy petting when I found out about Natalie's abortion. Soon after, Geoff and I were sitting on my parents' living room couch kissing. I was uneasy.

"What's wrong?" Geoff asked, pulling on his eyebrow.

"Nat had an abortion," I blurted. This was the first time I said it out loud. Words that had been crashing around in my head, sounded harsh and cruel on my tongue.

Geoff was sympathetic. "Poor Nat. Is she all right?" he asked.

"I think so. I mean she seems OK. We don't talk about it." Geoff put his arms around me. "I'm worried that could happen to me," I admitted.

"That won't happen to us because we won't take any chances," he said. "Cindy, I'm not going to pressure you into doing something you don't want to do. I have no interest in taking any risk whatsoever. When you feel you are ready, you can go on the pill."

"The pill?" I hadn't considered this before.

"That's the safest way."

I needed a prescription for the birth control pill. I wasn't comfortable talking to my mother about it; instead, I decided to seek the advice of Natalie. I suspected she would be able to help me. This conversation would be the closest we came to acknowledging her pregnancy and abortion.

I was in my bedroom and stopped her as she was going up to her room. I told her I had something to ask her. "How do I go on the pill?" I asked abruptly.

She was embarrassed by my assumption. "Why do you think I know how?" she asked, turning her blushing face away. Although we both knew the answer to her question, this was hard for her.

"Nat?" I asked more gently. "Are you on the pill?"

She chewed her fingernails. "Yes," she said. "Don't tell Mom. She doesn't know."

"I won't," I said.

"It was during my follow-up appointment with the doctor. She had finished examining me and Mom and I were leaving when the doctor asked me to step back inside the room - without Mom. She told me that she didn't want to say anything in front of Mom because it would upset her. Then she handed me a prescription already written out. It was for the pill."

"Are you on it?"

"She said to make sure I used it. She's a very wise doctor."

Then my youngest sister told me to make an appointment with our family doctor in town and ask him for a prescription.

It was the first time I made a doctor's appointment on my own. I didn't tell my parents. The doctor recommended to take the pill for three months before having sex as a matter of further precaution, to make sure my body was fully charged with estrogen first.

Dutifully, I took the pill for three months marking the time on my calendar. Geoff spent that summer at a Junior Forest Ranger camp in northern Ontario. I spent a long, lonely summer as a live-in nanny on a farm twenty five miles from our house. After living on the farm all week and spending my days with a nine year old, I couldn't wait for Mom to pick me up on the weekends and take me home. For the first time I found myself excited to be going into town. Mom said she couldn't understand why the mother, who was a nurse but was home for the summer, needed a nanny.

"She only has one child, for Pete's sake. What's the matter with her?"

"The child is a nightmare," I said.

"I knew it," she said. "I always wanted to be a nurse. But nurses don't make good mothers. Our neighbour on Whitman Street was a nurse and look at how her kids turned out."

I couldn't wait for the end of the summer and for Geoff to return. Before he left, he arrived at our house with an unexpected gift in his arms – a seven month old German shepherd. The puppy's owner couldn't keep him and Geoff thought our family might want him. We did. His name was Duke.

The high school gym teacher stood at the front of the classroom. "So, after foreplay, there is the climax," he said, pointing to the top of the rising chalk line on the board. "It is possible for a man and a woman to climax at the same time, but it is very rare. My wife and I have only done this once, and that was on our honeymoon." He smiled fondly at the memory.

I squirmed uncomfortably in my seat thinking about my teacher and his wife. What would she think if she knew we were all intimately acquainted with her sex life? I respected our teacher's honesty, but his comments confused me. I understood their dual-climax was the height of their sexual relationship and a defining moment in their marriage. I realized he was holding it up to us as an example of the ultimate sexual goal, but I also recognized an underlying tension, unavoidable frustration and likely disappointment in living up to this aspiration. The more I discovered about sex, the more complicated it became.

"Now, who knows what stage happens after the climax?" the teacher asked the class leveling off the arc and continuing the chalk line downward.

A boy in the back row who was repeating his year and a year older than the rest of us yelled out: "Clean up!" The class erupted in laughter.

My father had always told his children that when we turned eighteen years old we were old enough to make our own decisions. I had decided that I would lose my virginity on my eighteenth birthday. And I did. Quickly and quietly, without fuss, on the beaten up dog-haired couch in the mudroom while my parents slept upstairs.

CHAPTER NINETEEN

Truth

 Cindy

I had seen the way things were between my father and Natalie's boyfriend. I was home on one of the few nights when John was still coming by the house to pick her up. Mom asked John if he wanted to come inside, meaning past the mudroom, but he wasn't to be persuaded. He preferred to cling to the back door, as though he sensed danger inside. He left a few minutes later with Natalie.

I can't be sure if John ever made it past our kitchen door. I always thought my father didn't like John because he didn't think he was good enough for his daughter. But I couldn't put my finger on why he was so hard on him. My father was usually tolerant and open-minded, willing to accept people at face value. I couldn't believe he didn't like John because he was the son of a truck driver, or because he didn't like the fact he was a small-town boy. It didn't fit. My father would never hold an honest job against anyone, and he himself was raised in the country and appreciated the honesty of country folk. However, he didn't like the boy.

Several months later, he told me what he really thought. We were watching *Charlie's Angels* on TV when Natalie walked through the room and announced over her shoulder she was going out. My father exchanged glances between the television and the window watching his youngest daughter climb into a strange car. We didn't know the driver but recognized John in the back seat. We watched them drive away and then I swallowed and asked my father what he didn't like about John.

"It's not that I don't like him," he said frowning, taken aback by my question.

"But you don't want him to date your daughter, right?" I said.

He considered this at length and eventually said, "What I don't like is that I've invited him into my home, I've been nice to him. But he wasn't man enough to come and talk to me. He didn't have the balls to come and tell me what the situation was."

"He's sixteen" I pleaded. "He's afraid of you."

"Well, I can't help that now can I," he replied. "Am I so hard to talk to? I don't think so."

"Huh!" interjected a voice from the kitchen. My mother had been sewing quietly at the kitchen table. We had forgotten she was there. My father didn't seem to hear her comment as he kept his eyes on the television. From the kitchen we heard the sudden furious whine of the sewing machine. My father continued to stare at the television in silence.

Once I was safely on the pill, Geoff and I had sex whenever and wherever we could. We both still lived at home with our parents and so, out of necessity, became very sly about where we did it. His mother's car was a sure bet, but we also screwed recklessly in his parents' house: in his bedroom while his parents were out, in the basement on the couch with his parents reading upstairs, or on the floor in the bathroom next to the kitchen while his mother prepared dinner. We took chances - doors without locks didn't deter us. A favourite summertime location was on a grassy hilltop in nearby Alton with a view of the valley. Our old barn was another place we did it a lot, the hay providing a ready-made bed. We showed poor judgment and were careless, so when we finally were caught, it should have come as no surprise.

This particular time we used my bed. My parents were out at a Christmas party. We didn't hear them drive in. My mother walked straight into my room without knocking and turned on the harsh overhead light.

"Cindy Carey what are you doing?" she cried.

"Mother just turn out the light and leave," I said, surprisingly calm. My first reaction was more irritation than fearful as Geoff scrambled to cover himself up. My mother walked out of the room and we jumped out of bed and grabbed our clothes. My hands began shaking as I realized what we had done. We would have to face my father downstairs.

"What were you two doing up there?" my father asked angrily as I entered the living room first.

"Making love," I said.

This stopped him. The best tactic with my father was always the truth. His jaw unclenched a little. Geoff now entered the room.

"Well, I think Geoff should leave. I don't think he should come around for a while," he said as if Geoff wasn't there.

Geoff headed off for the back door. He told me in a voice loud enough for my father to hear that he would call me tomorrow. Following this bravado he left.

My parents were waiting for me in the living room. "What do you think you are doing?" said my mother. "How could you...What if...?"

"I'm on the pill."

"What!" said my mother like I had just delivered the worst news of all. I had kept my promise to Natalie and not told my mother that she was on the pill. The discovery that one of her daughters was using regular birth control came as a blow.

"Don't worry, Mom. It's safe. I've been on it for six months now."

"Oh, heaven help us!" she cried.

"You're lucky I've had a few drinks. Otherwise I might not be so easy on you," my father said. "I'm going to bed. I'll speak with you in the morning once I've slept on it." He crossed the room, stopped and turned back to me. "But I admire your honesty. I'll say that."

In the morning, I sat at my little crowded vanity table-turned-desk in my bedroom in front of the Smith Corona typewriter, trying to focus on my essay assignment. I spent the majority of the morning too upset to work and staring at my reflection instead in the mirror in front of me. I replayed the scene over and over while twisting my long gold flecked hair in the mirror. I worried that my father was going to react rashly. Geoff had ingratiated himself into our family and I didn't want our foolhardy mistake to now cause a rift in the relationship. I was afraid of igniting another Natalie and John scenario.

I waited nervously for my father to come through the door and talk to me. I remembered a time as a child when my father tried to console me. I had never been so devastated in my life. I had made such a mess of it and was so embarrassed. I had just returned from a ballet recital.

In one of the numbers, the Skater's Waltz, it was my job to lead the dancers in a grand balancé onto the stage from the wings. But for some reason, I had started on the left foot instead of the right. I had got it all mixed up. Everybody saw. I could never perform again.

"Remember, that movie that you and I like so much, *Cat Ballou?*" my father asked, pulling me onto his lap.

I nodded through my tears.

"Well, you know that actor who plays the drunken old gunfighter? Lee Marvin? There is an actor who struggled for years before he got his big break. No one wanted to hire him. All he could ever get was two bit parts in movies. Well, here if he doesn't up and win the Academy Award for Pete's sake. The point is, he never gave up. No matter how bad it got, he kept trying. And look what happened to him."

I stopped crying. Everything was going to be OK. I loved him for that.

But I wasn't sure how my father would react this time and by the time he finally came to see me I had worked myself into a tight ball of anxiety. He pushed open my bedroom door and I blurted out, "I don't think it's fair that Geoff can't come around any more."

My response caught him off guard and for a moment he wavered. I knew in his heart he saw a daughter he was proud of.

"I didn't say that," he said quietly. I waited for him to explain. "I said I didn't think he should come around for a while."

"What's a while?"

He considered. "A few days. At least."

I was relieved. I think my father was too. He needed to prove that he was a reasonable father.

My mother behaved like I had deeply wounded her. She was deliberately distant and calculatingly silent, her punishment for my misconduct. In a huff, she coldly informed me that Nana Darwen and Grampa Russ were coming for dinner implying that I was in her bad books and had better be on my best behaviour. It occurred to me that she may have told Nana about last night. When I asked if she had, she was offended that I could consider such a possibility.

"Of course not," she said. "It's not something I'm proud of. I don't want anyone to know," she said her chin quivering into a pout.

My cheeks burned with shame and we didn't discuss the matter further. But a few days later, Geoff was back at the farmhouse as though our indiscretion had never happened.

CHAPTER TWENTY

Hari Kari

Cindy

"Diane, your cows are out again," informed Mrs. Rose over the phone.

"What? Not again! Where are they?"

"Down the highway across from my place."

"Oh, for Pete's sake!"

"You better come quick. One of them has jumped the fence and is on the highway."

Mom hung up the phone and ran out the side porch peering down the field in the distance. She could make out the cows about a quarter mile down the road near the fence.

"Where the heck is your father when I need him?" she cried to the dogs, Duke and Toby, who were stretched out in the sun.

She knew what to do. She'd seen Harry do this before. First, she went to the new barn and filled a sack with oats. Then she quickly searched the garage for something to corral the cattle with. She grabbed the first thing she saw - her curling broom.

Armed and ready, she walked as fast as she could down the shoulder of the highway to rescue the cows. Sure enough, one had cleared the four foot fence, the other was still behind the fence in the farmer's field.

When her neighbour called to warn her that the cows had escaped again, Mom immediately flew into action. Reaching the cows, she shooed them along the fence back toward the farmhouse. It was mid-day on a warm summer Sunday and the highway was busy with people coming back from Church. She was wearing shorts, a white shirt and no jacket. She had also chosen not to wear a bra for the first time. She had read in *Chatelaine* magazine the previous day a story about women going braless and how it made them feel empowered and free. She now found herself chasing two cows down the highway with a curling broom, baiting them with oats, mortified that her bare boobs were bouncing up and down under her shirt.

She managed to get the cows safely back into their pasture, but cursed Harry for not being there to help. It was his darn fence after all that couldn't keep the cows in. She was determined he'd have to do something about that when he got back. In the meantime, her husband was down south on a golf trip with his buddies.

Natalie

The radio announcer mourned: "Today was the day Rock 'n Roll died". It was Tuesday, August 16, 1977. I turned sixteen that day, and the King of Rock and Roll was dead. Elvis Presley died from a heart attack caused by a drug overdose. John was devastated. He had all of the King's music and knew all the words. He had seen each movie Presley had ever made more than once. John had a poster of Elvis pinned up above his bed. He loved everything about the man - his clothes, his voice, his movies, his moves. John was an expert; he knew the biographical facts by heart from the star's childhood, to his first appearance on Ed Sullivan, to his dismal Vegas show days, and finally, his tragic death. His dream was to go to Graceland one day. His uncle had been there once and brought John back the original dancing Elvis that shook and shimmied on the dashboard of John's car.

My parents had never been big Elvis fans and there were no tears shed at our house for him, but I knew John would be grieving. He hadn't been by the house or talked to my parents since the day he had unsuccessfully tried to talk to my father over a year ago. I never spoke about John in front of my parents. The subject was off limits. They still didn't like me seeing him; however, I'd decided that enough time had passed and that my parents would just have to tolerate him picking me up to take me out for my birthday dinner.

When John came by the house that evening in his new 1973 Cutlass Supreme he didn't get out of his car, but waited for me in the driveway. My father was outside by the carport and strolled toward the car.

By this time, I had climbed into the passenger seat and saw John was upset and agitated. He certainly wasn't in a frame of mind to talk to my father. I shouted goodbye and we drove away. I could see my father in the side view mirror watch us drive away and shake his head. I was frustrated that he was disappointed with us again. I wished for the hundredth time that he would just lay off us.

Elvis crooned on the radio and John turned up the volume. I slid along the bench seat closer to him and laid my hand on his thigh. "Are you OK?" I said. Before he could answer, we were interrupted by a crackling voice over the CB radio, making me jump.

"Breaker breaker. 1/0. This is Bandit. How about y'a King?"

"Who is that?"

"It's Hewlett. Say somethin' back to him."

"Breaker, breaker," I said laughing into the transmitter.

"You have to hold the button down. Here give it to me." I passed him the transmitter. "Breaker, Breaker Bandit. This is The King. Let's switch to channel 19," John said into the microphone as he drove. He switched the channel frequency on the CB. "Bandit, what's your 10/20?"

"King, how y'a doin' buddy? I'm at Broadway and First."

"Meet us at the arena in five."

"10/4 good buddy."

I was disappointed. "I thought we were going out for dinner."

"We are. We just need to do somethin' first."

We pulled up in front of the sports complex and parked the car. The sun was setting and night was falling when a brown Plymouth drove up beside us. I saw the bulky shape of Grant Hewlett behind the wheel. Hewlett had gone to school with John, as had his passenger, Daniel Cocker.

"Let's get out of the fuckin' spotlight and park around the side," Hewlett said.

We followed him around to the side of the building and parked in the shadows. John reached around to the back seat for the bottle of rum. He reached for the plastic bag on the floor and pulled out a bottle of chilled Coke and two plastic cups. I opened the bottle, poured some into the cups and John added the rum.

Cocker and Hewlett climbed into the back seat each with a beer in their hands.

"Here's to Elvis," said John as we raised our glasses in a toast to the King.

"To Elvis," we chimed.

"Hey, you missed the action last night," Cocker said to John. He had long straggly hair that hung limply over pimply skin.

"You should'ov seen Cocker. He puked his bag off. Almost puked in my car. I had to push him out," said Hewlett.

"That's bullshit!" said Cocker, shoving his friend's shoulder. Hewlett glared at the scrawny boy beside him. Cocker slunk back into the corner, he knew better than to antagonize his brawny friend. "But you sure clocked that guy at the party," he said to appease him.

"He had it comin'. The little creep," Hewlett said puffing himself up so that his chest muscles popped out of his shirt.

"John, what time is our reservation?" I asked.

"Relax," he said and put his arm around my shoulders pulling me closer to him. "You look real pretty in that dress," he said. I could smell the liquor on his breath. His hand travelled down my front and flicked my nipple. I jerked and pushed his hand away.

Cocker and Hewlett jeered. John glared at me. "Come here, Baby," he said yanking me and shoving his mouth hard on mine. The boys hooted. He pulled away and I turned to stare out the window, embarrassed and angry.

"Did you bring the stuff, Hewlett?" asked John.

"Yep. It's in the back."

Hewlett got out of the car and popped open the trunk of the Plymouth. He removed what he needed and closed the trunk. I saw he had a couple of cans of spray paint. John and Cocker climbed out of the car and shut the door.

"Are you comin'?" he asked me.

"What are you doing?" I asked.

"We're just goin' to have ourselves some fun," he said.

From inside the car I watched them stride over to the wall of the arena. I looked around to see if anyone was watching. We were alone. John grabbed a can from Hewlett. "I have an idea," he said. He shook the can as he paced back and forth in front of the cinder brick wall. He aimed and fired red paint at the wall. I opened my door and stood by the car watching him. John took his time absorbed in his painting. When he was done, he stepped back to view his work.

He had depicted a life-size man bent over and shoving a long sword with a scrolled hilt into his stomach. Blood gushed out of the man's guts spilling onto the tarmac.

"Hey, cool!" said Hewlett.

"You're good!" said Cocker.

John wasn't finished. He wrote in big red letters angled beside the painting: "Hari Kari Sucks!"

"Who's Hari Kari?" asked Cocker.

"Her ol' man," said John pointing to me. They turned to me and I laughed nervously. They hollered.

A police siren sounded in the distance. The boys raced back to their cars laughing. John heaved the paint can into the ditch and climbed into the car, chuckling softly to himself. "Pretty funny, eh?" He put the car into drive and we drove off.

CHAPTER TWENTY ONE

CareyOn'77

───────── Natalie ─────────

In September of 1977, my parents were getting ready to throw a party. The barn party was my father's idea. He wanted to create a good old fashioned hoedown and invited all their new friends from Orangeville as well as old friends and family from out of town. My mother loved organizing the food. She went to a lot of trouble planning and preparing the menu. Long tables were rented and set up near the fire pit my father had dug a safe distance from the old barn. When the guests arrived, these tables was covered with big bowls of creamy potato salads, fresh green salads, devilled eggs, pickles, chips, plates of butter for the corn, and every order of condiments for the hotdogs. Hotdogs were boiled in the farmhouse and brought out steaming in their buns on large trays once the party was in full swing. On another table stood homemade chocolate cake, cookies, butter tarts, and apple pie. Between the tables were two large metal tubs filled with ice, one for pop, one for beer.

On the day of the party, my mother and I sat on the steps of the backdoor stoop shucking dozens of cobs of sweet local corn. We shoved the peeled cobs into potato sacks to be fed later that night into an enormous cast iron pot hung over an open fire. The day was hot and humid and the sun bouncing off the screen door made it scorching hot to the touch. Fred the cat meandered over to investigate. I wiped the sweat from my brow and peeled back the tough outer leaves. John was on my mind. I wished that he could come to the party, but I didn't see how that was possible.

"I know you are still seeing John, Natalie," Mom said. Out of the blue. It was spooky how she could sometimes read my mind. "I knew you probably wouldn't stop seeing him," she sighed. After a pause, she added, "You two have been together for a long time now."

"It'll be two years next week," I said stroking Fred's long Persian fur.

"That's a long time for someone your age," she said, carefully searching for the right words. She decided to get to the point. "Are there any boys at school you like?"

"No, Mom. I'm with John," I said exasperated at her complete lack of understanding.

She sighed again. "I don't even know the boy. We've never said more than a quick hello to each other from the back door. He's shy isn't he?"

She stood up and opened the screen door. She hesitated before going inside. "Why don't you ask him to come to the party."

"Really? What will Dad say?"

"I'll talk to him."

"You'd do that? Thanks Mom."

She disappeared inside the house. I smiled. I couldn't wait to tell John. I looked down at the piece of corn in my lap and ripped back the dry husk. I tore the leaves exposing the golden flesh inside and ran my fingers down the length of the hard cob.

"What are you thinking about?" interrupted Cindy. She was standing over me blocking the sun. "Or, should I say who?" she asked with a teasing grin.

"No one," I said blushing.

She sat down beside me. Cindy had started her first year at university, had followed Michael to the University of Waterloo, and was living on campus. She was home for the weekend for the barn party. "You still seeing John?" she asked.

Not her too, I thought. I had never spoken to Cindy about John. For a moment I thought I would confide in her. Tell her I loved him. How worried I was about him. Just then a yellow Gremlin drove into the driveway. It was Geoff in his new car. Cindy went to greet her boyfriend and they kissed. I heard him say he had come to help Harry with the barn floor. The urge to confide in my sister quickly passed.

That evening, I stood by the back door anxiously waiting for John to arrive. I left the porch and walked toward the barn where the party was already in full swing. The old barn leaned precariously at the back corner of our property. Technically, it was not even on our property; it hugged the other side of the lot line that divided our land from the neighbouring farmer's. Apparently, there really was a farmer who tended the fields around our property, although I had yet to see him for myself. I had come to think of him as an elusive character who planted and sowed and reaped when no one was looking. As he was rarely around, no one seemed to think he would mind if we used the empty barn for a party.

The stone footing along one corner of the barn had collapsed years earlier, and lay crumbling under the weight of the decrepit grey structure. Parts of the barn wall had broken off, leaving loose boards dangling in the breeze and gaping black holes where rotten boards had fallen away altogether like the missing teeth and grizzly mouth of my Daddy Bill. My paternal grandfather never went to a dentist in his life, preferring to pull out his own rotten teeth with a rusty pair of pliers from his workbench. The barn was top-heavy and tilted to the south, slowly sinking further into the earth as decay set in like the bent-over spine of an old man falling perpetually closer to his grave.

I walked up the slope to the entrance at the back of the barn. The large sliding door hung crooked on its hinges and flapped lightly against the stone wall. A white sheet hammered into the wooden door warned in big red letters: "No Smoking!" While the frame of the barn lay in decline, the expansive main level lay mostly intact except for a few missing floorboards. Inside, the barn had been transformed for our first barn party, CareyOn'77. The floor had been swept and checked for weak spots. Makeshift electric bulbs hung from the rafters throwing pools of light onto the guests dancing on the dance floor or reclining on bales of hay, which had been arranged in a semi-circle for seating. Swallows darted at reckless speed in between the rafters above.

My father had gone all out to arrange a corn shucking contest, apple bobbing, a wheel barrow race, and a wood chopping event. The corn shucking contest was well under way and still John had not arrived. I walked impatiently back to the house and went inside.

I entered the kitchen and walked through the living room. The house was empty. I climbed the stairs and looked out from the hall window on the second floor. The field before me was filled with dense rows of mature autumn cornstalks. (When had the farmer planted those?) The tall stalks brushed the bold evening sky, awash with vivid strokes of pink and orange and graced by the emerging face of a giant yellow moon behind the barn.

The music from the barn floated through the open window. The three-piece band strummed to the chorus of a thousand chirping crickets. The banjo, fiddle, and drum were loud enough to be heard up and down the highway. Cars were parked on the shoulder of the highway for a quarter mile in both directions. The raucous noise of one hundred revelers drifted over the fields, but still no sign of John.

Something caught the corner of my eye. I looked up and saw a black shape lodged into the top corner of the wall beside the window. It was curled up and appeared to be sleeping. A bat! I quickly jumped away from under it and moved down the hall watching it nervously. I'd never seen a bat up close before and I didn't know how long it would be before it woke up and started flying around my head. The thought made my skin crawl. I'd have to tell Dad to get rid of it.

I was standing in front of the framed print on the wall. As always, I was drawn into the haunting story of *Christina's World*. I had passed this painting a thousand times, and each time I found myself staring at the girl in the pink dress crawling across a brown field, a New England farmhouse in the distance. The artist, Andrew Wyeth, had captured her from behind so that her face was not visible, but her twisted body spoke of anguish and yearning. Her pain and longing gripped me with a striking intensity.

I heard someone outside and looked back out the window in time to see John getting out of Hewlett's Plymouth parked on the highway. I flew downstairs and out the back door. I stopped momentarily when I saw John coming towards me flanked on either side by Hewlett and

Cocker. I had expected him to come alone. He stood on the driveway hesitating with his hands thrust in his pockets.

"Where's your car?" I asked him.

"In the shop."

Hewlett pulled a mickey from inside his jacket pocket. Hewlett wasn't much taller than me, but he was wide and his thick chest and bulging upper arms poked out of his tight black T-shirt. He took a swig then passed it to Cocker who did the same and passed it on to John. John took his turn and offered it to me. The scotch burned the back of my mouth and throat and warmed its way down into my stomach. I handed it back to Hewlett who took another mouthful.

I wanted to get John away from his friends so we could be alone. "There's beer over near the barn," I said and motioned vaguely in that direction. I led the way and they followed me to the beer and the party.

My father was at his fire post, minding the corn and talking to friends. The log fire crackled and spit orange sparks into the falling darkness. Clouds of steam rose from the cauldron along with the sweet smell of steamed corn. I avoided my father, and grabbed a dripping beer from the tub while he wasn't looking, and two paper cups from the table. John and I walked away from the party and headed for the pasture beyond. We walked as far as the old fence that separated our property from the farmer's.

The light was quickly fading and soon we would be in the dark. I poured the beer into the cups and we drank watching the party from a distance. I was convinced my father had seen us. Sure enough, he was peering in our direction, his face a question mark. I wished then we had said hello to him. He headed towards us. John swore and stamped his feet nervously. Just before my father reached us, I tossed the beer bottle over the fence.

"Hi Dad," I said.

"Hello Nat," he said, looking at me in expectation. He turned to John. "John," he said in a strained greeting.

"Hello, Sir."

"You two wouldn't be doing something you shouldn't out here would you?" he said in a teasing manner, but his eyes were focused on us intensely.

"No, Dad," I said.

"Good, because we can't have you two getting into trouble."

Oh, no, I thought. Here it comes. I looked over at John and saw he couldn't look at my father. My father said, "So, John, what are you up to these days?" Maybe I was wrong; maybe he was going to be easy on us after all. "Are you at school?"

My father knew little about my boyfriend, I thought with dismay. John had graduated with his grade twelve that spring, but wasn't interested in getting his grade thirteen.

"No," John said, kicking the earth with the toe of his boot. "I'm workin'."

"Where do you work?"

"I'm drivin' a truck," he said and I could feel his eyes on me pleading for me to come to his aid.

"Is that so. How old are you now, John?"

"Eighteen."

"Eighteen," my father said mulling this over. "Natalie, how old are you?"

"I just turned sixteen, Dad," I said rolling my eyes. "It's amazing you got my name right," I mumbled.

"Huh! Don't be so hard on your old Dad!" my father said smiling. "So, do you own your own car then?" he asked.

"Yeah, I bought my first one a while back," he said proudly. It was a trap. He couldn't have known this wouldn't impress my father much.

"Is that right?" Just then we heard someone calling my father's name. "I have to get back," he said. "You two should come join the party. The wood chopping contest is going to start soon. We need you on the team, John." He started to walk away. "Make sure you go easy on the booze, eh?" he said over his shoulder.

"Dad! Wait!" I ran up to him. "I almost forgot. There's a bat in the upstairs hall."

"A bat? Well, I'll be darned."

"Yeah, can you get it?"

"Not tonight. It will be fine where it is til the morning."

"You can't just leave it there!"

He shrugged his shoulders and continued walking back to the barn. A few minutes later we could hear his loud party voice booming directions and stirring up fun from inside. For a slight man who never weighed more than 150 lbs in his life, my father could be very loud. Above the noise, I recognized the unmistakable high notes of my mother's laugh.

CHAPTER TWENTY TWO

Trouble

 Natalie

John and I finished our beer and wandered inside the barn, which was full of people, the air heavy with their heat and sweat. Guests were perched on the bales of hay around the barn's circumference, drinking and relaxing, while others danced and stomped to the music. Paul was whooping it up with his friends, ecstatic to be outside at night at a grown-ups' party. I spotted Christine with a couple of older guys she knew from town. Even in the dim light, I noticed her eyes and lips were dark with heavy makeup. Cindy formed a circle of her own group of friends. I saw Nana Darwen and Grampa Russ with an uncle and aunt I hadn't seen for years sitting stiffly on lawn chairs they had brought with them.

The band was playing a lively three step and several couples were swirling and sashaying around the dance floor.

"Do you want to dance?" I asked John.

"Not bloody likely," he said.

Geoff came up and yelled in my ear: "Let's dance!"

I hesitated, seeing John's glower. I really wanted to dance, and I followed my sister's boyfriend onto the dance floor. We spun and careened our way around the barn with the other wild dancers barreling around the dance floor.

135

When the dance was over, Geoff went to find Cindy, and I returned to John. I was breathless and happy, but I could tell by John's brooding face that he wasn't pleased.

"What's wrong?" I asked.

He ignored me.

"You're not jealous are you?"

John turned on his heels and left the barn. I followed after him. He began walking faster.

"Hey, what's wrong?" I cried. I grabbed onto the sleeve of his jacket to stop him from leaving. "John, what is it?" I said.

He spun around. "Don't you *ever* let me catch you dancin' with another guy again!" he yelled into my face. I let go of his sleeve and backed away frightened.

He reached for me. "I'm sorry, Nat. It's just that I love you so much. I can't stand to see you with anyone else."

"I'm sorry too, John. I didn't think you would mind. It's only Geoff after all."

"I know. You're right, it's just that I don't want to share you with anyone."

I was flattered. I thought he was so sweet and caring, wanting me all to himself. I put my arms around him. The harvest moon clung over the barn like an orange cut-out on a black felt board. John bent his mouth to mine and we kissed under the moonlight.

We were soon interrupted by angry shouts coming from the barn. We heard with alarm the raised voices of Hewlett and Cocker. A few moments later, we recognized Hewlett's barrel-chested shape emerge from around the corner of the barn. Cocker slunk close behind on his heels. The muscular youth stomped up to us swearing and swinging his arms, brushing off his friend's efforts to calm him down. John stood in their path. "What happened?" he asked.

"We're out'a here. This place stinks!" said Hewlett hawking into the dirt.

John looked at Cocker for an explanation. "He was refused a beer. Some punk told him he'd had enough," he slurred. They were both staggering drunk.

"We're headin' into town. Y'a comin'?" Hewlett asked John.

John hesitated, looking from his friends to me. "Yeah, OK, give me a minute," he said.

Hewlett scoffed. "Remember this!" he said menacingly and brought his hands together fist over fist in front of his torso. He lifted them up high in front of him before he plunged them hard under his ribs. He buckled over in a dramatic burst of agony, mimicking a Japanese death cry: "Hari-Kari!"

The friends reeled with laughter. Cocker and Hewlett weaved their way toward the highway. John turned to me. "I have to catch a ride back with them," he said, apologetically. He pulled me to him then, but I resisted.

"Just go with your buddies," I said. Our night was wrecked.

John shrugged his shoulders and went to join his friends. I walked slowly back to the barn feeling sorry for myself. I nearly bumped into Cindy who was coming out of the barn.

"Nice friends, Natalie," she said. "What rock did you find them under?"

"What's your problem?" I threw back.

"Dad's looking for you," she said, meaning I was in trouble and would be best to avoid him. "By the way," my sister warned: "If I were you, I wouldn't let on those guys are friends of John's. Not unless you really want Dad to never like your boyfriend in this lifetime."

"I don't care. Dad can think what he wants." I took my sister's advice and steered clear of my father that night, but the next day he sought me out and asked me if I knew the names of the two troublemakers at the party. I told him I didn't know who they were.

The bat stayed hanging upside down in the hall for two days. I raced by it my heart beating in my chest every time I had to go up or down the stairs. I was afraid of disturbing it. By the third day it was gone. I assumed Dad had finally got rid of it.

CHAPTER TWENTY THREE

Trespasses

 Cindy

The trespasses started after the barn party. I was home from university one autumn weekend when we were disturbed in the middle of the night by a car zooming into our driveway spinning around and speeding out. I found out this wasn't the first time my family had experienced a similar disturbance. The trespasses seemed to follow no apparent pattern; the randomness of their acts perturbed my parents. The incidents usually occurred over a weekend, but sometimes during a weeknight too. Once, a black pick-up truck wheeled in waking up the household. It sped out and everyone went back to bed, only to be woken again by a repeat performance later that night. That time, my parents called the police and reported the incident.

There was no rhyme or reason behind the visits. The actual vehicles changed: once it was a white sedan; a couple of times there were two cars at the same time; but mostly it was a brown Plymouth that squealed into our driveway in the middle of the night.

Sometimes, the morning after one of the disturbances, we found things missing: an electric bug zapper, an outdoor lounge chair, Paul's bicycle. We reported the thefts to the police as a matter of course; we knew we wouldn't retrieve them. The unpredictable nature of the disturbances fed our anxiety, while our ongoing inability to identify the drivers increased our frustration.

We weren't the only ones to feel victimized. Malicious property damage had escalated in the late seventies in the Orangeville area causing area residents to speak out about their concerns. We heard similar stories of vandalism that echoed ours and that left us feeling uneasy and powerless. A flurry of smashed storefront windows and car windshields prompted some residents to claim that vandalism was increasing all over their town. In an editorial in the *Orangeville Banner* entitled "Vandals are Sick", a resident expressed a growing sentiment that vandalism was getting worse in Orangeville as the town grew. The resident wrote: "Unless something is done, the antics of a few punks might give us a reputation of being a town where no one cares about the property of others".

A particular rash of violence occurred to area residents during the winter of 1977/78. I was attending a Christmas open house with my family. The party took place at the rural home of friends of my parents, near the village of Mono Centre. As we drove along the rolling snow-covered back roads, the picturesque setting was blemished by strangely misshapen mailboxes leaning awkwardly into the snow banks by the roadside. Some looked like they had been smashed with a heavy weapon. When we arrived at the driveway of our destination, I noticed the owners' mailbox had also been hammered out of shape and teetered drunkenly over.

Inside the front hallway we were greeted by our hosts, the Tibbles. Both husband and wife were short and plump with pudgy round cheeks and an overbite. Their similar physical appearance, together with their sweet but constant fussing, reminded me of Alvin and the Chipmunks. My father asked what happened to all the mailboxes.

"Isn't it horrible?" said Mrs. Tibbles taking our coats and making a "tsk"-like sound with her tongue. "That just happened last night. We found it like that this morning."

My mother shook her head. "Isn't that awful?" she said.

"Yes," Mr. Tibbles agreed hanging up the coats. "In the last month alone, over 300 mailboxes have been pulled down and smashed. These characters are verging on maniacs. There have been three cars wrecked around here in the past two weeks. Windows and doors smashed with a crowbar."

"I think they must have been high on dope or something. No human being in his right mind would want to do anything so stupid," said Mrs. Tibbles.

By this time we had removed our dripping winter boots and placed them on the grey rubber floor mat. We pulled our good Christmas shoes, cold and stiff, out of plastic bags carried in from the car. Balancing stork-like to avoid stepping in a puddle of melting snow, I caught Christine and Natalie roll their eyes at each other as they bent over to fasten their shoes.

"Is anyone doing anything about it?" asked my father.

"The Mono Council is actually offering a reward, $500.00 to anyone who comes forward with any information leading to an arrest and conviction," said Mr. Tibbles.

"Do you think the reward will work?" my father asked as we followed our hosts into the living room where several other guests were mingling around the Christmas tree.

"It's got to help," Mr. Tibbles said. "Eggnog and rum, Diane?" he said handing my mother a glass from the silver tray. "Some of our neighbours have threatened to take the law into their own hands. And that's not right."

"We had trouble of our own," my father said, watching his two youngest girls join a cluster of teens across the room. He turned back to his host, "We've had cars pulling off the highway and tearing up and down our driveway and lawn."

"It's a serious problem," Mr. Tibbles said mixing a drink.

"It's serious allright," agreed my father, his eyes darting to Natalie. She felt him looking at her and started biting her nails.

"I think their parents should be made to pay for the vandalism," said Mrs. Tibbles, passing a cheese ball. "At the end of the day, the parents are the ones responsible."

"I agree," said my mother. "Someone's got to pay."

In late April our farmhouse was once again a target. We'd had one of those "freak" late spring snowstorms. (I don't know why they insist on calling them that as though they hardly ever happened; to me the only thing freakish about a big snowstorm in April is that it happened with regularity in that part of the country.) The skies dumped so much snow in twenty-four hours that, much to the students' delight, the school announced another "No Bus Day", which meant the high school was virtually shut down. While most people were happy to stay nestled indoors and avoid going anywhere, trespassers were determined to vandalize our property that night.

In the morning, we found deep tire tracks carved into the snow on the driveway and spilling over onto the lawn across a border of delicate primulas my mother had planted experimentally that spring. We had anticipated the tracks, but were completely unprepared for the toppled trees. The tracks ran right over them.

"Ah, for Christ's sake!" said Dad, bending down to get a closer look at the newly planted maple saplings. Their young slim trunks had been ripped out of the ground. The branches that had only just sprouted new spring growth lay crushed and crippled across the mangled lawn.

Lifting a trunk a few feet above the ground, Dad said, "Go tell your mother to call the police." He gently placed the sapling back down on the ground.

Before his daughters rushed off for the school bus, Dad called an unprecedented family meeting in the living room. He was not blind to the possibility that one of his children might have information about the vandalism, or even be involved. He directed his questions to his two high school daughters.

"Is there anybody at school who may be angry at you and taking it out on our home?" he asked.

Both girls denied there was anybody mad at either of them. The room was silent as he digested their response and gave them ample time to reconsider and speak up. He realized he was potentially asking his children to betray their friends or siblings. Breaking the silence, he said, "We are all going to have to pull together to find out who is doing this to us. Keep your eyes and ears open and let me know if you hear anything suspicious."

Then he asked Christine and Natalie one at a time if they knew who was responsible for wrecking our property. Christine looked down at the floor and said she couldn't think who it could be. Natalie looked straight at her father and said she didn't know.

Natalie

The day we found the trees run over, John came by after school to pick me up.

"Oh, John, it's you," said Mom, coming out the backdoor and finding him in our driveway. "I didn't know it was you."

"I'm waiting for Natalie," he said, leaning against his car.

"Did you see what happened? Isn't it awful!" He watched her walk across the lawn to inspect the maple trees that lay beside two ugly holes in the earth. Their exposed roots hung shamefully naked in the bright daylight. "My poor trees," she said.

"It's bad," he said.

"Who would do this?"

I came outside and we climbed into the car. "My mom called the police again this morning," I said once we were on the highway.

"What for?"

"She's scared. Look what they did. Harry is so angry."

"She didn't have to call the cops for Christ sake!"

"They're fed up. They want to catch the guys."

"That won't happen."

"It was you in the car wasn't it?"

"Did you see the car?"

"No, I was asleep."

"Farrell was driving. We was just foolin' around."

"Oh, my God. It was you guys all along?"

"No, no that was our first time. I don't know who come before."

"Whose idea was it to run over the trees like that?"

"No one's. Just happened."

"Harry wanted to know if I knew who was in the car."

"What did you tell him?"

"Nothing. What should I tell him?"

"There's nothin' to tell. I ain't done nothin' wrong.

"Just be careful John. My father is really upset."

"Don't worry. I've got it under control. Yer ol' man don't scare me."

CHAPTER TWENTY FOUR

Decision

 Cindy

On May 15, 1978 I packed up my dorm room and moved back home for the summer. It was my first night in my old bed and I was just falling asleep when I heard the slow crunching of tires on gravel. We weren't expecting anyone at this time of night. I sat up in bed and caught the car's headlights slice through my room. I went to my window at the front of the house in time to see a car creep into our driveway. It made me uneasy the way it tried to sneak up on us. The reverberating hum of the idling engine left an icy metal taste in the back of my mouth. It reminded me of something dark and repugnant I had experienced before. A flash from my childhood of a red car crawling up beside me.

My heart beating quickly in my throat, I crossed the hall into my parents' bedroom. "Dad," I called urgently at his side of the bed, "they're back."

He woke with a start. "What?"

"The car's back," I said. He jumped out of bed to the window.

My mother stirred. "What's wrong, Harry?" she asked groggily from the bed.

He pressed further into the window straining to see into the night. As if on cue, the car's engine roared announcing its arrival.

"Cripes! It's them again all right," my father cried, and bolted from the room and down the stairs. I hesitated for a moment, glancing at my mother who was throwing on her housecoat. The alarm clock beside my parents' bed read 11:09 p.m.

I followed my parents downstairs. From the living room window I saw the car race across the lawn and brake suddenly sliding into a stop. Duke and Toby were herding the car, chasing and barking at it furiously. I was distraught they were going to be hit. I hoped they were quick enough to stay out of the way of the car. The vehicle did another full circle and then sped across the grass past the attached garage toward the old carriage house. My father opened the door off the living room and teetered on the edge of the cement verandah, undecided whether to stay put or chase after the car.

The car headed for the driveway and now my father was off the porch and running after it. It was too late; the car reached the highway and took off.

From the shoulder of the highway Dad watched the car follow the long bend in the road turning into town. I pulled a coat over my nightgown and joined him at the side of the road. After the car had disappeared from sight, he remained staring toward town, the lights in the distance nothing more than a few pinpricks in the dark. Turning my head in the other direction, I saw the sleeping, undisturbed silhouette of Mrs. Rose' farmhouse a quarter of a mile away.

My father continued to stare silently toward town. It was a cool spring night and the damp cold settled over my bare legs. I shifted impatiently from foot to foot to create some warmth. I wanted to go back inside, but was reluctant to leave my father alone in the dark. The night wrapped the earth in shades of grey turned to deepest black under the shadow of the old barn. The bulk of the barn stood solid and reassuring, its tattered walls and sinking roof concealed. It appeared larger than life and towered over the horizon, dwarfing everything around it. For the moment, I felt comforted by its watchful permanence.

"Come on Dad, let's go inside," I said, urging him into the house. I was now trembling in my nightgown. "It's freezing out here," I said.

"Did your mother call the police yet?" he asked.

"I don't know. Let's go inside and find out."

Finally Dad turned away from the highway and headed back toward the house. Inside, my mother was already on the phone in the hall. "Yes, this is Diane Carey. The car was here again."

"Tell them you need to file a report, a complaint," interrupted my father as he entered the living room.

"I need to report another complaint. About the car. No, they have left already. Did you get the license plate Harry?" she asked him, holding the phone away from her mouth. He shook his head crossly.

"No, he didn't. It was too dark. They were too fast."

"Tell them it was the same car, the brown Plymouth," my father said fed up.

"You're coming? Now? Please hurry!" my mother cried into the phone. She hung up and shoved her hands deep inside her housecoat pockets. She wore foam pink and green curlers in her hair, the kind that weren't supposed to hurt in bed. One had come loose and dangled above her right ear threatening to come undone. "They said they'd get here as soon as they can," she said, to be soothing but sounding unconvinced.

We knew from past experience that it could be quite a while before the police arrived. Living outside the town boundaries, we had to report to the Snelgrove Ontario Provincial Police which was stationed about fifteen miles away. We had called them before but they never showed up until long after the vandals had sped away.

I went over to the window and peered out. The wind gently stirred the branches of the mature maple trees that bordered the fence. Everything else was quiet.

I couldn't prevent my teeth from chattering. My mother came and stood beside me. "Cindy, why don't you go to bed," she said. "You must be tired after your move. There's no sense in staying up. Your dad and I will deal with the police when they arrive."

I wasn't ready to go to bed yet. "Who do you think it is, Mom? Who do you think is doing this to us?"

She hesitated and looked around for her husband, but he had left the room. "I don't know. But whoever it is they are very angry." Her voice cracked and she began to weep. She reached for a tissue in her housecoat pocket. She sank down exhausted in the rocking chair.

I looked for my father and found him seated at the kitchen table. He was contemplating the space just beyond his hands, which laid clasped on the tabletop. If I didn't know better I would think he was praying. But my father was an atheist. He had told us often enough that he had been completely turned off religion after his grandparents made him attend church three times every Sunday as a boy for several years. He was made to go to Sunday school at the United Church followed by a mid-morning service, and then forced to join his grandmother at the Presbyterian church service in the evening. When he was old enough to make up his own mind, my father stopped going to church altogether and became a non-believer.

The only time my father went to church with us was on Christmas Eve and that was just to please his wife. When I was a little girl and hyper with excitement for Santa to arrive, having my father come to church and sit with us in the pew, made the special day perfect. I knew he didn't feel right about being there, and the fact he came just for us, meant everything. My father sang the hymns alongside us, but when we kneeled to pray, he remained sitting on the bench. Even then he hadn't prayed with us.

"Dad?" I said. It struck me what a private person he was. He was becoming more mysterious as I got older. I really didn't know this man.

"Oh, Cindy, you still up? Don't worry, we'll catch those jerks. I'm not going to let them get away again," he said.

"What are you going to do?"

"I don't know yet. But I've got to do something. I can't sit here anymore and have them continue to...to harass us like this. Your mother's nerves can't take it."

"I hope the police get here soon."

"Little good they're going to do now anyway," he said, looking out the kitchen window. My image was reflected in the glass - long hair parted down the middle, wide eyes studying him, mouth drawn in as I chewed on my lips. He caught me looking at him and pushed back his chair from the table and stood up. "But I'll take care of it. You go to bed. Don't worry; I'll make sure those idiots don't bother us again."

I kissed him on the cheek and climbed the stairs to my room. But less than an hour later, I was disturbed by the car again.

CHAPTER TWENTY FIVE

Nightmare

———————————— Natalie ————————————

The baby was wrapped in a blanket and I rocked him back and forth in my arms cooing softly:

"Down in the Lee Hi Valley
There lived a little Hindu.
He didn't have no clothes,
So he had to make his skin do!"

My fingers fumble for the touch of my baby's soft skin and find only air. I tear open the blanket but it is empty. My baby has vanished! Now I'm in a huge cornfield running frantically through a maze of tall cornstalks, searching and calling for my baby. My father appears and helps me look. I ask him where my baby is and all of sudden there is a big bang!

I awoke in a sweat, my heart thumping against my chest. Lifting my hands to my face to drink in the smell of the baby that still clung to my skin, I sat up in panic and realized I was in my attic bedroom. I'd had the recurring nightmare again. And there was no baby.

A blast woke me. Later, I thought maybe it was the sound of the car as it gunned its engine, or perhaps I was woken by an actual shot. I'm not sure what I heard, but I didn't get up. I lay back down and pulled the covers tight to my chin, concentrating on the window across the room as if expecting something to crash through it at any minute.

I listened for clues. Something was wrong, but I didn't want to know. I held my breath and willed myself to stay in bed. I lay there listening, but not wanting to hear, as Christine slept on in the single bed beside me undisturbed. She was in a deep sleep and I marked the time by the rise and fall of her every breath. I wanted more than anything to sleep like her. I heard the car leave. An ominous stillness settled around me.

After a while, I felt the old familiar sensation of my body growing lighter and smaller like it didn't belong to me anymore. Like I had shrunk into a tiny weightless matter that I could hold in my fingertips. I touched my thumb gently to my middle finger and my fingers felt strangely numb. I stared at them and they seemed unattached. I lay there unmoving in an unnatural silence, feeling restrained as though wound in a tight cocoon. I waited for the feeling to pass. I heard my parents come up to bed one floor below me. That was the last thing I remembered before I finally drifted off to sleep.

In the morning, I had to get up for school, but I was tired and my stomach was upset. I pretended to sleep while I snuck peeks at my sister's reflection in the mirror as she patiently held a hot curling iron to her hair. The iron hissed and sent off little wisps of steam flipping her bangs back into long wings that framed her face. I turned over. I didn't want to talk. Christine eventually left our room and went downstairs. I waited for the bathroom to be free and every-one to go downstairs for breakfast, before I came down from the attic.

I used the bathroom and walked down the hall noticing the door to Cindy's bedroom was shut. She was not up yet. I hesitated at the top of the stairs feeling anxious and afraid. My eyes shifted to the painting on the wall and once again I felt myself pulled into *Christina's World*. There was a strong feeling that the girl remained fiercely connected to the farmhouse and her life there, but found herself estranged from it. She longed for a world that had ceased to exist and to which she could no longer return.

I wanted desperately to avoid my parents, but eventually I had to go downstairs. I tried to creep out the kitchen door without seeing them, but when I entered the kitchen my father was waiting for me. His appearance confirmed my suspicion that something was wrong. He didn't look like he was ready to go to work. He was wearing his old moth-eaten-outdoor-chores clothes instead of his comfortable business attire of slacks and a sweater. His thick hair, normally brushed neatly back from his wide forehead, was disheveled with deep ruts like he had just rubbed his hands through it. His eyes were weary and red rimmed with lack of sleep. Mom was standing at the stove in her housecoat making oatmeal. He told me to follow him into the dining room so he could speak with me alone.

He closed the shutter doors to the kitchen with deliberation, and my foreboding from the night before returned in full force. I hadn't just imagined it; something serious had happened.

I stood before my father chewing on my fingernails, as he told me last night he used his old shotgun to shoot at the car that kept terrorizing us. He said the pellets from the gun had sprayed and accidentally wounded two of the passengers.

"I'm going to ask you again, Natalie" he said, "Do you know who was in that car?"

Outside the window a truck passed us on the highway, a dog barked, branches rustled in the breeze, but I felt the world had stopped. I couldn't believe what I was hearing. "You *shot* them?"

"I didn't mean to hit them," he said. "I was aiming at the *car*."

"With a *gun*?" I asked.

He waited for me to answer him. "Well, do you know who they were?"

I shook my head slowly.

"The police told me their names. The driver was Grant Hewlett. He wasn't hurt. One of the passengers was Daniel Cocker. I don't know these boys," he said looking at me pointedly. He took a deep breath, "But I know the other passenger. It was John."

I felt as though the room was one giant vacuum and sucked all the air out. I couldn't breathe.

"What have you done?" I choked. "Is he o.k.?"

"He's fine. He has injuries to his head, but they are minor. You know I never meant to hurt anyone."

Relief surged through me. John was going to be all right.

"Natalie, why didn't you tell me it was John?" my father said in anguish.

I felt trapped and confused. I knew John and his friends were guilty of at least one incident, maybe more. I had known and I had kept it to myself. My father couldn't find out about this.

"I didn't know," I said. Then because I knew he saw through me and I was scared, I accused him. "You never believe me!" My words had the intended effect - he winced. Honesty and trust were paramount to my father.

"Nat, I want to believe you, I really do, but you are making it very hard for me."

"Well, it doesn't matter what I say. You'll just believe what you want anyway."

He crossed his arms over his chest and sighed. With one hand cupped under his chin he stood heavy with disappointment and seemed to weigh his options. I felt my side of the scale tipping downward. I had been revealed and found unworthy. I had not been able to admit, even to myself, that my boyfriend was the one behind the trespasses. My will to stand up to my father weakened and I waited with resignation for my father to deliver the inevitable punishment.

After a minute he said, "We'll talk about this more tonight. You need to go to school now." He started to walk out of the room, then paused. "You should know," he said, "I spent last night in jail."

Jail! The tears I had been holding back finally came. My father had shot and wounded two boys. What would happen to him? What would happen to the boys? To John? I saw my father look at me like he was seeing for the first time who I really was. I felt vulnerable and ashamed.

I grew lightheaded and I felt myself slipping away like the balloon I had once let go outdoors. Released, I had watched it climb higher and higher into the sky until it became a barely recognizable speck in the distance. Like my balloon, I felt myself suddenly unfastened and disappearing.

"Dad," I said, "I'm really sorry you had to spend the night in jail."

"So am I," he said, and walked away. It seemed to me he was sorry I was involved, but not really surprised. I saw how it was going to be from now on between my father and me.

I was afraid I would be swallowed up by the atmosphere like my balloon and not be able to return.

I wiped my tears and headed through the kitchen for the back door. My mother was standing by the stove stirring the pot of hot oatmeal. When she saw me, she accidentally knocked over the salt shaker. "Uh-oh," she gasped quickly, tossing a pinch of salt over her left shoulder to overthrow the bad luck. "Here. Take this," she said, shoving a paper bag lunch into my hands. Her eyes were red from crying.

I stepped outside to a dazzling spring morning, the bright sunlight hurting my eyes. The sun reflected harshly off fluorescent orange police tape strung across our lawn and driveway. I had to step over it. I walked down the driveway and saw Christine standing across the highway, waiting for the school bus to arrive. She turned her head away when she saw me, choosing to look down the highway rather than at me. I was suddenly so tired and heavy it took all my strength to cross the road and join my sister on the other side. I dragged my feet, hanging my head low. Looking down, a part of me became aware that I was walking across the painted white line on the highway that marked the quarter mile. It seemed to me now more grey than white, its boundaries indistinct and blurred by my tears.

CHAPTER TWENTY SIX
Damage

Natalie

We waited at the side of the highway. The sun glistened on the dewy grass, freshly sliced with tire marks. The rumbling bus lumbered up and stepped on squeaky brakes in front of us. The folding doors sighed open as the high whistle of a cardinal sounded from the branches of the maple tree. Christine and I climbed up the steep stairs. We still hadn't said a word to each other.

The kids on the school bus stared out their windows at our lawn and driveway zigzagged with official crime scene markers. As the bus drove down the highway, they turned and gawked at us. I ignored them. I looked over at Christine who was sitting across the aisle from me. She kept her eyes focused out the front window of the bus. I couldn't tell what she was thinking. I would make an effort to talk to her later when we were alone.

I didn't expect to see John waiting for me when we pulled up in front of the school. Normally, he would have been at work by now. I climbed down from the bus and fell into his arms. "I'm so sorry, John," I said pulling away to examine his face. Surgical tape lay across a gash high on his left cheekbone. I wasn't prepared for the shock of seeing him wounded. I would never forgive my father for hurting him.

I hugged him to me. "Oh, my God, John, I'm so sorry. Your poor face. Are you OK?"

"Yeah. The nurse said I was lucky. Any higher and I could have lost my eye."

"Does it hurt?" I asked.

"A little. I got ten stitches altogether. I got hit up here too." He lifted his bangs back and revealed a second wound also covered in surgical tape from where a pellet had grazed his forehead. My stomach lurched.

"I can't believe it. I just can't believe it," I said beginning to feel like I was going to be sick. I walked away from the tarmac holding my stomach. I walked toward the grassy area between the school and the neighbouring house. John huddled beside me, his shoulders hunched up by his ears, his hands clenched into fists in his pockets.

"The cops fuckin' arrested me, Nat."

"Oh my God! When?"

"Last night at the hospital. They said I could be charged. I'm goin' to have a fuckin' record."

"Charged with what?"

"Some shit about trespassin' and vandalism."

"Everything's out of control. My father spent last night in jail!"

John punched the inside of his left palm with his fist. "Fuck!" he said enraged. "He shot a goddamn shotgun at us, Natalie. He's a madman." Something occurred to him and he threw me a dark, suspicious look. "Did yer Dad know who he was shootin' at? Did you tell him it was us in the car?"

I resented his implied accusation. "Of course not. How could I? I didn't even know for sure it was you," I said defensively. But the possibility that my father had known who was in the car planted itself like a deviant seed under my skin. "Why didn't you tell me what you were up to?" I asked, my voice rising.

"I just wanted to see you. I asked Farrell to drive out to your place. You were supposed to call me, remember? If you had, none of this would of happened."

"It's *my* fault because I didn't call you?"

"I never meant it to come to this. We was just havin' a little fun in the beginnin'. But it got carried away. I thought you must have known it was us all along."

"Why, John?"

"I can't believe you're asking me that," he cried, pulling away from me. "You of all people should know why. Yer dad deserved it. He brought it on himself. He's never wanted us to be together."

I reached up and gently smoothed the lock of hair across his bandage. His scars ignited my anger. How could my father have done this? At that moment, I silently accused him of everything that had happened. The angrier I was with my father, the more I wanted to protect John. I stood on tiptoe and brushed my lips across his cheek. "I'm so sorry," I said again. "When did they let you out of the hospital?"

"I left after I got the stitches. That was about four o'clock this mornin'."

"Where did you go?"

"I crashed at Hewlett's place. Cocker was still in the hospital when I left." He started to get worked up again. "His head was hit pretty hard. It's all cut up. He was bleedin' like a stuffed pig last night. He got hit in the leg too. We took him back to Hewlett's place and tried to clean him up but we couldn't get the bleedin' to stop so's we took him to the hospital."

"What a disaster," I moaned. "You could have been killed!"

"At first I thought it was Hewlett revving the engine," he said. Then everythin' fell to pieces inside the car. It was smokey ... glass was flyin' everywhere. I got hit on the side of the face. I turned around an' there was blood an' stuff rollin' out of Danny. I knew then what had happened."

"I can't believe my father did this. I won't defend him, it's inexcusable what he did, but I don't think he would have done what he did, used a *gun*, if he knew it was you in the car," I said to appease him and hoping I sounded convincing.

"The cops want to talk to us again. We're probably goin' to be charged. All three of us. We might even lose our licenses. My ole man is goin' to be furious."

Everything was spinning in a downward spiral. I sat down on the grass my legs crumbling under me. I didn't know if I could take any more bad news. I certainly didn't want this to cause a rift between John and his father.

The first time I met Gus Ranberg was on the long, asphalt driveway in front of his house where he was washing his monstrous eighteen-wheeler. He was standing on a ladder so he could reach the power hose over the roof. I remembered his complete absorption in his task so that at first he didn't notice us standing below him. From inside the mammoth red and chrome cab, wailed C.W. McCall's *Convoy*, a hokey trucking tune and Gus' anthem. John's father spotted us and climbed down from his perch. He was a gentle, soft-spoken man despite his large frame. He had a neatly-trimmed dark brown moustache and sentimental chestnut eyes.

Gus was passionate about his truck and his job as a truck driver. His devotion to maintaining and driving his truck brought him comfort and solace, like another man's dedication to religious pursuits. It seemed to me the only thing Gus loved more than his truck and the independence and freedom of being on the road was his only son, John. Gus was as proud and dedicated to his son as he was to his truck. He told us as we stood on his driveway admiring his truck that day that the best day of his life, besides his wedding day, was the first time he handed the keys of his "baby" to John to drive. He said it filled him with pride to be able to entrust his son with the one thing he loved more than anything else. He looked forward to the day he would pass on his truck to his son.

John sat down beside me. "I'm sorry too, Natalie," he said hoarsely. "I really blew it didn't I?" He drew me to his chest and nestled his face in my hair. "You smell so good," he said.

"It'll be alright," I told him trying to sound reassuring when I wasn't at all sure of anything.

"Nat, if you had known for sure it was me in the car would you have told yer dad?"

I looked into his face and his eyes looked back at me with tender vulnerability and desperation. "Of course I wouldn't have told him," I said. "But if he'd known you were in the car he wouldn't have fired a gun on you." I hoped this was true.

CHAPTER TWENTY SEVEN

Exposed

 Cindy

I was awoken by the raucous cawing of a crow outside my bedroom window. I had only been asleep for a few hours. I opened my eyes disorientated, not yet accustomed to sleeping in my old room. Then I remembered where I was and the horror of the night rushed back to me.

I stayed in bed and stared at the olive green floral wallpaper peeling away from the wall near the ceiling. The room had been papered over several times by previous owners and underlying hints of tattered old patterns yellowed with time snuck out from behind the latest decorating attempt. The peeling wallpaper begged to be picked at. There was one piece near my bed that had come unglued and urged me to peak at the hidden layers. I knew better. I knew once I started peeling it back, it could only lead to more temptation. I was afraid once I started, I would find it impossible to resist ripping and tearing until the pieces became bigger and uglier, and I would eventually manage to pull down the huge sweeping mess, revealing the hideousness underneath. I wondered what would become of the raw ugliness once it was exposed.

I got up and went downstairs. No one was around. It was a school day for my brother and sisters. I supposed they were at school; however, I couldn't believe my father had gone to work. Entering the kitchen, I found Toby lying on the floor in a patch of sunlight, thumping her tail happily on the coiled braids of the rug. I remembered hearing her and Duke barking vigorously last night at the trespassers from their bed in the mudroom. "Good old Toby," I said as I bent to pat her. "You'll protect us, won't you girl."

There was no scribbled note offering any clues to where my parents might be. We had never gotten into the habit of leaving messages for each other when we went out, there was no magnetic message board stuck on the fridge, or chalkboard tacked to the wall. Today was no exception.

Looking around, I tried to get my bearings, to see if I could detect any changes. Last night was only my first night back home from living away at school and, with the dramatic events that had taken place, I hadn't had a chance to yet make the adjustment to being back home again. Before leaving university, I had imagined what it would be like to live at home after being on my own for several months. I anticipated things might look different now that I had a fresh perspective. This morning, still shaken by last night, home was not exactly as I remembered it.

I took comfort in the fact that everything looked the same on the surface. The kitchen looked as it always had. My mother's cheesy china rooster Michael teasingly called her "big cock" was still perched on the long, butter yellow pine table built by Daddy Bill. The same am/fm clock radio sat on the window ledge by the table within easy reach of my father's chair so he could listen to the news.

The kitchen was quiet and I could almost believe peaceful. I opened the fridge and surveyed the possibilities.

Nothing amiss here, except for the unexpected tub of yogurt beside the bag of milk. Yogurt was the new "good for you" food product that I had tried at the school cafeteria, but had never seen in our fridge before. Yogurt was something you bought in a health food store, the likes of which didn't exist in Orangeville. I was glad to see that my mother was trying out new things.

I shut the fridge door. Despite the everyday appearance of the kitchen, I couldn't shake the feeling that all was not as it seemed. The electricity of last night sparked a current of unrest and anxiety as real and dangerous as an exposed live wire. I followed a hairline crack on the wall that ran up to the ceiling. I hadn't noticed it there before. Now that I had detected the fine crack, I knew I would always see it from now on. Our foundation had shifted last night and the effects of the long term damage were just starting to surface.

A buzzing sound drew my attention to the windowsill where a housefly was spinning on its back trying to upright itself. The warm weather was waking up the flies from their long winter sleep. Soon our house would be crawling with them as they made their way groggily from inside the cool brick walls. I remembered how repulsed I had been when I realized our walls were the nesting ground for hundreds of flies laying thousands of eggs. I was used to them now. A person could get used to almost anything if they had to.

The flies had been just another reason to hate the farmhouse when we first moved here. Almost three years later, I still found the farmhouse deficient and the small town dull and depressed, but now this was my home. We belonged here. This was the place we came together as a family.

The telephone rang interrupting my thoughts. I answered to a stranger's voice, identifiable as a local by his accent. "I just want to say I'm real sorry about Harry. I curled with Harry last season an' he's a good man. Hell, he must'ov had good cause to do what he did."

What exactly *had* he done? "Yeah. Thanks," was all I said.

"Well, if yous need anythin', you call me," he said.

I went outside to the porch letting Duke out with me. I found my mother on the front lawn talking closely with the same burly grey-haired officer from last night. Duke ran up to him barking and growling.

"Off, Duke!" I yelled at the German shepherd.

Mom and the officer were standing beside tread marks gouged into the spring grass. The lawn furniture lay crushed and twisted beside the driveway. The middle of the garage door was dented where the car had hit it. Two seven foot maple trees lay toppled across the lawn wrenched out of the earth, torn and broken. But it was the glaring orange tape used by the police to stake out the restricted area that hit me hardest. That, more than anything, declared our home a scene of violence and crime.

The officer was showing my mother something he was holding in his hand. Then they both started walking away from each other heads bent down studying the ground.

My mother found something. She cried eagerly, "Here it is! Is this what you're looking for?" and held up a brass cartridge shell. She was excited like a little girl at an Easter egg hunt. She held in her hand the second shell discarded by her husband when he emptied the casing from his double barreled shotgun. She handed the empty cartridge over to the policeman who thanked her politely.

I walked toward her. "Cindy, this is Corporal Bryant," she said smiling. "You'll never guess. He plays the banjo in a band!"

I couldn't believe it. My mother was actually flirting with the cop! She couldn't help herself. My mother was drawn to men like bees to honey. Duke started up his growling again.

"Sorry," I said. "He's very protective. Especially of my mom."

I watched Corporal Bryant toss the empty cartridge lightly up and down in the palm of his hand, enjoying the weight of it. The sound of the shot being fired echoed in my head.

"Where's Dad?" I asked.

My mother frowned and looked away. "He's gone to the lawyers."

"When did they let him out?"

"Early this morning. They released him," she said her voice starting to break. "They said he wasn't at risk - neither dangerous nor likely to flee. Isn't that crazy?" She let out a sob and retrieved a tissue balled up in the sleeve of her sweater.

"It will be OK," the Corporal said.

"Where's Nat?" I asked.

My mother's face hardened. "At school," she said.

I thought the police probably knew by now it was my sister's boyfriend in the car, but I knew better than to mention it. I looked at the damage. We had seen our lawn plowed up before by tire marks but never this bad. The ravaged grass would take longer to heal this time.

"Why? Why would they do this?" I asked in frustration and anger.

My mother shook her head despondently. She bent over to pick up a mangled lawn chair and leaned it against the garage door. We watched her as she walked over to the maple trees lying by the side of the driveway. Stroking their leaves, she asked the cop if he thought the trees would live if we replanted them. He said all we could do was try. Then he bent down searching for something in the grass. He found a lead pellet and placed it in a plastic bag along with the brass cartridge.

I walked to the end of the lawn to the fence and gazed across the highway where new green shoots of cattle corn poked up through the dirt field. Despite the bright sunshine, a winter chill lingered in the air. A lone patch of grey snow still clung to the shadow of the hydro pole by the highway, the last remnant of a massive mound of snow piled there by the snowplow during the late spring snow-storm. We lived two hours north and west of Toronto and smack dab in the middle of the province's snow belt. The snow always lasted at least a month longer than in the city's milder temperatures. Another reason for hating this place when we moved here. I resented the long winters.

I recalled this particular section of the highway had earned its own reputation of crime and violence before we lived here. The white line running across the highway in front of our driveway was faded, but still intact marking the infamous "quarter mile". I remembered the story Mrs. Rose had told me about the boy, Brian, who was killed road racing on this piece of highway.

A car grinding over gravel behind me made me jump, but it was just the policeman leaving. Corporal Bryant pulled out of the driveway while my mother waved enthu-siastically like she was saying goodbye to a close friend.

A frigid breeze blew over the field, flattening the grass on our lawn and whipping my hair across my face. I tucked my arms across my chest and turned my back into the wind. I inspected the toppled trees. It surprised me how disproportionately large the root beds seemed compared to the size of their tender trunks. On their own, each root was weak and fragile, incapable of offering support, but wrapped together into a tight, intricate mass, they became a tough, secure base capable of sustaining a tall tree.

I looked up at our red brick farmhouse toward my sisters' attic window. I wondered how much my sisters knew. It was inconceivable to me that Natalie had known all along who was in the car. I couldn't believe she wouldn't have told our father if she'd known. If she had told him, none of this would have happened. I didn't know then the worst of it.

CHAPTER TWENTY EIGHT

Choice

 Natalie

I stood at my locker telling Bev what happened last night. I was at the part where John had been hurt, and was pointing to my cheek to describe his injury, when a group of younger boys sauntered by. At first, we ignored them, but they were intent on interrupting us.

"We better be careful," one of the boys taunted loudly so we could hear, "I hear her old man is wicked with a gun."

"Yeah, we wouldn't want to get on his bad side," jeered one.

"We wouldn't want to date his daughter," scoffed another.

The little pests were beginning to irritate me. "I could eat you for breakfast," I said dismissing them.

"Ooooh! I'm scared!" said the first boy.

Bev raised her arm straight from her shoulder and fired an imaginary pistol with her hand - "Pow!" She started laughing and I joined in. Once we began, we couldn't stop. We laughed until there were tears in our eyes and we couldn't catch our breath. By the time we pulled ourselves together, the boys had long since disappeared.

After school I was helping coach gymnastics in the gymnasium when John came by to ask me if I wanted a lift when I was finished. His bandaged face still startled me and my stomach lurched. I told him I'd meet him outside when I was done. He left to wait for me in his car. Five minutes later my father appeared in the gym asking me if I wanted a lift home. I hesitated. Then I told him I'd like that.

When I was ready to leave, I walked out the front door of the school and saw my father sitting in his parked car to my left. John was sitting in his parked car to my right. I walked straight ahead not at all certain which way to go. Then I walked to the right and got in John's car. I didn't look back as we pulled away.

We drove around for a while in John's Cutlass listening to Elvis Presley eight tracks. We headed outside of town and pulled over into a favourite parking place. Here, a small u-shaped section of road curved off the town line, shielded by trees and bushes from the main road. A canopy of branches overhead formed a natural camouflage, suggesting the perfect place for a secret rendezvous. We turned the car off and John went around and opened the trunk. When he slid back into the driver's seat, he had two cold beers in his hands. He found a bottle opener in the glove box, pried off the caps and handed me one.

"I'm scared, John. What are we going to do?"

"Don't be scared, Baby. I'm goin' to make sure nothin' bad happens to you. It's not safe at your house. Not now."

"Not safe?"

"You have to trust me, Natalie. Do you trust me?"

"Yes."

"You are goin' to have to move out."

I was shocked. "I can't move out. Where will I go?"

"You and I can get a place together. I'm makin' good money. We'll find a place in town. I can take care of you."

"I wish we could just stay together now. I don't want to go home."

"I know. It'll just be fer a little while longer. I'll look into gettin' us a place of our own." He flicked dancing Elvis with his finger making his white sequined bellbottoms jiggle. "Did you know Graceland has twenty three friggin' rooms?" he said. "Not bad fer a guy who grew up in a two room shack, eh?"

With his sultry hazel eyes and pouty lips, I thought John resembled a young sexy Elvis. They had other things in common too. Sometimes, when he'd had enough to drink, John would croon Elvis-style to me. He could even move his hips like Elvis. Elvis had been a truck driver, and they were both the sons of truck drivers. No one thought, including themselves, they would ever be anything else.

"Why don't you sing for me, Elvis?" I said coyly.

John smiled at me. He touched my cheek where my dimple flashed at him. "Maybe later. Right now I have other things in mind."

"Really? Like this you mean?" And I reached over and kissed him on the mouth.

"Yeah, somethin' like that."

We drank our beer and necked until the windshield grew steamy and the shadows lengthened over the road. It was getting late, and I should have been home by now.

"You better take me home, John," I said.

He reluctantly turned the car on and drove me toward home. He pulled over to the shoulder of the highway before the farmhouse and I got out.

"I'll call you tonight at eight o'clock," he said. "Oh, and Natalie, better not tell anyone about our plans just yet. Let's keep it our secret until I find a place. OK?"

I nodded my head and he drove away.

It was close to dinnertime by the time I arrived home, but as I entered the kitchen I was surprised to find no signs of a meal prepared. Usually my mother would be busy by the stove, the table would be set, and I would be told to wash my hands before I sat down, but tonight I was greeted instead by loud German Oompah Pah music. Although she didn't know a word of German, my mother had always had a passion for German music. (Well, actually any vaguely eastern-European-sounding music would do.) I was used to her singing and dancing around the house. Coming home from school I had found her on more than one occasion marching and twirling to the foreign radio station, volume pumped up, as she did her housework. She would pick up bits from the chorus and sing them with increasing gusto like she understood what she was singing. When she ran out of words, she would sing la, la, la or ah, ah, ah, or oo, oo, oo. I'm not sure where her love of this particular kind of music came from. We are of English, possibly Welsh and/or Scottish, descent; no German that we know of flows in our genes. Yet this fiery, cymbal-crashing German dance music always resonated deeply within my mother.

I poked my face into the living room and found Mom rocking in her rocking chair feet tottering back and forth on the little wooden stool. She had her eyes closed and was in a far-off-German-castle-kind-of place. Her subdued reaction to the music was uncharacteristic and ominous. I thought it best not to disturb her and crossed the room quietly to head up to my bedroom, when my father spotted me from the dining room. He was sitting in my spot at the table playing solitaire. Our dining room had hosted count-less family meals over the years, but never before had I seen my father sit in there alone. He was waiting for me.

"Natalie, I'd like to speak with you," he said for the second time that day. I reluctantly entered the room and stood beside him. He made me wait as he played out his hand. I looked straight ahead at the large family portrait hanging at the far end of the room. This was the focal point of the room. I took in the pastel drawing of the seven of us thinking how much we had changed since it was done. I recalled how excited I was at eight years old to have my own private sitting for the portrait. I had promised not to tell my father about it because it was a surprise Christmas present for him. The artist was a friend of my mother's and had sketched each of us separately; my father she had drawn from a photo. I thought it was miraculous how she had managed to capture us individually and put us altogether.

My father was looking down at his cards deep in thought over his next play. He was sucking on a toothpick, wiggling it between his lips. Finally, he cleared his throat and took the toothpick out of his mouth.

"Where did you go after school?"

"I was coaching gymnastics."

"Don't be coy. I know that. I was waiting for you. Where did you go after that?"

"Nowhere." I said talking to the floor. When I looked up at him he averted his eyes from me. He considered my response at length staring out the window to the highway for so long I thought maybe he hadn't heard me.

Then he turned to me with a sigh and said, "Natalie, I don't want you seeing John anymore."

I could feel myself slipping away again. I saw the image of the balloon rising in the sky. I wondered how high it got before it succumbed to pressure and burst. "I'm not going to stop seeing him, Dad. You can't make me."

"If you continue to see him, you are no longer welcome in this house. While you live under my roof, you live by my rules."

"I hate you!" I cried and stormed out of the room. I thumped up the stairs running into Paul, who halted in his tracks, mouth flapped open. He must have overheard us. I brushed past *Christina's World*, a blur of a pink dress in a bleak field, and stomped up to the attic. I flung myself facedown on my bed prepared to hate my father forever. He couldn't stop me from seeing John, I vowed.

I heard Christine climbing up the steep attic stairs. Turning my face, I saw her enter our room, throw her macramé handbag on her bed, and turn on the transistor radio.

"What's wrong?" she asked.

"Dad said I can't see John anymore," I said into the bedspread.

"Well, that's not surprising. As if that will stop you."

"He also said I can't live here if I keep seeing him."

"Ouch. Classic move, Harry. What's the man thinking?"

Christine plunked down on her twin bed opposite to mine under the low slanting roofline. When we first moved here, my father had the attic turned into a fourth bedroom for my sister and me. A built-in desk with dresser drawers ran the width of the room, topped by a long, horizontal mirror. The walls were covered in burnt orange shag carpet that ran up to the slanting roof line. It was our own little haven. Our parents seldom came up here, the steep narrow stairs created a physical barrier that separated us from the rest of the house. From our place at the top, we enjoyed the illusion we reigned supreme and nothing could reach us.

"By the way," she said, "I thought it was John all along. In the car, I mean." I rolled over and sat up. She said, "You knew didn't you?"

I gave a slight shrug.

"What are you going to do?"

I twisted the blue sapphire ring on my finger. I held it up to the light exposing the flame of white deep inside the dark blue gemstone. "I can't stop being with John. We are thinking about getting a place together."

"I don't understand you. What do you see in that guy, anyway?"

Now she was against us too. I flew off the bed in a temper and lashed out at her. "You're one to talk. At least John loves me. Not like the greaseballs you've slept with!"

I stormed over to the window. Now I'd done it. I had never told her what I really thought before. Over the past year, Christine had dated one guy after another, high school drop-outs who worked in town as auto mechanics and had a bad reputation. They were tough guys known for causing fights. The way she had thrown herself at them had scared me. Overnight, she went from being the family angel and straight-A student to a bitchy slut. I missed the old Christine, the sister who was kind and gentle.

I took a deep breath. "I'm sorry, Chris. I didn't mean it."

From across the room she said in a small, hurt voice, "Yes, you did." She stared up at the ceiling. After a moment she said, "And, you're right. They were losers. Big time."

She got off her bed and came to stand beside me at the window. "But at least I've moved on."

She was referring to her new boyfriend, Rob. He was tall with blonde hair, broad shoulders and a six pack from lifting bails of hay on a farm all summer. He was a departure from the rough and tough guys she had tried on for a while. I hoped she held on to this one.

"I have to admit Rob is a hunk," I said, ignoring the insinuation and offering a chance at reconciliation.

Christine moved away from the window and crossed to the other end of the room where she leaned into the mirror and puckered her lips into a dainty circle, a reflexive action she did whenever she checked her mirrored image. She reapplied heavy dark eyeliner and examined a pimple on her chin close up in the long horizontal mirror that ran the width of the wall. "Anyway, Dad will probably calm down in a few days and then you can try talking to him," she said.

"You know I can't. He doesn't listen. He'll just lecture me about how he expects so much more from me and how I've lied to him and let him down."

She picked up a brush from the built-in dressing table and dragged it through her long, thick chestnut hair. "I know the speech. How he's raised us to think for ourselves and how we need to stand up for ourselves."

"That's the one."

Christine began searching for something in the bottom of her dresser drawer. She pulled out a baggy and some rolling papers. I watched her roll a joint. We opened the small window and stuck our faces outside, blowing the sickly sweet smell of weed over the branches of the maple tree. In the farmer's field across the highway, between neat rows of plowed up dirt, a groundhog poked its head out of its hole, sniffing the air. A mile above the field a hawk circled a dull sky in expectation.

Dad never gave John a chance, I thought. Now it's too late.

Harry wearing a WWII helmet, Whitman Street, North York, circa 1969

REBOS breakfast Whitman St, North York, circa 1972,
Left to Right: Cindy, Harry, Natalie

Left to Right: Cindy, Michael, Natalie at the Farmhouse 1975

Christmas at the Farmhouse, 1975, Centre:
Diane; Left of Centre: Natalie

CHAPTER TWENTY NINE

Murder

Cindy

The night I watched my father being taken away to jail was the night he became a local celebrity. It was also the night he was charged with attempted murder. For the next couple of days, news reports of: "Orangeville Man Charged with Attempted Murder" were aired on the morning and evening news on both radio and television stations. The *Toronto Star* covered the story, as did several community newspapers, including our own *Orangeville Banner*. On Wednesday May 17, 1978, the front page of the *Orangeville Banner* headlined: "Youth Is In Hospital", and under in big bold letters: "Attempted Murder is Charged". Ironically, this was the second time within a few weeks that my father's name had made the *Banner* headlines. Earlier that month, he was photographed smiling alongside my mother holding substantial curling trophies. They were being recognized for winning the Sutton Trophy for three consecutive years. (They would go on to win it the next two years as well.)

The morning after the shooting was the morning the phones started ringing. It seemed everyone who knew my father, or knew of him, was calling to see if it was really their Harry Carey on the news. The first couple of days we

179

took turns answering the calls. My mother was the first to buckle under the stress. The night of the shooting was the culmination of several sleepless nights my mother had spent in fear of the anonymous cars terrorizing our property. Her nerves were already frayed. Now they were sliced. She grew increasingly agitated and weary of the well-wishers' questions and concerns. Unable to keep going, she went to her bedroom, pulled the blinds down, and climbed into bed. It was three o'clock in the afternoon. She stayed there for three days. We left the phones off the hook then.

My father was charged with five criminal counts: use of a firearm in the commission of an offense, three counts of aggravated assault, and attempted murder. Everyone said he was lucky he didn't kill someone. When he fired his one hundred year old shotgun that he had kept hidden on the top shelf of his bedroom closet (I had never seen it before) he aimed at the car's tires. The last time my father had fired the gun he was a young boy shooting at ground-hogs on his grandparents' farm. Like the gun that was rusty and stiff from lack of use, my father was long since out of practice, and he missed, hitting the rim of the tire instead. Pellets from the cartridge pierced the tire but did not cause enough damage to flatten it immediately, and the car was able to drive on. Fearing that the car was going to get away again and he would have failed once more to identify the intruders, my father ran after the car and dislodged a second cartridge at the rear tires. This time the pellets smashed out the back window. Several lodged into the head and leg of Daniel Cocker in the backseat. Others seared Natalie's boyfriend's face, narrowly brushing his left eye.

My father received a great deal of support from relatives and friends as well as the general populace of Orangeville. Although he had lived in Orangeville for less than three years, he had been active in the community as both a business owner and community service volunteer. We were amazed by the dozens of well-wishers who called to express their sympathy and show their support. Encouraged by the positive reaction he received, my father decided to attend his weekly Rotary meeting that fell just two days after the shooting. He was resolved, however, not to discuss who was in the car if he was asked.

He went to the meeting fully expecting to be confronted by fellow Rotarians about his story, which was now all over town. But to his surprise, no one mentioned it to him. The meeting adjourned, people were starting to leave and still no one had said a word, when a loud voice called out, "Hey, Shotgun! Just a minute, I want to talk to you". The room grew suddenly quiet as everyone held their breath and waited for my father's reaction. He looked directly at the man who had addressed him, and without a hint of reproach for the stinging acknowledgement, replied with an honest, "Yes?"

The tension in the room was broken. The fellow Rotarian had addressed the elephant in the room and, in doing so, paved the way for others to come forward to talk to my father about what they had heard. My father was grateful for the chance as he wasn't ashamed of what he had done. (He would eventually become the President of the Rotary Club.) For now, for those who knew him, and those who knew of his reputation, he was henceforth known as "Shotgun Harry".

The following weekend my parents were playing in the finals of the last curling bonspiel of the season. My mother called from the curling club between games to see if I could pick up Paul from the club and take him home as it was getting late and they had to keep playing. I entered the dim lounge area behind the long glass windows facing the rink. There were a few clusters of curlers relaxing at tables and chairs between games, watching the ice and talking amongst themselves. As I passed a group of men I didn't know I heard one of them say, "It's so unlike Harry. So out of character for him."

I stopped short behind them and pretended to watch the action on the ice.

"I know. It's so dramatic. I can't believe he fired a *shotgun* at them," another man said in a low tone. "What was he thinking? You can't just go around taking the law into your own hands. Someone could have been killed."

I sat down quietly nearby without drawing attention to myself so I could continue to listen.

The first speaker said, "I wonder why he just didn't get the license plate number and report it?"

"He did that the first time but the police didn't do anything," said a Scottish accent.

"I'm not so sure I would have used a gun though. Maybe a bat. Guns are asking for trouble. Where did Harry get a gun anyway?" asked a raspy voice.

"I would have done the same thing if I had been vandalized. Especially if the police did nothing about it," said the Scot. "I think it's great someone finally stood up to those delinquents. We need to be able to protect ourselves. We can't just let them walk all over us whenever and wherever they please. I think it shows real heroism."

"Did you hear it was his daughter's boyfriend driving the car?" said the raspy voice.

"What a nightmare. Harry better have a good lawyer," said the first man.

I got up from my chair then and found Paul. By this time it was a couple of hours past his bedtime, and he had fallen asleep in one of the chairs facing the ice. He had his feet propped up on the window sill, his head tucked into his chest, and his arms loosely hugged his knees. Fondly, I noticed how big he was getting. I tapped him gently on the shoulder and he stirred, rolling back his fair head to reveal soft freckled cheeks. He woke up and, together, we watched our parents curl for a few minutes.

My father was the skip. He was yelling at his teammates so loudly we could hear him through the thick glass, "Sweep! Sweep!" If I didn't know better, I would have thought he was angry; however, it is the skip's role to call out clear orders to their teammates. My mother swept vigorously until he yelled at her to "stop!"

"You know, Paul, some people think our father is a hero," I said.

"I know," he said simply, without hesitation. "He stands up for himthelf."

A few days later I was at home with my mother in the kitchen while she was making date squares. My favourite. "Did you see this Mom?" I asked, showing her the editorial section from today's *Orangeville Banner*. "It says:

'Harold Carey's reaction to try to stop the vandals so he could identify them should be applauded. The real crime here is that an honest man who tries to protect his property and family when the police failed to do so, is punished like a common criminal when he should be treated as a hero.'"

"It's unbelievable, peoples' reactions," she said, popping the baking dish into the oven. "I have people I don't even know stop me on the street telling me how proud they are of Harry. They say I must be so proud of my husband because of what he did to protect his family and his property. They say he was justified in doing what he did."

"Do you think he was?"

"He was only trying to protect us. People are still sending us gifts and cards. Their encouragement is touching. Yesterday I got a phone call from a man I've never even met who invited your father and me to dinner at his farm so we could 'get our minds off things'. He said he and his wife wanted to extend an invitation to us for 'taking the bull by the horns'".

"Are you going to go?" I asked.

"I think so, he seemed very sweet. And next week we got invited to go flying. A couple who owns an airstrip near here has had their airstrip torn up a few times recently. They've never been able to catch the culprits. They are so frustrated that when they heard what your father did they wanted to show their support so they asked if we wanted to go up in their plane."

"Wow, that'll be fun."

She winced. "Ewhh," she said holding her soft stomach. "I don't know. I don't think I'd like being in a small plane. You know me when it comes to planes."

But when the day came, my mother surprised everyone and went up in the plane. Before she left home, she told us to watch out for her flying over our house. It was a clear, sunny day, the bright blue sky creased with slivers of white cloud as Paul, Christine, Natalie and I saw the plane approaching. We ran outside waving our arms over our heads and yelling, jumping up and down like we were signaling to be rescued. The plane circled low over our house and dipped its wings at us. Maybe, I thought, everything was going to be all right after all.

The next day Mom and I returned from a shopping trip in town to find Geoff alone outside and hard at work shoveling gravel onto the floor of the new barn my father was building. Judging by the diminished pile of gravel, he had been at it for a while.

"What are you doing this for?" I asked when I reached him.

Geoff paused and leaned on the shovel. Wiping the sweat from his brow, he said grinning, "Thought I'd help Harry out. I don't want to get shot".

CHAPTER THIRTY

Blame

Natalie

I was forbidden from seeing John, but I continued to be with him. I thought my parents had no idea I was still seeing him. He never came to the house, but I would meet him in town or at friends' places. It was never a problem to get a lift with someone else. Unfortunately, we no longer had the use of my grandparents' home. After the abortion, my parents put two and two together and had asked me to hand over my duplicate key.

If my parents had their suspicions about John and me, they kept them to themselves. They chose to look the other way and avoid confronting me, afraid perhaps of where a confrontation might lead.

The secrecy made our meetings even more exciting, the romance more magical. The more I saw John behind my parents' back, the further I distanced myself from them. I was traveling a new highway and I didn't care if I forgot my way back home. I tried not to think of the possible impact of my deceitful behaviour on my parents. I didn't want to consider how they may be hurting. Communication between us had virtually shut down, making it easy to avoid having to deal with them. If it weren't for my mother's eczema returning again, I probably would not have known how stressed she was.

My mother has always been a nervous person. She's the kind of person who shrieks loudly if she almost steps on the dog she didn't see lying by her feet, or you accidentally drop the ketchup bottle beside her, or enter a room without her hearing you. Her stress was most often demonstrated by the state of eczema on her hands. When I was in the hospital, her eczema flared up; after the shooting, it returned more fiercely red and raw than ever before.

My mother's hands had a life all their own. Her hands had cradled and nursed five babies, cooked our meals, sewn our clothes, grown our morning glories, tended our vegetable garden, and caressed our foreheads. They were busy, nurturing hands; however, they could also be sharp and angry. Occasionally her hands were responsible for swatting a stinging spatula at a naughty bottom. Sometimes they harboured pointed finger nails that accidentally poked and scratched when I got in the way. It was never intentional or malicious, but it hurt more because she never seemed all that apologetic.

Now my mother's hands were forced to lie idle and itchy in her lap. She knew she shouldn't scratch, but she couldn't help it. Once she started she couldn't stop. She'd scratch and scratch while moaning in pure sensual relief. She said anything that felt so "gorgeous" couldn't be bad for you. On doctor's orders, she wasn't supposed to get her hands wet, and had to wear rubber gloves all day and soft, flannel gloves to bed over a greasy layer of Vaseline and cortisone cream. When she took the gloves off to reapply more cream, I couldn't look at the brittle and blistery hands, the dry and flakey fingers grown redundant with lack of use like prehistoric appendages. I felt responsible for those hands.

John and I weren't welcome at my house, so we went to his house. The Ranbergs lived in a modest brick bungalow on Airport Road about twenty miles outside of town. The first time I went with John to his house after the shooting I was apprehensive about meeting his parents again. I thought they might be angry with me for being the daughter of the man who shot their son. However, my fear subsided as soon as I saw them.

John's mother was in the kitchen making tea. Barbara Ranberg was a tall, slim woman with a sallow smoker's complexion. Judging by the massive tower of teased brown hair on top of her head, she hadn't changed her hairstyle in over a decade. She greeted me with a hug. "How are you holdin' up, honey?" she asked.

"Fine," I replied, surprised at the sudden knot in my throat.

"We just sat down with a pot of tea. Come join us," she said, pulling out two chairs for us. "You two sure have been through a lot lately," she said as she poured our tea. She rested the tea pot on the table and bent over her son's chair to examine his scars. A red line ran across his cheekbone. She lifted his bangs and traced the second line with her finger. "They're healin' nicely. Shouldn't leave much of a scar at all," she said. She stood up and crossed to the other side of the room, but not before I saw tears in her eyes.

"Parents can make it awfully tough on their kids sometimes," said John's father. "Too bad you don't need a license to be a parent," he said.

Such unexpected compassion from John's parents unglued me. I had to fight back the tears. I was fine until someone showed me sympathy, and then I had to struggle to hold myself together.

"Did John tell you he is thinkin' about going to school in the fall?" John's mother asked me changing the subject. She had dried her eyes and turned a bright, brave face toward us. Gus frowned at her.

"That's wonderful. John, why didn't you tell me?" I asked him.

John had heard the hopeful plea in his mother's voice at the same moment he saw the disappointment cross his father's face.

"I haven't decided yet," he mumbled.

"Well, there's still lots to be done," his mother urged. "We need to call for the applications. And fill them out." She was gaining momentum. "I'll help you. We'll need to get the deadlines. If we get on top of it now, you can start in September. You don't want to miss out."

Gus glared at his wife. She smiled back at him. "More tea, honey?"

"It's a big decision, Son," he said. "You'll need time to think about it."

"Time he doesn't have if he is to start in the fall," said Mrs. Ranberg.

"The fall is our busiest season, Barbara. I will need him."

Barbara bowed her head and sipped her tea. John pushed back his chair to leave. "Thank you for the tea," I said standing up.

"You're welcome, dear," said Mrs. Ranberg. But she wasn't ready to let us go yet. "By the way, how is school goin' for you?" she asked me.

"Can't you see the kids are tryin' to get away?" Gus said.

"You are smart to stay at school, Natalie," continued his wife.

John cringed. Gus turned to me. "Just so's you know, you are welcome here anytime. Our door is always open."

"Thank you, Mr. Ranberg."

"Call me Gus."

Somehow, my friendship with Bev had managed to endure through my relationship with John, and we were still best friends. Bev was my lifeline. She listened endlessly to me when all I could do was talk about how I was going to continue to see John despite my parents' wishes. Bev was direct and forthright and I could always trust her to say exactly what she felt. She never seemed to mind me complaining about how uncomfortable and tense it was at home.

We were sitting in her bedroom listening to CHUM FM on the radio. The song, I *Shot the Sheriff, but I did not Shoot the Deputy*, came on. Bev turned it up. "Oh, my God, Nat. What a riot. This song could be your father's new theme song!" She crooned, "I shot the boyfriend, but I did not shoot the driver!"

"Shut up," I said, suddenly not wanting to talk about it. I gave her shoulder a light hit.

"Relax. I'm on your side, remember."

"Sorry." Bev had light blond hair cut in a sensible short bob, a heart-shaped determined chin, and large grey eyes that never lied. "I don't honestly know what I would do without you," I told her.

"It's so unfair that your parents blame you for what happened. I don't know how you put up with their judgmental attitude. You'd think they were living in the Dark Ages the way they are always trying to control you."

I agreed with her. When she invited me to spend the night, I gladly accepted. I shared in confidence that John and I planned to move in together as soon as he found a place. Bev suggested I move in with her and her mother until that time. She said her mother was fine with having me stay with them for a while until I figured out what I wanted to do. I decided Bev was right. It was time to leave home.

CHAPTER THIRTY ONE

Leaving

 Cindy

"Oh, Cindy, it's you. I was just thinking of you!" my mother said over the phone. I rolled my eyes. Without fail, she told me the same thing every time I called her. She was convinced it was just another sign of her clairvoyant tendencies.

I was living at my friend Judy's house in my old neighbourhood in North York for the summer. I had a job at Ontario Place, the new waterfront entertainment complex erected under the provincial government of Premier John Robarts to showcase the province. I was glad to be out of Orangeville for the summer. Besides, I had pretty much used up all the employment opportunities in town. Since moving to Orangeville, I had had a string of part-time and summer jobs. Without question, my best job to date was being a hostess at Ontario Place. It was a highly-coveted summer job restricted to Ontario university students only. One of the highlights was providing security on stage for the entertainers. I got to see many famous performers up close from the stage, including live performances of The National Ballet Company.

I hadn't talked to my mother for a few weeks. "I'm glad you called. Natalie's run away," she told me.

"What do you mean she's run away?"

"I came home from grocery shopping and she was gone. Some of her clothes are gone too."

"When was this?"

"Two days ago. The day the twister touched down over in Erin Township. We got the tail end of it. What a terrible storm we had! The wind was so strong I couldn't drive. I had to pull over."

"And you have no idea where she went?" I asked with growing frustration.

"No."

"And she didn't leave a note?"

"No."

"What did Dad say?"

"You know your father, he hasn't said anything. Just keeps it all inside."

My father's words rang in my head, "He wasn't man enough to come and talk to me." Who wasn't doing the talking now?

"Did you try at John's place?"

"No! I don't want to call that boy."

"Well, maybe you should. She's probably there."

"After all I've done for her."

"Mom, I have to catch my bus for work. Just find her please," I said.

Natalie

I didn't really mean to run away. I just meant to stay at Bev's house for a few days, but after a week passed and I hadn't heard from my family, I decided I was happier where I was.

I know I should have called home but I guess I wanted them to worry about me. I wanted them to get good and upset and angry. I wanted them to miss me. Besides, if they really wanted to, they could find out where I was and call me.

Bev lived with her mother in the downstairs apartment of a one hundred-year-old house in town. Bev's mom, Lara, was cool with me staying with them. Lara was not like other mothers. She lit incense and played the guitar. She went barefoot and braless and wore flowing pink caftans over white cotton petticoats that showed underneath. Lara was a vegan. She laughed when I asked her if she thought vegetarianism was safe. Coming from a person whose family regularly stocked half a cow in the freezer, I was shocked to learn that there were people who actually preferred a meatless diet. One night while Bev was working, Lara taught me how to make vegetarian pizza and we sat on her bean bag chairs in the living room balancing our pizza on our knees and listening to the Beatles and Carol King.

Lara studied yoga and greeted most days with a deep breathing salutation to the sun in front of her living room window. I was fascinated; the only time I had seen yoga was when I was home sick from school one morning and, searching the television channels, had come across a husky-voiced eastern European blonde in a white leotard contorting her sixty-year-old frame into positions that only young children should be able to achieve.

One morning, after I had been living with Bev for almost two weeks, I spread open the beaded curtain that separated the front hall from the living room, and found Lara deep in meditation. She stood in front of the floor to ceiling window and the brass potted palm with her hands to her heart in silent prayer. I tiptoed around behind her, trying not to disturb her concentration, but Lara heard me, and turned around.

"Sorry. I didn't mean to interrupt," I said.

"No problem." She stopped me on my way into the kitchen. "Do you know how to breathe?" she asked.

"Last time I looked."

"No, I mean really breathe. Like this." She put her hands on her abdomen and, with eyes closed, inhaled with a long "aaah" that filled her body with air. Then she exhaled with a loud "soooh" and her stomach contracted. "Now, you try it," she said.

"No, it's OK."

"Come on, there's nothing to be afraid of," Lara said putting her hand on my shoulder and leading me in front of the window. "It's very important to breathe. Buddhists use the same word for both breath and life – prana. Without breath there is no life."

She directed me to sit on the red and gold Persian rug beside her. I crossed my legs and let her guide my inhalations and exhalations. She had me sit up tall, put my hands on my stomach and inhale into first my navel, then ribs, chest, shoulders and finally my throat. Then, I retraced the flow exhaling into my navel feeling my stomach press against my spine.

I found out I had never truly breathed before. As I breathed, she told me it was really important to breathe fully to increase the circulation, improve the posture, and expand the mind. She said if I practiced regularly I would soon be able to slow my breathing down to the point where I could take long pauses between breaths. It was during these still moments, she said, that the third eye became all-seeing and the soul was most open to experiencing new images and receiving revelations. Well, I didn't know about that, but I continued to exhale deeply.

"That's good," Lara said. I realized I had been holding my breath for a long time. It felt such a relief to breathe. I had been working so hard to hold myself together for such a long time. With the release came tears.

"That's OK." Lara said gently. "It's all right, just let it come. Don't fight it." She stroked my back.

"I'm sorry," I said. "I don't know why I'm crying."

"It happens sometimes. Don't worry about it. It's best to let it out. Some people will go through their whole life holding their breath, keeping everything locked up inside, so that they can't ever let go."

It felt good to cry. Lara said she would make us some coffee. I followed her into the kitchen.

"So, do you want to talk about it?" she asked while the coffee brewed.

"I don't think I can go home again."

"You can't or don't want to?"

"A little of both I guess."

"Your parents must really miss you. Why don't you give them a call?"

Lara handed me the phone. I dialed the number nervously. I'd had no communication with my family since I moved here. "Ma? It's me."

"Natalie!" She started to cry. "We've been so worried about you."

"Ma, I'm fine," I said, my voice cracking.

"What? Where are you?"

"I'm at Bev's."

"When are you going to stop this nonsense? When are you coming home?" I didn't answer her. "Natalie? Are you there?"

"Yeah, I'm here.

"Will you at least come for supper tomorrow?" Another pause. "Your dad won't be home," she said pointedly.

"OK. Bye, Ma."

"What did you call me?"

"Bye." I hung up. Lara was watching me.

"You going to see your folks? Well, there is something I need to tell you. I was going to wait until tonight when Bev was here, but I might as well tell you now. I'm moving. I've decided to move to Oshawa to be with my boyfriend. So, it's just as well you are going back home."

"But I'm just going home for supper!" I cried. "I haven't decided to move back." I was in a panic. I thought about Bev. "What's Bev going to do?"

"Bev has decided to stay in Orangeville and finish her high school here."

"Where will she live?"

"She is supposed to be looking at a place this week. Maybe you could move in with her if it doesn't work out for you at home."

When Bev got home that evening we talked about renting a place together. She had heard about a two bedroom place that sounded perfect. My new job at McDonalds would cover my portion of the rent – fifty dollars a week. It was settled.

I went home for supper the next day. I told my mother that Bev and I were moving out on our own in a couple of weeks. Her reaction was as I imagined - she was horrified by the idea. She tried to talk me out of it. She clearly didn't think Bev and I could pull it off. She wanted me to live at home, and suggested I at least move back home until my new place was ready. I told her I would consider it.

I moved back home for a week. At the dinner table the first night, the strained silence between us was punctuated only by certain unavoidable requests.

"Pass the salt," said my father without looking up from his plate.

"Pass the bread please," my mother said.

My father stopped eating and raised an eyebrow.

"What?" she said to him.

He put his fork down. "Pass your mother the bread, children. Look at her, she's wasting away."

My mother chewed her bread slowly, throwing daggers with her eyes at her husband across the table.

While I was living back home, my mother couldn't do enough for me: she whipped up my favourite dessert - strawberry cheesecake; made a pair of shorts and matching top for me; drove me into town whenever I wanted; and let me talk for hours on the phone. Harry, on the other hand, acted like I had never returned. He talked to his dogs more than he spoke to me. He never asked where I had been, how I was doing, or where I was going.

John thought I had made a big mistake moving back home. The first night home, I sat by the phone waiting for him to call. It rang at last, but it was for Christine. I couldn't get her off no matter how hard I pleaded. I knew John would be upset if he couldn't get through. By the time she got off the phone, I was frantic. When John finally reached me, he was in a terrible temper. He had tried calling every ten minutes for an hour and a half. He yelled and cursed at me and there was no reasoning with him. The next evening, my family was going to the movies and wanted me to join them. I told them I had already seen the movie. I stayed home by the phone. I didn't dare miss his call again.

I left home officially on a sunny day the first of July. Bev came and helped me stuff the rest of my belongings into her little Pinto. My father sat outside in the shade of the deep side porch pretending to read. My mother folded laundry in the mudroom, fretting between the kitchen and the back door checking our progress. Mom hadn't tried to talk me out of moving out since her initial reaction a week ago. Dad never spoke to me about leaving home. Maybe they thought it wouldn't happen if they just let it rest, didn't make a big deal about it. I guess they underestimated me. Now that I was actually leaving for good, they didn't know what to do. But they didn't try to stop me.

We finished loading the car. My mother was now visibly upset, scratching long and hard at her hands. A horse neighed from the back pasture. It was Abbey, Christine's new horse. I looked toward the back pasture to see if Christine was coming to say goodbye. The wind came up and whipped the long grass in the field around the old barn. It whistled through its vulnerable walls, sending shivers along its fragile roof. The barn trembled and shook, and for a moment it seemed close to not being able to hold up much longer. But then the wind died down and the barn gave one last tremulous sigh before it settled once more into its enduring foothold in the earth, worn and stooped, but still standing.

Christine was not coming. She was too busy working out the yearling. Abbey was very green and my sister spent many hours training her so she could ride her. Paul had crept outside to say goodbye. He was watching me from the back stoop, his face bleak and wan, highlighting the freckles across his cheeks and nose. He started to cry. I didn't want him to worry about me, but I didn't know when I would see him again. I felt my own tears coming and averted my face from him bending down to pat Duke goodbye. Our eleven-year-old terrier, Toby, not to be outdone, wiggled over for some attention too. "Wiggle Bum," I thought, remembering how I had laughed when Dad called her that.

My mother, watching from the back door, finally realized I was actually leaving and quickly scooped up the grey and white bundle from around her ankles and threw it at me. She yelled, "Here, take the damn cat with you!" I grabbed for Fred as she landed by my face, scraping her claws down my cheek. (The ugly red scratches would last for weeks.) I hugged her to my chest and gathered us into the car. As we pulled out of the driveway I felt my father's eyes on me. I forced myself to look at him. He sat unmoving and erect, his piercing blue eyes boring into me. I could not tell what his expression might conceal. I smiled uneasily and looked down at the cat in my lap. As we drove past the farmhouse I looked up at my old bedroom and saw a bat fly across the attic window.

CHAPTER THIRTY TWO

Coping

 Cindy

Like most of her peers, my mother stayed at home while she was raising her children. After we had lived in Orangeville for a few years, she started working part-time for The Banner Book Store on Broadway. I, too, had worked at this store part-time for a while. Mom was good with the customers, much better than I was, and she enjoyed working at the stationery store. She also liked earning a little extra personal income. My father kept my mother on a shoestring budget. The managing, or mismanaging of funds as my father saw it, was a constant source of irritation in my parents' marriage. Out of necessity, my mother had become adept at creating ways to stretch her very limited budget.

To look at her, no one would suspect she was wanting. Once, when she was ringing up a bill on the cash register, her customer exclaimed: "Look at all those diamonds on your fingers! I guess you don't work here for the money!" My mother basked in the compliment, and was flattered by the notion that she could be construed as wealthy. Who was she to point out the origin of the diamonds was the inheritance of several inconsequential diamonds forged together?

Mom had always shown a craving toward all things expensive and luxurious: diamonds, mink coats, Mercedes. After twenty three years of marriage, she felt she had done without long enough and deserved the luxuries she sought. She was on a mission to accumulate her most-wanted possessions and, eventually, she got what she wanted.

After my grandfather retired from the office supply store he and Helen had started in 1957, and which they left to my father to run, Diane quit working at the Banner Book Store and joined the family business. When Dad invested in Darwen Office Supply, it had grown from a small store on Mill Street, to a small business on a warehouse lot in the new industrial area of town. The new office was five times the size of the previous store, with a large warehouse in the back, a boardroom, a loading bay and ample parking. After Dad's first year in business with his in-laws, my grandmother was ready to retire, but my grandfather stayed on for another four years. Gradually, the company's target market changed, and the focus shifted from general office supplies retail to office furniture and commercial interior design. It was a progressive move and, over the long haul, proved successful as the business expanded.

My mother didn't particularly like working at Darwens. More accurately, she didn't like working for her husband. She didn't like the way he treated his staff, including her, barking orders at them, managing from a superior distance. Adding injury to pain, my mother was indignant about the amount of money she was paid. She found the $5.00 per hour her husband paid her insulting. On one of the few times that my mother criticized my father while they were still together, she complained that: "Harry orders me around like a dog, and only pays me minimum wage". However, she had no aspirations to manage the family business, and despite being unhappy working with her husband, she continued to work there part-time for several years.

One autumn weekend I was home from university when I found Christine in the field behind the house working out her horse. "Hey Lou!" I yelled over the fence calling her by her nickname. She dropped the lunge line and came over to greet me.

"When did you get home?" she asked.

"A little while ago. Abbey is so pretty."

"Yeah, but she's a brat."

"Do you think I could ride her?"

"She's not ready. She'll throw you off." Christine rubbed her hand over her hip and leg and winced in pain. I've been bucked off so many times I've stopped counting."

In appeasement for making us live in the country, our father had promised his daughters a horse. Christine got the horse. She saved her money and bought her own horse. She'd only had one year of riding lessons, once a week, before we moved to the country. She taught herself theory from library books, and the rest she picked up from discussions with other riders. Although I never told her, I was impressed with my sister's perseverance and courage, and proud that she was able to train the animal so she could get in the saddle.

The same perseverance had enabled my sister to learn how to drive a standard car. Convinced it was a good skill to have, Christine was determined to take her driver's test in a standard, something everyone had tried to talk her out of as it was more difficult than driving an automatic. She took the test in a standard car and passed. In the end she was right to persist – I never learned to drive standard.

"I better get back to her," Christine said walking back toward the middle of the field.

"Have you seen Dad?" I called to her.

"Nope. He's not around much these days," she yelled across her shoulder.

I retraced my steps and headed back toward the farmhouse. As I walked by the new barn, the pungent, earthy smell of fresh hay and horse engulfed me. I stopped to breathe in the perfume of the country, the wonderful penetrating aroma of the outdoors. The front door of the barn was open and Toby ambled outside to greet me from her warm barn bed.

My father built the barn to house his cows and Christine's horse. It was fashioned from recycled scraps and salvaged parts. The front door and windows were from a wreckers he'd found in Toronto. The walls were made with lumber and steel from the old piggery that had formerly stood on this site. Only the corrugated steel roof was new, and it stood out like a beacon against the dark evergreen trees, trapping the sunlight and blinding the eyes. Inside the barn, my father crafted double stall doors that split in half so the animals could look out from their containment. The barn included four stables - there was hope for another horse one day - and storage room for bales of hay, feed and supplies.

I walked by the old carriage house and my mother's vegetable garden, past the single car garage attached to the farmhouse, and reached the back door. Inside the house, I found my mother busy in the kitchen. A delicious smell of brown sugar, spices and apples filled the room. I leaned against the warm oven door, always my favourite spot in the house, while inside the oven an apple crisp bubbled and baked. "Where's Dad?" I asked.

"What's today? Saturday?...he's golfing," she said preoccupied.

"But it's almost November. The golf course is closed," I said.

"Oh, I meant curling. Golfing, curling, whatever. He's not here."

My father had always enjoyed the camaraderie of the men he golfed and curled with, but now he was with them more than with his family. A few evenings a week he could be found at either the clubhouse or rink lounge telling jokes and sharing stories with his cronies. For such a social creature, my father craved large doses of privacy. He was happiest working alone on outdoor projects on his hobby farm, like building the barn, or repairing the old fences around the property. In the winter, he liked to cross-country ski with his dogs in "the back forty" behind our property. He would arrive back home invigorated from the fresh air and exercise and settle into his chair alone with a good book.

"You missed all the excitement here a couple of weeks ago," Mom was saying. "We had a herd of horses show up. They were in the pasture with the cows."

"Where did they come from?"

"Don't know. It's the strangest thing. There were about seven or eight of them. Someone said they might have come from Teen Ranch."

"But that's more than five miles from here! How long were they here?"

"A couple of days. They seemed quite happy to be with our cows."

"What happened to them?"

"I called Town Hall and they sent someone to pick them up. A reporter from the *Banner* came and took photos. They were in the paper. Your father missed it all."

"Where was Dad?"

"Down in South Carolina again. Golfing."

My father was not around as much as he used to be. When he was around, he was withdrawn from us. He folded layer upon layer inward like the prayer plant that hung in the crocheted basket in our kitchen window and tightly gathered in its leaves when it didn't receive enough light. At home he became less obtrusive, more unassuming. He slipped in and out of the house without interruption and shuffled about inside between rooms in his worn slippers like someone who didn't wish to intrude. He still had our respect, but he didn't demand the same attention and authority he once had.

He never appeared stressed, he didn't rant or rave or even complain. I had seen him lose his temper only a few times in my life. For the most part, it took a lot for my father to get excited about something. His standard response to most things was: "Not bad". He used this reply consistently when asked his opinion on anything from the meals my mother cooked him, to the movies he saw, or the books he read. But when something impressed him, it *really* impressed him. He raved for years about the western *Shane*, he exclaimed enthusiastically over Mitchener's *Hawaii*, and he couldn't say enough about my mother's homemade soups and her bare shoulders.

However, with Natalie gone, perhaps for the first time in his life, Dad had to consciously make an effort to remain calm and collected. As a rule, my father liked to keep a lid on too much emotion, believing to reveal too much of oneself was dangerous. Perhaps he was afraid if he let too much slip out he wouldn't be able to prevent a havoc of unleashed emotion descend upon him.

Accustomed as we were to our father's reluctance to share his feelings or thoughts with us, we relied on any external clues for information we could get our hands on. When Dad returned from his trip down South that November, I had a glimpse into how he was feeling.

I found my mom in the kitchen baking hermits. She slid the cookie trays into the bottom rack of the oven and closed the oven door with a flourish. "There! Now let's have a cup of tea," she said to me.

She busied herself with putting on the kettle and washing the dishes. A spoon accidentally flung out of her hand and bounced onto the floor. "Oh, it's a child," she said, bending down to retrieve the spoon. A dropped spoon meant we should expect a child visitor, a dropped knife meant a man, a fork a woman.

She set the teapot on the table and sat down wearily. She removed her glasses and vigorously rubbed her forehead and eyes as she did when she was tired. Just then my father walked into the kitchen. He took one look at us and blurted out: "What's wrong now?" My mother jumped and quickly put her glasses back on. She looked nervously to her husband and then back to me puzzled by his interruption. He crossed the room and went to the sink where he washed his hands under the tap, and dried them on a tea towel. He glanced our way sheepishly as he left the room.

His comment caught me off guard. He had mistakenly assumed we were upset. This behaviour coming from a man careful to avoid overreaction, and unusually tolerant of external stimuli, was completely out of character. This was the closest I had heard my father admit we were having difficulties, and that he might perceive things may be out of control. With his simple statement, "What's wrong now?" I caught a glimpse of the doubt and anxiety my father was feeling, as well as an admission of previous trouble. I realized how heavily I depended on him to make everything all right. In a moment of panic I wondered if he was having trouble keeping it together, how were we expected to?

My parents didn't argue, but they didn't necessarily get along either. They just didn't communicate much. I have often thought if they had argued more they might have saved their marriage. My father had always been prone to sarcasm, but after Natalie left, his insensitive remarks became more frequent and more harmful. He began to harangue my mother about her weight. She was never slim enough for him. He would look across the dining room table at her affectionately after finishing his supper and declare, "Children, your mother is a beautiful woman. I've always said that. From the waist up, she's beautiful".

We grew accustomed to his comments, anticipating them before each meal was done. If there was pasta leftover, or one piece of pie left on the plate, he would ask one of us to finish it saying, "Better you than your mother. Better finish it off kids, heaven knows your mother will be into it later if you don't."

He would use laughter to get us on his side. He would say things like, "Watch out kids, if your mother puts anything else in her mouth, her buttons will go flying!" He invited us to laugh along with him, and, wanting to please him, we did.

Meanwhile, Mom had trained herself to barely flinch. She rarely spoke back and when she did it was with a "Ha ha...very funny!" making it into a joke she tried to laugh at with her family for her family's sake.

But after Natalie was gone, my mother could no longer bring herself to pretend to laugh along. We were sitting in the dining room, Natalie's place at the table conspicuously empty. Our dining room was furnished in a low budget version of Canadiana antique – an eclectic assortment of hodgepodge relics and homemade furnishings. An old wagon wheel wired for lighting was strung up over the maple dining table. (The same table that Mom had accidentally gouged when Michael was a boy and she threw a bowl at him in frustration. She missed, hitting her new table instead.) A wooden beam ran the circumference of the room displaying my father's vintage bottle collection. A clumsy oak desk sat in one corner covered with black and white family photos under a glass top. A cluttered tea wagon, a wobbly deacon's bench, and an antique buffet table clamoured for the remaining space. The walls were hung with two paintings by the same artist. One was our family portrait, the other painting was Homer.

Homer was an original portrait of an old hillbilly farmer inspired by a photograph of Daddy Bill. Homer, as we had christened him, was elfish with a bulbous nose, long grey beard, and a ridiculously tall farmer's hat perched on elephant-size ears. Over the years, Homer had become an honourary member of our family.

As we had come to expect, my father made a typical derogatory comment about my mother's diet. But this time, watching her at the end of the dining room table, I noticed she couldn't manage more than a tight-lipped grin. For once, she couldn't bring herself to find humour in my father's verbal attacks. She sat there fighting back the tears. "Laugh all you want, you silly bugger," she told her husband. "But the joke is on you". We stopped laughing then.

CHAPTER THIRTY THREE

Grandparents

 Natalie

Nana Darwen and Grampa Russ were neutral territory. They made it easy for me to spend time with them. They refrained from making judgmental comments and asking too many probing questions. They must have wondered what made me move out, but they never asked. They encouraged me to visit. I think they were lonely; they didn't talk much to one another. I recounted stories about my co-workers and customers at McDonalds, and they listened attentively and doted on me. We talked about hockey, something both grandparents were passionate about, and looked forward to the beginning of a new season for the Toronto Maple Leafs. I don't know what, if anything, my parents had told my grandparents about my boyfriend, but I had the impression they knew about the pregnancy.

It was July 26, 1978, not long after I had moved in with Bev, and I was visiting my grandparents. We were sitting in their smoky den, watching the news about the world's first test tube baby, which had been born the day before. My grandfather was appalled.

"Imagine a baby conceived in a test tube," he said alarmed. "I'm not a religious man, but it seems sacrilegious to me," he said.

"I don't know," said my grandmother on one of the rare occasions she spoke her mind. "It might not be such a bad idea. To make a baby outside of a woman's body."

"The woman still gets to carry it. They implant the embryo into the mother's uterus," I pointed out.

"Well, next thing you know they'll tell us men can have a baby," Grampa Russ huffed, adjusting the waistband of his trousers that lay snug across his bulging stomach.

"You'd never be able to take the pain," Nana Helen said icily. Then turning her back on her husband, she said: "Right, Natalie?" It was an innocent enough remark. My grandmother was simply looking to me for endorsement, but as soon as she said it, she looked at me like she wished she could take it back. Right then I knew she knew.

With his generous silver moustache and eyebrows, his abundant silver hair, and thick, stout shape, Grampa Russ was a dead ringer for Santa Claus. He never played Santa though - he never liked to be in the limelight. He left that up to my father. Grampa Russ was a person you could depend on. A loyal husband, a responsible father, a person who didn't ask for much. He was the kind of person you almost forgot was there, he blended so well into the background. My grandmother preferred it that way. Most of the time she ignored the man.

I don't know if she ever loved her husband. The story, as far as anyone could piece together, was that my grandmother married Russell after her first husband, a Scot named Robert Dagleish, died of tuberculosis. Russell and Helen had met while speed skating in the Beaches neighbourhood in Toronto. When my mother was eleven years old, my grandparents had a child together, Heather. I knew Grampa Russ was my mother's stepfather and that my mother never knew her birth father. I didn't know why Nana Helen would never talk about him.

Nana Helen was still a good-looking woman in her senior years, but her face was molded into an habitual expression of bitterness and resentment. She hadn't always been a sour, unhappy person. There were glimpses of the person she once was. Apparently, and quite incongruously, my grandmother had always wanted to be a tap dancer on the big stage. There was always a tragic disappointment about her as though she had once known true love and had never got over losing her lover. She was a suffering soul, who had withdrawn behind her enforced walls long before I was born.

The only time my grandmother expressed herself was when she was drinking. The effect of alcohol gave her the permission to let go her guard, a welcome relief; otherwise, she held herself together in rigid control. She was a pretty, petite brunette, with a creamy complexion and delicate features who was prone to vanity and hated the effects of aging on her fine features. She was forced to wear false teeth that never fit her properly, and humiliated her with their incessant clacking. It wasn't all vanity however. Her ill-fitting dentures hurt and made it impossible for her to chew anything that wasn't stewed or soft. The dentures turned the corners of her mouth down even further so that she wore a perpetual grimace.

Nana Darwen was never a gushing grandmother. As a child, she had never paid much attention to me - Cindy was her favourite, just like Michael was our paternal Grandfather, Daddy Bill's, favourite. For the first sixty five years of her life, my grandmother's name was Ellen. But when she received her birth certificate in the mail that she had requested in order to apply for her old age pension, she found out her real name was actually Helen. I think this may have bothered my sister since she was supposed to have been named after her: Cynthia *Ellen* Carey. (Coincidentally, Daddy Bill, also experienced a name change revelation. He had gone through his life believing his first name was Albert until he, too, received his first birth certificate at the age of sixty-five to discover his name was officially registered as Charlie.)

I stood at their sink drying the dishes and looked out the window into their backyard. I saw the plum tree at the back of their garden. The tree reminded me of the first time John and I were together alone in this house. I flushed thinking about it. My grandparents must have known what we'd been up to in their home. I was grateful that they had never asked me about it.

I realized I was more comfortable now with my grandparents than I had ever been. They didn't avoid mentioning my parents or my siblings, they were too much a part of each other's daily life to do that, and so I continued to hear news of my family through my grandparents. They told me about the barn dance I missed that September. And, in December, they told me my parents and Cindy were going to court.

CHAPTER THIRTY FOUR

Court

—————————————— Cindy ——— ————

It was snowing and we tracked melting slush from the parking lot along the warm halls of the Brampton Courthouse. We stomped along corridors in our heavy winter boots making small pools on the marble floor until we came to a set of tall double doors. My father pulled one open and held it for us as my mother and I filed in. We stepped aside for him to lead the way, conscious of our every move in the imposing silence of the room.

The courtroom was a large, graceful room with a vaulted ceiling and vestiges of Greek architecture, worthy of upholding law and order. It was intimidating and I began to wonder if the crime being tried here was perhaps of greater magnitude than I had believed. Fragments of hushed conversations from the few people in the benches resonated in the air, reminiscent of church parishioners whispering from their pews. Only the first few rows of the courtroom were occupied. We trudged up the long aisle to the front, our boots echoing loudly in the nearly vacant chamber.

Unexpectedly, my father stopped, forcing my mother to pull up short to avoid knocking into him. He stared toward the row on our left. I followed his gaze and was shocked to see Natalie. She was sitting with her back to us wearing a bulky winter coat and talking to John in the row ahead of her.

To Natalie's right was a young girl who looked about twelve years old. On her left sat a woman and a man. I realized with a start this must be John's family. John was half turned around to the back of the room and spotted our arrival first. He said something to Natalie who stopped talking and looked over her shoulder at us. Apprehension at seeing us there flashed across her face before it was quickly wiped away by a smirk. Her smirk stung like a slap across the face. I felt she had denounced us and proclaimed her new allegiance to John's family. I was stunned by her blatant cruelty. Dad began humming a little tune under his breath, a melody between clenched teeth. We followed him to a row behind our lawyer and sat down on the other side from Natalie.

I hadn't expected to see her there. My parents hadn't warned me that Natalie would be in court. By the looks on their faces, it seemed they hadn't expected to see her there either. I hadn't seen Natalie since I dropped her off at her yellow house last July.

I was only there once. She had come back home to collect some of her clothes she hadn't been able to fit into Bev's car when she moved out. She had called ahead of time to see if she could come by in a couple of days. Bev could drop her off, but she wondered if someone could give her a lift back into town. My mother made sure she would be home. My father would be at work.

My mother spent the next two days preparing comfort food for Natalie to take with her: a frozen shepherd's pie, beef and pasta casserole, a pot of homemade soup, raisin spice muffins, and oatmeal cookies. She was showing Natalie the meals she had made for her and giving instructions how to reheat the shepherd's pie when my father walked into the kitchen. He was as surprised to see Natalie as we were to see him.

My mother said, "Harry, you're home early."

"What is she doing here?" he said to my mother.

"Natalie has just come by to pick up some of her things," she said too brightly.

My father's eyes narrowed. "I thought I told you she wasn't welcome here anymore."

"I was just leaving," said Natalie. She scooped up her bundle of clothes and headed out the back door. Natalie piled her clothes in the backseat while I helped load the prepared meals into the car. My mother jammed the rest of the food into a plastic bag and hurried outside with it, deliberately not looking at her husband, who was standing in the kitchen taking it all in.

"Here, Natalie, don't forget this," Mom said handing her the last bag.

Natalie looked at her and said, "I won't, believe me."

We got in the car and I drove her to her new home. She had rented the first floor of one of the original rambling homes that graced Orangeville's central streets. Built by prosperous townspeople in the early 1920s and subsequently divided into a rooming house, it had endured several metamorphoses. The most recent involved a coat of falsely optimistic lemon yellow paint.

As I parked the car on the street in front of the walkway, I thought I saw a dark head in the front window. My pulse quickened. I was afraid it was him.

"Is there anyone home?" I asked.

"Bev's at work," she said.

I was certain John was inside. I helped her carry her stuff to the front door. Up close, I noticed the paint was cracked and peeling. She hesitated at the door with her arms full, but she didn't ask me in.

"Look, Natalie, don't be a stranger," I said, uncomfortable leaving her there.

"Yeah, well..." she said into her shoulder. I waited for her to say something. "I didn't have a choice."

"Dad can be so stubborn," I cried.

She pushed open the door. "So can I," she said.

I peered past her into the musty hall but all I could see inside was gloom and darkness after the bright July sunshine.

I left her then. She seemed to have it all figured out. I had to give her credit - at sixteen she was already living the life I intended to have for myself when I graduated from university. She didn't seem to need us. I found myself thinking that for someone who was so easily frightened, she was being very courageous. I also wondered if she could pull it off.

Now, watching my sister in the courtroom, I looked for signs of fear or anxiety, but was disappointed. I wondered what had happened to the little girl who'd clung desperately to the swaying bridge, too terrified to move. I recognized Grant and Daniel sitting beside John, along with another man I assumed was their lawyer. The boys were each accused with mischief causing damage to private property. We were in court as witnesses for the Crown against the boys.

I was told I may have to testify because I saw what happened the night of the shooting. I had just come home for Christmas break the previous night and I had no idea what was expected of me. I was apprehensive; no one, not my parents nor our lawyer, Douglas Maund, had prepared me. Provincial Court Judge J.D. Ord entered the room and we all rose.

The Crown Attorney, Stephen Sherriff, called my father up to the stand. Dad swore on the bible and stated his name. He looked grey and shrunken, but he spoke clearly. He was asked to identify photographs of tire tracks on our lawn following the May 15 incident, answered the lawyer's questions about the history of the trespasses to our property, including when and how many times the incidences occurred, and the nature of the damage and the thefts.

"According to the police report filed on November 1, 1977, the vehicle you describe as responsible for trespassing on your property was a black pick-up truck. Did you know the owner of this vehicle?"

"No."

"Later, on two different incidents on March 13, 1978 and April 25, 1978, you reported a brown Plymouth entered your property and ran over your lawn. Did you know the owner of this vehicle?"

"Not at the time, no."

"Did you think the three incidents were related?"

"I thought they could be. We had a few different vehicles trespass on our property over the years, but it was the brown Plymouth that we saw the most."

"I am going to show you a photo of a vehicle like the one you describe. Could you please tell the court whether this vehicle bears resemblance to the car you saw on your property?"

He examined the photo. "Yes, it looks like the car."

"For the record, this is a photograph of a 1970 Plymouth registered under the name of Mr. Grant Hewlett."

"Mr. Carey, thinking back to the night of May 15, 1978, could you please tell the court what happened starting from when the car first entered your property."

"We had just gone to bed when we heard a car in our driveway. It was shortly after 11:00 o'clock. I ran downstairs and saw the car run over the grass and spin around on the lawn. By the time I got outside it had run over the lawn by the garage, turned around and took off out of the driveway. This had happened before. It scared Diane. Her nerves were bad."

"Then what happened?"

"We called the police."

"And that was the end of it?"

"No, the car came back later that night."

"The same car?"

"Yes, the Plymouth."

"And what did it do the second time it came back?"

"Spun around on the lawn again. Ran over a couple of lawn chairs. This time it backed up right onto our side porch. I thought it was going to crash through the window."

"Did you see who was in the car?"

"I could only see what looked like three dark heads."

"Could you identify anyone in the car?"

"No, I could not."

"Now, Mr. Carey, when did you decide to use a shotgun to shoot at the car?"

My father hesitated. The judge said, "May I remind you, Mr. Carey, that you are here as witness to the Crown and protected under the Canada Evidence Act. Whatever you say today cannot be used in future legal proceedings against you."

"Thank you, Your Honour. I decided to use an old shotgun I had kept hidden in my closet. I hadn't used it since I was a boy. I decided to use it after the boys got away again on the night of May 15. After they damaged our grass again and ran over a couple of trees."

"Now, it is true, is it not, that one of the passengers in the car is the boyfriend of your daughter, Mr. Carey?"

"Yes, it is true."

"But you still maintain that you did not recognize him the night of the incident?"

"Yes, that's right."

"Do you know why your daughter's boyfriend would want to damage your property?"

"I have thought about that a lot. I wish I knew. I can only guess that he was mad."

"What would he be mad at?"

"Objection," said the defendants' lawyer. "Counsel is asking the witness to speculate about a possible cause. He is leading the witness away from the proceedings at hand."

"If it please your Honour, I am attempting to show possible motivation for the defendants' actions."

"Overruled. Answer the question Mr. Carey."

My father paused and glanced over at Natalie before he continued. "I think he was mad about the aborted pregnancy," he said quietly.

There was a stir in the courtroom. I looked over at Natalie who was staring down into her lap. Beside me, my mother scratched viciously at her hands.

"Thank you, Mr. Carey. No more questions Your Honour."

The boys' lawyer approached my dad. "Did you know, prior to the incident on the night of May 15, 1978, who was responsible for the acts of vandalism on your property?" he said.

"No, I did not."

"Now you claim the car returned a second time later that same night, during the early morning of May 16. Correct?"

"Yes, it did."

"You have said that you were unable to identify the driver and/or passengers of the car the second time it returned. Can you explain how you failed to recognize the passengers and the driver of the car?"

"It was dark. I couldn't see their faces clearly through the car windows."

"Are you able to identify any similarities to the passengers and driver you saw in the car and the men in the courtroom today?"

"Other than three dark heads, and the fact they looked young, I can't recognize any similarities."

"You have stated you did not know who was in the car prior to the early morning of May 16, 1978, when you shot at the car. So, is it safe to say that on the alleged previous occasions in November of 1977, and in March and April 1978, and again on the night of May 15, you cannot be sure if the occupants of the car were the same as those involved in the early morning shooting incident on May 16?"

"No, I am sure."

"But how can you be sure if you could not see them clearly?"

"Sorry for the confusion. What I mean is I could see enough to realize they were the same boys who had trespassed at my house before, but I could not identify them. I didn't know who they were."

"No more questions Your Honour."

"That will be all. You may step down, Mr. Carey," said Judge Ord.

My father took his seat. He looked straight ahead as he passed Natalie's row.

Then my mother was asked to testify. She nervously took the stand. Her voice quavered as she took the oath.

"Please state your name for the court," Crown Attorney Sherriff said.

"Joan Diane Carey," she said clearing her throat.

"Please state your husband's name."

"Harold Albert Carey."

"Please state your daughters' names in full, starting with your oldest."

"Cynthia Ellen Carey. Christine Louise Carey." She looked over at Natalie.

"Go on."

"Natalie..." she whimpered. The lawyer asked her to repeat Natalie's name. She couldn't say it. Her face crumpled into a fragile, childlike version so that she looked like a little girl who had just lost her favourite doll. She was handed a tissue and we waited for her to gain her composure. The sound of her blowing her nose echoed in the courtroom. Sherriff patiently asked her if she was able to continue. My mother tried again and then bowed her head and cried softly into her chest, her shoulders shaking up and down.

I looked over at the back of my sister's head. John looked over his shoulder at her and grinned.

There was a long pause as the attorneys consulted their notes and whispered quietly amongst themselves. Then my mother was told that was all and she could step down. She blew her nose again and looked up bewildered at the Crown Prosecutor and then at the judge. She didn't seem to comprehend what was asked of her. The lawyer repeated his request for her to step down. She looked over at her husband for verification and he nodded his head. She slowly stood up and climbed down from the witness box.

CHAPTER THIRTY FIVE

Barricade

 Cindy

As it turned out, I was not needed to testify. I was more disappointed than relieved. I wanted to be called on to say what I knew. I wanted to feel useful. At the conclusion of the proceeding, our lawyer, Douglas Maund, gathered with us for a quick debriefing. He mistook my disappointment for anxiety over the outcome and tried to reassure me.

"Don't worry," he said. "Everything went as well as could be expected. Harry is one of my favourite people. The whole thing was out of context. When we go to trial, the judge will take this into account."

On the night of the shooting when Dad needed a lawyer, he had called the only lawyer he knew in town, Douglas Maund. He had used Maund to help him file his income tax. Maund was a soft-spoken young lawyer with a mustache and a bushy beard. He was inexperienced; however, he knew my father and knew he was well-liked in town for his community service.

In the car driving away from the courthouse, I asked Dad if he was going to plead not guilty.

"I'm sure as hell not going to plead guilty," he said.

"What will happen if you are found guilty?" I asked.

"Doug said I could be asked to pay a fine. Either that or go to jail."

"What would you do?"

"I'm not going to pay a fine when I'm not guilty. I'll go to jail first."

We drove home in silence after that. I was confused and angry with my sister. I couldn't understand how she could sit there and smirk at us like we were the enemy. She had become a stranger to me. I blamed her for upsetting my mother so much that she broke down on the stand and couldn't answer the questions. A part of me hoped Natalie felt really guilty.

I was also ashamed of my mother for being weak and unable to pull herself together to get through the questioning. I was angry at my father for creating this disaster in the first place and forcing my mother to testify against her daughter's boyfriend.

I sat in the backseat looking out the window of our station wagon. I had learned to drive in this car. Dad taught me. The first thing he had me do was back out the driveway being careful to avoid the fence posts. We practiced driving around town, three point turns and parking. Mom let me drive her into town once, but she was a nervous passenger – she screamed at me when she thought I was going to sideswipe the cars parked on the street. She left it up to my father after that. My parallel parking was weak but Dad said I was ready to take my road test.

The driving examiner handed me a copy of my driver's test. It indicated I had failed to stop at a railway crossing, had driven 50 mph in a 30 mph zone, and had demonstrated erratic steering. "You'll need to work on those things," he said. Then he said, "Congratulations! You passed." Turns out it wasn't hard to get your license in Orangeville.

Not long after I got my license, I was headed into town alone in the station wagon. I pulled out of the driveway onto the highway and stepped heavily on the gas. It was a hot, dry summer afternoon and the car windows were down. The station wagon was the Darwen Office Supply vehicle and company papers sitting loosely on the front passenger seat threatened to fly out the window. I looked down and quickly put my hand over the papers to trap them. When I looked up I was in the other lane. I jerked the steering wheel to the right but overcorrected. I spun around doing a complete 360 in a matter of seconds. I slammed on the brakes and screeched to a halt in the middle of the road. My heart was pounding. I looked up and down the highway but there were no cars coming in either direction. I looked back at the farmhouse over my left shoulder expecting my dad to come running out shouting. But the house was quiet. No one had seen me. I took my foot off the brake and slowly stepped on the gas and headed into town like it never happened.

In a few weeks my father would trade this car in, ending a series of family station wagons we had owned over the years. First, there had been Bessie, the ruby red Classic Rambler; then came Nellie, the faux-wood side- paneled Country Squire; and lastly the no-name lusterless Darwen Office Supply wagon. We had been one of the last suburban strongholds of the one-car family and the last ones on Whitman Street in Willowdale to acquire a second car. My father gave my mother the keys to Nellie, and drove home with a sporty fire-red Ford Mustang.

He got the Mustang at a time in his life when he had five children, a wife, a home in the suburbs, and a mortgage. It was his expression of FUN! His custom license plate, HAC, was a bit of a novelty, made long before personalized plates were popular. My father liked to stick toothpicks he collected from restaurants still wrapped in their paper envelopes in the vent holes in the dashboard. It reminded me of playing at building forts, and I pictured my father playing with the little walls, redesigning his wooden pieces while driving to work every day. My father drove the Mustang into the ground, and then my mother got it.

By the time my mother inherited the Mustang, it had neither horsepower nor heater left. There were holes in the doors and one right through the floor where years of driving on wintry Ontario salted roads had corroded the panels. I'll never forget driving from Orangeville to North York one cold and snowy night with my mother to one of her Sweet Adeline chorus practices. We were bundled up with blankets on our knees and rags stuffed in the holes. We were freezing and, despite the rags, the snow blew in on us as we slid and slipped about in a light weight sports car with bald tires that should not have been on the road.

When we lived in North York, Mom joined the North Metro Chorus, a chapter of Sweet Adelines. In 1973, she sang with this group of one hundred women barbershoppers when they earned first place in the Regional Competition. (The North Metro Chorus would go on to place first at the International level in 1996, and again in 1999, making it the World's Premiere Sweet Adeline's Chorus.)

My mother was determined to stay with her chorus when we moved, and for several years she made the long drive to North York once a week to attend practices. The fact that my mother drove the two hour mission from Orangeville to her Sweet Adeline's practice, and then back again the same night, sometimes along slick winter roads, is testimony of her sheer determination to do whatever it took to get to her weekly Sweet Adelines' practices. The group was nourishment to her and the therapeutic bouts of Sweet Adelines made living in Orangeville bearable. The camaraderie of the women in the chorus and the pure delight in achieving perfect harmony through singing, was my mother's balm.

Mom was a nervous driver. She got her license at the age of thirty four. We were so proud of her studying her driving manual at night in bed. "It's been such a long time since I had to write an exam," she fretted, worried about passing the test. She was never comfortable behind the wheel.

Once, we were driving along a country road with our Christmas tree that we had chopped down tied to our roof. The road was gently rolling, filled with unexpected dips and bumps that wrenched our stomachs like the roller coaster at the Canadian National Exhibition. Only this time, my mother was driving, and she drove slower than my father so that we couldn't feel the bumps as much. My mother had just gotten her license and my father was letting her drive to gain experience.

She had never driven on snow-covered roads before. We crested a hill, my mother threw her hands up into the air, letting go of the steering wheel completely and moaning: "Ooowwwhh!" My father quickly grabbed the wheel but not before the car plunged into the ditch at the side of the road.

"What the hell kind of driving was that!" he cried.

My mother's chin trembled. Dad got out of the car and walked around to the driver's side. He drove after that.

We had left the city of Brampton behind and were in farm country now. I watched the million dollar farms and horse stables roll by outside my window as we continued our journey north. Steadily climbing uphill, we passed the turn-off for the Chinguacousy Country Club (in three years I would hold my wedding reception there) where the highway shifted more intensely upward until we reached the giant hill that harbored Orangeville. We geared up and climbed, gaining elevation until I had to swallow to unplug my ears. The surrounding hills formed a natural barrier insulating its residents from the faster pace of the city and urban influences. Free from the peering eyes of neighbours, the people of the Caledon hills developed over the course of several generations their own unique customs and dialect. The hills were responsible for creating more severe weather conditions than the milder regions to our south - colder in the winter and hotter in the summer. As we reached the summit, it occurred to me more than ever how the people living behind the hills were cut off from the rest of the world.

The light faded and it started to snow again. Flurries of miniature tornadoes whirled and whipped across bleak fields. A car with skis on its roof passed us heading for Hockley Valley, the nearby ski resort. The Hockley Hills produced a natural fortress protecting the Hockley Valley. Without the Hills, there would be no lush and beautiful Valley, no mecca for outdoor enthusiasts and nature lovers, no extensive terrain for skiers, hikers, and horseback riders.

We drove into town and churned through heavy snow on Broadway Street, spewing grey mucky slush up to the car's windows. Although it was only late afternoon, it was already dark and the streetlights were on. Striped candy canes hung limply and cheerless from the streetlights announcing Broadway was ready for Christmas. The lonely sidewalks had disappeared under drifts of snow and concealed treacherous coats of ice. There was no one in sight.

We passed the turn-of-the-century storefronts locked up tight for the night - Sproule's drugstore, Korsten Jewellers, Mark's Work Warehouse, Harkness Women's Clothing - each window dark and covered with drooping awnings weighed down by snow. I watched the old Town Hall roll by outside my window. Built in 1876, it looked tired and rundown, in need of a facelift. We passed the lone Chinese restaurant in town. Its dark red drapes closed behind a front window haphazardly framed in white Christmas lights. The sign in the window stated in yellow letters: "Chinese Canadian Restaurant". For a few months I had been a server at this family-run establishment, the only Chinese restaurant in town, serving up doughy sweet 'n sour chicken balls along-side greasy cheeseburgers and fries. I'd felt like an intruder on the occasions when I'd come upon the family taking their dinner breaks in the backroom huddled around each other digging chopsticks into shared steaming bowls of noodles while they spoke Cantonese.

We passed through town and soon reached the farm-house. We hadn't said a word to each other since we left the courthouse. We pulled into the driveway and the privacy and safety of our own home. I pictured my sister sitting on the courtroom bench across from us. The aisle between us an impenetrable barricade, keeping her estranged from us. I saw her dwarfed and crammed between the members of a strange family, the walls around her growing larger, impris-oning her. I saw her sneer again. She had seemed so tough. My little sister had crossed the line and I didn't know how to get her back.

CHAPTER THIRTY SIX

Ranbergs

Natalie

When I saw my parents and Cindy in court that Christmas I hadn't seen them since July. I felt like a stranger as I sat on the other side of the courtroom from them. For the most part, I was afraid to look at them fearing their disapproval and alienation. When Mom broke down on the stand I was overcome with misery and guilt, although I tried not to show it. I was distraught and angry when Harry said John's actions were motivated by my abortion. How dare he say this in front of everyone in court! I wanted to be anyplace but there at that point and was relieved when it was over and we could leave.

I'd recently moved in with John's family. Bev had gone to visit Lara in Oshawa. She phoned me from her mother's place and said she wasn't coming back. Lara's boyfriend had left and Lara wanted her daughter to live with her again. Bev said her mother was kind of messed up and needed her. She hoped I understood.

With Bev gone, I couldn't afford the rent on my own, not with working only part-time. My problem was solved when John's parents offered me a place to stay in their house with free room and board. They even said I could bring Fred.

John and I couldn't believe our good luck. No more sneaking around. Now we could be together whenever we wanted. It was what we had always dreamed of.

My first night in John's house I got up from bed to get a water glass from the kitchen. I noticed the kitchen light was still on. John's parents were talking quietly at the table. I heard my name and stood still in the hall holding my breath.

"I don't know how long Natalie will be here, Barbara. Long enough I expect. But we can't have her on the street," said John's father.

"I know, it's just I can't help thinkin' it's not right she has to live here with us. I can't believe her own mother let her leave in the first place. She is still a child! It's inexcusable that her parents didn't make her come back home."

"It doesn't really surprise me after everythin' else they've done. Her father basically made it impossible for her to stay. Anybody knows you don't give your teenage daughter an ultimatum, for Christ's sake. That was his first mistake. He should never have said: 'Either you stop seein' John or you leave!' He just showed her the door when he did that."

"His first mistake was taking a shotgun to our son!" she cried.

"I know. He's made his share of mistakes. Well, it's our job to do our best to make Natalie feel at home here."

"She must be awfully mad at her father."

I crept back along the hall, giving up on the glass of water, and returned to the bedroom I shared temporarily with John's little sister, Michelle. I climbed back into my twin bed beside her careful not to wake her. I was sharing a room with Michelle until the bedroom in the basement was finished for John and I would have his old room. In the meantime, Michelle had cleared part of her cupboard for my clothes and I had been given a dresser for the rest. I still felt like an interloper. I wasn't really wanted here, that was clear. The bed was strange and, in the dark, the room became claustrophobic, crammed as it was by Michelle's stuffed animals and dolls. I didn't belong here.

Gus and Barbara were wonderful to take me in, but who were they to be so judgmental? They had it all wrong. I wasn't angry. It was my decision to leave home. I could have stayed, but I chose not to. I had never felt so homesick. I just wanted to go home. The problem was I didn't belong there either.

I felt a numbness settle over me. The familiar, eerie feeling of becoming small and weightless like the balloon descended on me again. I felt I was in a void where I couldn't move, or speak or hear. I felt totally unable to act, and helpless to make a change.

When I finally fell asleep, I had the recurring dream. The baby was wrapped in a blanket and I rocked him back and forth in my arms cooing softly:

> "Down in the Lee Hi Valley
> There lived a little Hindu.
> He didn't have no clothes,
> So he had to make his skin do!"

My fingers fumble for the touch of the baby's soft skin and find only air. I tear open the blanket but it is empty. My baby has vanished! Now I'm in a huge cornfield running frantically through a maze of tall cornstalks, searching and calling for my baby. My father appears and helps me look. I ask him where my baby is and he says, "I'm so sorry, Pepperpot".

I woke up as I always did at this place in the dream. I was sweating and my mouth was parched. I really needed that water now.

For the second time that night I crept along the hall to the kitchen. The house was quiet and I tiptoed into the kitchen to get some water. At the sink I was startled by a noise behind me. I turned sharply and saw a silhouette sitting at the kitchen table in the dark.

"Oh my God, Mr. Ranberg , you scared me!" I said.

"Sorry, Natalie. I didn't mean to. Can't sleep?"

"I just need some water."

John's father got up from the table and ran the cold water tap. He filled a glass from the cupboard and handed it to me. "Here you go. I'm really sorry for scarin' you like that," he said kindly. "Here, sit down for a minute," and he crossed over to the nook and pulled a chair out for me. He settled back into his chair at one end of the oval table.

The white laminated table was bathed in moonlight from the large picture window. I noticed that Mr. Ranberg was still dressed in his day clothes. I drank my water and thought it strange he was sitting here alone in the dark in the middle of the night.

He knew what I was thinking. "It's funny, when I'm on the road and drivin' all day, I have no problem sleepin'. I sleep like a baby in my truck. But when I'm home, I just can't sleep."

I noticed then he was nursing a drink. I remembered John had told me his father had a mean temper when he drank. It seemed hard to believe this soft-spoken, gentle man could have a temper. All the same, I felt the need to shift back into my chair and crossed my arms over my chest.

Mr. Ranberg held up his glass and the dark amber liquid glistened with sparks of gold in the moonlight. He raised the glass to his lips and smiled at me over the rim. He swallowed and replaced the glass on the table with satisfaction. "How are you doin', Natalie?" he said warmly.

"Fine, sir," I said.

"Call me Gus." He noticed me watching his drink. "Would you like some?" he asked sliding the glass towards me on the table. I shook my head. "Go on. Have a sip. It will help you sleep."

I raised the glass to my lips and felt the warm liquid stream down the back of my throat. He smiled at me reassuringly and settled back into his chair. I was relieved to see that, for the moment, he appeared calm and not the least threatening. I uncrossed my arms and released some of the tension in my chest.

In the soft moonlight he looked younger and I caught a glimpse of the good looking guy he must have been.

"It must be difficult for you to live away from yer family. To move in with another family like this, under these circumstances," he said.

"I'm very thankful to you and Barbara for letting me stay here."

"It's our pleasure." He took another sip and then continued, "John's a good kid. His heart's in the right place, he's just young. His mother has always been a little too... well, she only wants what's best for him."

He took another sip of his brandy and I waited for him to continue, curious to hear him speak about his son.

"He needs someone like you to keep him in line. I can see you know how to handle him. I can see you know where you are goin'."

I was confused. I started biting my nails. I couldn't see where this conversation was going. A silence fell between us and I was just going to stand up and excuse myself when he said, "You remind me a lot of Barbara when I first met her. Did you know Barbara and I were high school sweethearts too?"

"No."

"Yep, we met at Orangeville High, just like you and John. And we've been together ever since. Except for six months when she went to California after we graduated. She had to get it out of her blood, so to speak. I guess it was a good thing. When she got back, we got married."

He leaned forward and rested his elbows on the table. "Of course, back then we didn't behave like you kids do nowadays," he said giving me a long look. I was suddenly aware of only my thin white nightgown between my body and him.

"How are you and John doin' anyway?"

"Good. We are good."

"Good." Was he mocking me? I wondered. "Treat this house as it was yer own," he said.

"Thank you."

"We are glad to have you, Natalie," he said. "Please don't bite your nails." I removed my hand from my mouth and lay it on the table. He laid his hand over mine warmly.

I felt his heat flood across the back of my hand and pulsate up my arm. I grew hot and flushed and was thankful for the cover of the dark.

"You are so..." he paused. "Young."

He pulled his hand away reluctantly and said, "Well, I guess you should be gettin' back to bed".

I stood up and said goodnight. As I walked out of the room I could feel his eyes on me. I could still feel them as I climbed into bed and turned over.

CHAPTER THIRTY SEVEN

Responsible

 Cindy

My father's new royal blue Buick Park Avenue was a Christmas present to himself. The day he drove home in a luxury vehicle was the first time I ever knew him to own anything high-end. Where the Mustang met his middle-aged need to feel young, the Park Avenue symbolized my father's need to feel he'd arrived. Such extravagance was not typical of my father. Normally, he did not cater to the American creed of materialism and greed. He was a practical man who rarely acquired more than what he could use. (The in-ground swimming pool he built in the city he justified as the reasonable alternative to avoiding endless miserable hours caught in traffic jams heading north to cottage country every summer weekend. Not to mention the additional expense of gas.)

My father preferred to save his money. He was secretive about how much he had. Over the years his wife, having no idea how much her husband was actually worth, had speculated he must have hordes of cash stashed away. His kids concurred it must be a lot more than he was saying because he sure wasn't spending it. So, for my father to arrive home in style in a wide, buoyant boat of a car with a smile just as wide, was totally uncharacteristic. While the acquisition of a luxury automobile would not prove to be trend setting - the Park Avenue would remain my father's sole claim to frivolous luxury items - it was perhaps an indication that he was in need of something extraneous to get his mind off his troubles at home.

"Michael's bringing a girl home for Christmas," my mother told me, raising her shoulders excitedly and clasping her hands together in merriment. "He's in love!" she sang.

Michael met Marie when he worked with Katimavik, a national youth volunteer service program. He joined Katimavik after completing his second year at university and spent nine months working on various community projects across the country. One of his team members was a somber, dark-haired, twenty-year old Métis girl from Edmonton, named Marie Charbonneau. As the program wrapped up, Michael phoned from Nova Scotia where he was learning the science of beekeeping, to tell his parents he would be coming home for Christmas with his girlfriend.

It was our first Christmas without Natalie, and having my oldest brother and his girlfriend home helped to distract us from worrying about how our little sister was doing, and where she was spending her Christmas.

Like my mother, Marie loved to sew. But that's where any similarity stopped. Marie was unexpectedly reserved and severely earnest. Unlike my mother, whose creative talents at the time were leaning toward designing silky, sexy lingerie, Marie had conservative tastes. She sewed only practical polyester pants and plain crimplene dresses. Her natural reticence attracted my playful brother who, in keeping with the way in which he treated all the females in his life, took every opportunity to tease and embarrass her.

The more he plied and stretched her out of her element, the happier he was. She was always rolling her eyes at him and reprimanding him.

Michael was planning to go back to school to finish his degree in urban planning. There was talk of he and Marie renting an apartment in the married students' complex on campus. My mother started leafing through wedding dress patterns she found in her sewing closet.

When Michael brought Marie home for Christmas to meet his family, my mother washed the sheets on Natalie's bed in the attic. My parents assumed Marie would sleep there, and Michael could bunk in with Paul. This was not what my brother had in mind. Michael and Marie had already been living together for several months; he had every intention of keeping it that way. Michael argued with our father, accusing him of being completely unfair in not allowing him to sleep with his girlfriend. My father said it was his roof and his rules and he didn't think it was right they should sleep in the same bed when they weren't married. My mother worried about the effect on Paul if they let them. Michael threatened to leave and take his girlfriend elsewhere.

Marie, demonstrating a sober maturity beyond her years, said they should stay. "It's your parents' house, after all," she said. In the end, Michael surrendered to his girl-friend's sensible plea and decided he could put up with his parents' wishes. But not without a teasing jab at Marie first.

"OK," he said, hugging Mom. "We'll stay. But I'm warning you, Marie snores like a train. She'll keep Christine awake."

"Oh, Michael," Marie cringed turning red. "I do not."

"And she sleepwalks too," he said, rubbing the palms of his hands together gleefully.

"Oh, we can't have that. She'll fall right down the stairs," my mother said, genuinely worried.

"Oh yeah, she sleepwalks all the time," said Michael enjoying embellishing his own joke. "Once I woke up and found her in the fridge and she'd eaten a whole lemon meringue pie in her sleep," he continued, widely grinning, accentuating the dimples in his cheeks.

"Don't listen to him, Diane," said Marie, her arms folded stiffly across her chest.

Michael hugged his girlfriend to him. "I don't know how you put up with him," Marie said exasperated, but her smile gave her away. She was in love.

My brother had learned new life skills while he was away and he couldn't wait to share his new knowledge with us. He had developed an interest in culinary pursuits, among other things, and felt the need to instruct our mother in the basics of cooking. For example, he told her it was essential to rinse the spaghetti with cold water once it is cooked to wash off the starch. My mother was thrilled to hear her son speak her language of domestic activity. Normally, my mother would not have tolerated anyone interfering in her kitchen, but she liked to spoil the men in her life and humoured her charming, oldest son's sudden flair for cooking.

My brother also acquired new tastes during his travels. We sat stuffed with turkey dinner around the dining room table when Michael stood and brandished a bottle of after-dinner liqueur from the buffet cabinet. While away, he had discovered a new liqueur that he was excited to share with us - Amaretto Di Amore. He was the same dark haired, square faced brother with my mother's dimples, but now he seemed more worldly for his adventures.

"Christine, would you like a glass?" he asked his sister who was sitting next to him. "You'd better drink up while you still can, seeing your drinking days are short-lived."

The Ontario government had recently announced the drinking age would be raised from eighteen to nineteen years on January 1, 1979. "It's so unfair," Christine lamented. "I've been drinking legally for almost a year already. How can they just take away that privilege?"

"You'll have to dig out your old fake i.d. again," Michael quipped.

"Shh," she said, mortified that someone might have heard.

Michael continued pouring a round of the almond-flavoured liqueur into little crystal glasses. He held a glass out for Nana Darwen when he was stopped by mother's stern expression from her place at the head of the table. The slight shaking of her head indicated Nana had had enough. Michael withdrew his arm and offered the glass instead to Grampa Russ who eagerly took it. He put the liqueur to his lips while his wife curled her upper lip at him. Still holding the bottle, my brother looked around the room for more takers. Marie; Aunt Heather; her husband, Alex; and son, Christopher, were seated at the table with the rest of us. Michael was searching for something as his eyes travelled round the room. It appeared the realization that Natalie was missing fully sunk in.

He slowly lowered the liqueur to the table as he realized what he had lost. My brother hadn't lived at home for over three years; it had come as a shock to him to learn that Natalie wouldn't be home for Christmas. He found it difficult to understand how things could have deteriorated to the point where his little sister was gone and any communication with her had ceased.

When Michael was in high school he had made a film for a school project. His inspiration for the storyline and background music was the Beatles' forlorn song, "She's Leaving Home". I played the girl leaving home. Michael filmed our parents sleeping in bed while I snuck out the back door and down the street. When they awoke in the morning he filmed them devastated to find the note their daughter had left telling them she was leaving home. We knew it was a sad story, but we couldn't have predicted that the film would become our real life family story.

Michael also didn't understand or tolerate the unwritten family code of silence that we all seemed to accept and obey. "So Dad," he said, "When are you going to stop this nonsense and tell Natalie she can come back home?"

The room fell silent as everyone looked at Michael. No one had dared say that to my father before. My heart raced in my chest. Not only had Michael brought up the topic of Natalie, he openly suggested our father was responsible for her not being with us.

Dad looked at his son for what seemed a long time before replying. "It's not up to me is it, Son? She should know she can come home whenever she wants. I didn't tell her to leave."

"Well, isn't it up to you to tell her to come back home?" Michael persisted.

Dad leaned back in his chair and swilled the amber liquid in his glass. Behind him, the wise sad eyes of Homer looked down at us. My father placed his liqueur glass on the table. "I don't think so," he said and got up from the table and left the room.

The lines etched on Homer's face seemed to lengthen and his melancholy expression deepen as a silent void followed our father's departure.

When Michael went back to school in January, Marie surprised everyone and went back home to Edmonton. The wedding bells stopped ringing and my mother put away her wedding dress patterns.

CareyOn '78, Harry facing forward.

CareyOn '78

Christmas at the Farmhouse 1978; Left to Right: Aunt Heather, Nana Darwen, Marie Charbonneau, Cindy, Harry, Grampa Darwen. Portrait of Homer behind Cindy.

Diane and Harry, REBOS breakfast at the Farmhouse, 1978.

CHAPTER THIRTY EIGHT

Guilty

―――――――――――――― Natalie ――――――――――――――

I was behind the counter serving a bunch of Orangeville Crushers, fresh from the locker room, their hair still wet from the showers, when I saw my mother's oval face poking out from behind their bulky hockey jackets. I could tell by the hair sprayed curls on her head that she had come directly from her weekly appointment at the beauty salon. My mother had bad hair - extra fine and hardly any of it. "I'm cursed with my mother's hair," she would lament by the end of each week as her professional wash and set toppled and lay limp on her scalp. "You girls are so lucky," she'd say watching us brush our shiny, rich, full-bodied tresses in the bathroom. "You got your father's full head of hair."

The hockey players loaded up their Big Macs and fries and left. There she was, directly in front of me, her smile as stiff as her hair. She had changed her glasses again. My mother changed frames like other women changed shoes. Like most people who are condemned to wearing glasses all their life, my mother had a love/hate relationship with her specs (she tried contact lenses once but couldn't get them to fit her narrow crescent-shaped eyes). Her latest version was in the new fashion - big and round. On my

246

mother's small face they appeared like the gigantic eyes of a mutant insect. With her padded, yellow ski jacket and black slacks, she looked like a giant bumble bee. The jacket was all wrong. I thought it clashed miserably with her fancy hairdo and, despite the glasses, pretty face.

My mother belonged in satin and sequins, lace and feathers, not insulated outdoors wear. She believed she was an old soul whose many past lives stretched far back to the glittery days of King Louis XIV where, she once told me, she lived as a member of the royal court. Her roots were embedded in regal extravagance and splendour. She looked out of place in a line-up at McDonalds.

As she stood across the counter from me, I saw her face was wan and pinched with worry. "Hello, *daughter*," she said like she needed to remind me who I was.

"Ma. What are you doing here?"

She cringed. "Can't I come and see my own daughter, for Pete's sake?"

"It's just that you've never come before."

"I didn't know I could. I mean, I didn't know when you worked or if you even still worked here."

My mother had never called me in the seven months since I moved out. "What do you want Ma, cause I'm kind of busy," I said, indicating the customer behind her.

"I just wanted to see you," she cried in anguish. "I came here hoping to find you. But now I wish I hadn't bothered." She moved down the counter shaking with indignation to make room for a customer to place his order. I took the order hoping my mother would not make a scene. By the time the customer left with his meal, she seemed to have composed herself.

"Look, Natalie, I couldn't come before. Your dad doesn't want me to ...he doesn't know I'm here."

"Can I get you something, Ma?"

"I didn't have any other choice."

"You do what you have to, Ma."

"Listen, Natalie, I just wanted to see you," she repeated.

"It's not right that you have to come here to see me, Ma."

My mother stared at me. "Huh," she said looking away. When she looked back at me, her eyes had crinkled into moist slits behind her glasses.

"Are you going to order something?"

"Is it OK if I come and see you here again?"

"Sure, Ma."

"No, I don't want anything," she said adjusting the strap of the large handbag slung over her shoulder. She set her shoulders back. "Well, maybe just a coffee. And stop calling me 'Ma'!"

Cindy

I was living and working in Toronto on my first university co-op work term when I found out Grant, the driver of the car, had been sentenced to time in jail. The passengers, John and Daniel, were given a conditional discharge. I learned that the judge's decision for a conditional discharge was based on several factors: it was the boys' first-time offense; they were tried in a criminal court as adults (it would be several years before the Young Offenders' Act would be created for youths between the ages of sixteen and eighteen); and, being a property crime, the nature of the crime was not considered or treated as gravely as it would be in the matter of a crime against a person. The boys were let off on probation with a warning to stay away from the Carey property, to keep the peace and be on good behaviour. However, they did have their drivers' licenses removed for one year. For John, who worked full-time driving a truck, this was debilitating.

Meanwhile, my father had five charges against him including attempted murder. In January of 1979 Dad once again made the newspapers. This time he was photographed alongside four other men being honoured for their role as past presidents of the Orangeville Curling Club. Dad was the current president of the Club. At the beginning of the season, he had been approached by the Club executive to be the president. He appreciated the gesture, but didn't feel right about accepting the position in light of the criminal charges pending against him. The members told Harry they felt he was the best person for the job, and the charges did not sway their opinion. My father accepted the position.

As he had told me on the day of the trial against the boys, Dad originally pleaded not guilty to the five charges against him. But as the months wore on and he saw the lawyer's bills mounting, he had second thoughts to proceeding with a not-guilty plea. The case had already cost him more than $8,000, and to continue in court with a jury would cost him another $10,000. He was also worried about putting his wife on the stand again. After her breakdown the first time, Dad didn't think she could handle testifying a second time.

Although my father was confident he would win and believed he was not guilty, he decided to change his plea to guilty in accordance with his lawyer's advice. While Doug Maund believed a jury would be sympathetic, he felt the risk was too great. The minimum penalty for criminal negligence involving a firearm was one year in jail.

My father showed no remorse for what he'd done. He said he'd rather go to jail than pay a fine out of a matter of principle. I was under the impression that he'd been given a choice and he'd chosen jail time over a fine because he genuinely didn't feel he was guilty and, therefore, should not have to pay a fine. In fact, although he never indicated he felt he had acted wrongly, he changed his plea to guilty out of financial obligations and responsibilities to his wife.

He thought he was doing Diane a kindness by saving her from going to court. Unfortunately, he never discussed it with her, and she didn't see it that way.

I was in the living room when I heard my mother raise her voice in the kitchen. "I can't believe you," she cried. "Why didn't you tell me you were going to plead guilty!"

I went to the doorway to see what was going on. I was alarmed. My parents never yelled at each other. My father was sitting in his chair eating his lunch with his back to her. He shrugged his shoulders and continued chewing. He cleared his throat and said, "I thought I was doing you a favour, Diane. I know how you hated being on the stand last time."

Standing behind him by the counter, she said, "How do you know how I feel about it? You never asked me."

My father drank his milk. "You never said anything."

"Well, I'm telling you now, I'm still ashamed of my performance on the stand, but I would go through it all over again if I thought it would make a difference. Now it's too late."

"I didn't think you'd feel so strongly about it," he said picking up his fork again.

"Once again, Harry, you've gone and decided something without consulting me first. You've robbed me of my chance to help." She turned her back and began vigorously wiping the counter with a dishcloth. "It keeps me up at night," she said, releasing a moan. "All I can see is Natalie's face looking at me from her seat across the courtroom."

I was shocked. My mother never mentioned Natalie's name out loud.

Now my father was angry. He put his fork down. "I'm not the only one who has done things without consulting the other," he said, in a dangerously low voice to a spot on the kitchen table in front of him.

"What are you talking about?"

He pushed his chair back and slowly stood up. "Don't think I don't know you've been to see her."

"So, why shouldn't I? She's my daughter. I miss her."

"I forbid it," he cried, turning to face his wife.

"It's your fault she's not here with us where she should be."

My father picked up his dinner plate which contained his half eaten lunch of baked beans and toast, prepared and served by his wife, and hurled it at her. We watched in shock as the plate slammed into the kitchen cupboard. It hung suspended for a moment before it slid, bounced off the counter and crashed upside down on the floor, leaving a brown smear in its wake.

The three of us stood motionless, staring at the sauce running off the broken pieces into the braided rug. My father walked out of the room.

CHAPTER THIRTY NINE

Jail

 Cindy

Dad's preliminary hearing took place over two days, March 21 and March 29, 1979. This time, Mom and I were in court to observe only; we would not be called as witnesses. I was relieved to see that Natalie was not in the courthouse. Doug Maund, began his cross-examination with Grant Hewlett. He asked Hewlett if he'd been to the Carey property on April 25, 1978.

"Now, Mr. Hewlett, I suggest to you that on that occasion you vandalized the property and you drove on the lawn, is that not correct?

"That's possible, yes."

"Now would you not recall if you drove in your vehicle to a property and drove about a lawn area and did property damage?"

"Yes, I would recall."

"It must be a very difficult driveway to drive on to keep ending up on the lawn," interjected the Crown Attorney, Stephen Sherriff. "I might make it very clear Your Honour, that I'm not endorsing the evidence of this witness. I shake my head in wonderment myself."

"Were your headlights on?" continued Maund.

252

"As far as I remember yes."

"Was it difficult for you to see where the driveway ended and the lawn started?"

"No."

"Now in fact Mr. Hewlett, you were conducting a vendetta against the Carey property, were you not?"

"Pardon me, I'm sorry."

"You were conducting a vendetta against the Carey property, were you not?"

"Pardon me, I'm sorry."

"You were conducting a vendetta against the Carey property, were you not?"

"A vendetta? I'm sorry. I don't understand."

"You were trying to get even with him."

"No."

"Was somebody else prompting you to get even with him?"

"Could have been, I don't know."

"You were aware that John Ranberg had something against Mr. Carey?"

"Yes."

"You were aware that there was some friction between Mr. Carey and John about his daughter, Natalie?"

"Yes, something like that."

"And you went along with this plan to try to harass the members of the household, isn't that what really happened?"

"No, I wasn't trying to harass anyone."

"Just another social visit. Is that what you are saying to the court?"

"Well, just went up on the lawn I guess."

"You just went up on the lawn did you?"

"Yeah."

"Have you ever gone up on anyone else's lawn?"

"No."

Maund called John up to the stand next.

"Mr. Ranberg, do you know Mr. Carey, the accused before the court?"

"Yes."

"And do you know the other members of the Carey household?"

"Yes."

"You don't much like Mr. Carey do you?"

"I don't know."

"I didn't hear that. Could you please speak up?"

"Everybody has their differences I would imagine."

"You don't know what your feeling is about Mr. Carey, is that what you are saying?"

"Well, some things I like and some things I don't. There's things he's done that I think are a little bit much."

"Is there anything about him that you don't like that's sufficient to try to frighten him in the middle of the night?"

"No. If I was going to frighten him, I wouldn't do it in the middle of the night."

"As far as you're aware, Mr. Hewlett has nothing against Mr. Carey at all?"

"Well, nothing that he's...Like I guess the only thing he's got against him is what he's heard."

"Isn't it true Mr. Ranberg that this whole idea about going to the Carey property late at night was your idea? You told Hewlett to act in this way? Isn't that what really happened?"

"No."

"You deny that do you?"

"Yes."

The outcome of my father's sentence was dependent on Maund's ability to prove intent. He built his case around my father's intent to stop the car so he could identify the vandals. He had to convince the judge his client's intent was not to cause bodily harm. Maund argued in my father's defense that his first shot misfired and he missed the tire, hitting the tire-rim instead. He fired a second shot as a "human reflex action to prevent the trespassers from getting away". He further argued that, given the personal history and unblemished character of the accused, his client's reaction was "out of context" and unlikely to reoccur.

The judge, however, had to make a ruling in regards to the new law governing the use of a firearm in connection with an offence. The fact my father used a shotgun escalated the case involving criminal negligence. The Crown sought a ninety day sentence and defense sought a non-custodial sentence. Maund arranged a plea bargain in which the original five charges were dropped to one charge of criminal negligence causing bodily harm (two offences). My father was sentenced to thirty days in jail to be served on weekends.

It took sixteen months from the day of the incident to the day of the sentencing hearing, and a few minutes for the sentence to be delivered. My father appeared alone in court with Maund. My mother stayed home. At the close of the hearing, my father was taken away by a guard and placed in a jail cell. He hadn't expected that. After two hours of being locked up, his lawyer came, and he was allowed to go home.

My father served his time intermittently on weekends between Fridays at 9:00 pm through Mondays at 6:00 am. The evening before his first weekend as an inmate, he did what he would normally do - he cut the grass. Cutting the grass was something my father did a lot. There was a lot of grass to cut, over two acres, and he did not believe in the convenience of ride-a-mowers. He preferred the exercise of walking behind a gas-fed mower.

Cutting the grass relaxed him. Like golfing or curling, it calmed his mind and was a kind of meditation. This had to be true as no one would otherwise want to cut grass as much as my father did. The fact was, however, that not all the grass was ever cut at one time - there was just too much of it. As a result, our home was regularly surrounded by an odd patchwork of uneven plots of lawn, grasses in a variety of heights and various shades of green.

At dinner that night, my father was quiet, which meant we all were.

"Dad, can I come and vithit you in jail and talk through the thpeaker at you?" asked Paul.

Dad chuckled softly and said, "I won't be in long enough for you to need to visit, Son."

"Are you afraid about going to jail?" asked Paul, innocently voicing what was on everyone's mind.

"Yes. I'd be lying if I said I wasn't a little apprehensive."

Paul looked around the table to his mother and then to me. I was home for the weekend; Michael and Christine were away at university.

"Well, at leath you'll like the chorth you get to do," Paul said.

"What Son?" my father asked puzzled.

"You'll like the digging. You thaid you liked digging outthide. Now you can dig on the chain gang."

For a moment we stared incomprehensively at Paul. He turned white and shrunk down in his chair. Then my father started to laugh. A deep, hearty, uproarious laugh. Followed by my mother's melodious and grateful laugh. I joined in next. Paul rubbed his hands together briskly and bounced in his seat.

A warm smile spread across my father's face. "Hells bells! I don't think I'll be digging on any chain gang, Paul, but I'll sure as heck be the luckiest son of a gun in jail," he said hugging his youngest child to his chest.

After dinner and the kitchen was cleaned up, I found myself climbing the attic stairs to my sisters' empty bedroom. The room was hot and stuffy, the air stale and heavy on my skin. The house below was unusually still and quiet. I opened the window grateful for the fresh breeze. Turning around, I saw Natalie's face in the long, low mirror under the sloping roof. I put on a record of the musical *Chicago* and danced my heart out.

The next morning, my father packed his bags and drove himself south to the Mimico Detention Centre.

The prison guard took one look at the new rookie with the toiletry bag tucked under his arm, and snickered, "You think this is the Ritz Carlton?" Shaking his head like now he'd seen everything, the guard opened the kit to find to his amazement a razor and fresh razor blades. He confiscated the bag and told my father, "You get it back when you leave."

Dad was then asked to strip down. He was butt searched and shown to his bunk. This procedure was repeated each time he entered the prison. It was something my father never spoke about until many years later when we were watching a prisoner of war movie together. In a sudden outburst he blurted, "No one should be made to go through such disgraceful treatment".

My father shared a cell with two men in their early twenties who were doing weekends for drinking and driving. My father was by far the oldest inmate. At least half of the men were repeat offenders. He said it broke his heart to see so many young men going wrong. He decided the least he could do was teach his new roommates some new card games and help improve their bridge skills.

Dad played a lot of bridge in jail. His bridge partner was a 250 pound, steely-eyed inmate who went by the name of Butch. Butch had a way of staring that was "a little unnerving at first, but he turned out to be a nice guy". They'd already played several games of bridge together when Harry forced his partner to play his hand. Butch wasn't accustomed to taking such risk, and for one "fearful moment" my father thought he may have pushed him too far. But his partner played his hand and captured all thirteen tricks. It was Butch's first ever Grand Slam. The inmate was thrilled by his win and, carried away by the moment, he clasped his giant hands over my father's, engulfing them in his powerful grip.

"Thanks, a lot, Harry. I never would have gone all the way without you," Butch said, pumping my father's arm heartily.

"Well, you guys play some pretty good bridge, here," said my father, congratulating him.

"You think this is good," said his partner, "you should try Guelph!"

Dad was philosophical about his whole jail experience. He considered his time in internment an opportunity to learn something new and, rather than complain, he tried to make the most of it. His worst complaint was about the "terrible food," and he was critical of the blatant lack of any serious attempts at rehabilitation. He felt playing cards to while away the time, though enjoyable, was a waste of both tax payers' money and inmates' time.

Throughout the whole ordeal, my father retained a sense of humour. He had a new audience to tell his stories to and new stories to tell his old audience. There was the one about the Hells Angels who came in while he was showering. My father admitted he was quite nervous, but once he saw the men weren't going to bother him, he relaxed and curiosity prevailed. He had never seen anyone covered from head to foot in tattoos before.

He spent a total of fourteen weekends in jail (he got a week off his sentence for good behaviour) including the weekend of his fiftieth birthday. When he got home that Monday, he chuckled as he told us his latest story of his new friends singing "Happy Birthday" while they served him a bowl of tapioca pudding with an unlit candle.

CHAPTER FORTY

Enough

 Natalie

Moving in with John's family was difficult at first. For several months I had lived without anyone telling me what to do. I was accustomed to being on my own and being account-able to only myself. Not that John's family wasn't accommo-dating. They took me in like I was their own daughter. They didn't impose many rules on me, and respected my privacy. I soon grew used to their ways and habits and they to mine.

John had told me about his father's volatile temper and, at first, I was wary and worried he was going to explode any day. But after several weeks had gone by and his father showed no sign of losing his temper, I stopped being con-cerned. I wondered if his father's temper could be as bad as John had made it seem.

The schoolbus dropped me off and I let myself in the front door. John was lying on the couch in the front room. An empty bottle of beer, and an ashtray overflowing with cigarette buts cluttered the coffee table in front of the television set which droned on with the melodrama mono-logues of a soap opera.

"Hi," I said walking over to the couch.

"Hi," he said not taking his eyes from the television. He gripped a half empty beer on his chest. I moved away from him.

"Hey, where you goin'?"

"I've got tons of homework to do."

"Why don't you come an' watch some TV with me?" he said, shifting his long body onto his side.

"Maybe later. I have a lot of homework. I have a huge assignment due..."He flopped back down on his back. I was torn. I knew that he would have already spent most of the afternoon watching TV. For weeks, John had taken to sleeping in late in the mornings so that I didn't see him at breakfast, and when I got home after school I always found him lying in front of the television. I knew he'd gone from his bed to the couch where he stayed all day.

"John," I said, "how come you never draw anymore?"

"I don't have time," he said.

"Not enough time? You don't do anything except watch TV. And drink beer."

"Who are you, my mother?"

I began to walk out of the room again. "Well, what do you expect?" John said, raising his voice. "I don't have a job anymore cause I can't drive. And I can't go anywhere cause I can't drive. Do you think I *like* bein' stuck here all day long by myself?"

I swiveled around and stood beside him. "Well, why don't you draw?" I tried again.

"What's the point? I just don't feel like it anymore."

"Maybe you just need some inspiration. Why don't you go to art school?"

"Art school? Yeah, right. I can really see *me* in art school," he said sardonically.

"Well, why not? You're good."

"Why don't you stick to your own goddamn business and stay out of mine!" he sat up angrily and took a swill of his beer swallowing hard.

I waited a moment for him to calm down. "What's the matter, John?"

"I'm never goin' to go to art school, Natalie. I'm a truck driver. That's what I do. I'm not like you."

"What does that mean?"

"Nothin'. Forget it. Come here." He patted the cushion beside him. I perched on the end of it. "Did you miss me today?" he asked stroking my hair.

I smiled at him. "You should have seen it. We've been reading this book called *Lady Chatterley's Lover* and Mr. Simon read aloud one of the really sexy parts from it. When the book first came out, people thought it was evil and treated it like pornography, but it's not. Anyway, Mr. Simon started talking about how it is one thing to have sex with someone but the really intimate act is sleeping beside someone and waking up with them in the morning. He said that you really have to trust someone to spend the night with them."

"Is that right? Who is this moron?"

"Just my English teacher."

"He's just tryin' to get into your pants with all that shit. Trust you to fall for it."

"It wasn't like that."

"You chicks are all the same. All a guy has to do is tell some shit about a book he's read or tell you you're beautiful and you'll jump into bed with him."

I got up to leave. John grabbed my arm. "Where you goin'?"

"I told you, I have homework."

He tightened his grip on my arm and stood up. "Let go. You're hurting my arm."

"I bet you got good and turned on by your Mr. Simon, didn't you?"

"You're being ridiculous. Let go of me!"

He shoved his face into mine. "I thought I told you I don't like it when you wear makeup to school." He pushed me away with contempt. "Go do your precious homework."

I stumbled shakily from the room. An hour later, John came and stood at my bedroom door. He told me he was sorry for being such a jerk. He said he never meant to hurt me. He came across the room and put his hands on my shoulders. "It's just that I love you so much...and I'm afraid one day I won't be enough for you."

"You will always be enough for me, John."

He kissed me.

"Are your parents still out?"

"Yep. They won't be back til six o'clock," he said, a little grin playing at the corners of his mouth.

"What are we waiting for?" I said pulling him with me as I stepped backward toward my bed.

"I thought you had lots of homework."

"I do. But it can wait."

CHAPTER FORTY ONE

Ghosts

 Cindy

My mother eased the pain of losing Natalie by pouring more energy into her home. She had always been most in her element at home. In this way, she was a true Cancerian, the sign of the zodiac that is most strongly aligned to creating a home. She loved making a home, the true epitome of a "homemaker". Now she lavished it with even more attention. She never tired of rearranging the furniture, or pasting up another flowered wallpaper, or sewing new lacey curtains. She relied on her work to sustain her and fell back on her role of homemaker to keep her busy and occupy her mind.

As further distraction and compensation for her loss, she focused on the acquisition and hoarding of collectibles for her home. She believed she could never have too many Royal Dalton figurines, or Kaiser porcelain pieces, or fine bone china miniatures. These treasures wrestled for space amongst cheap and cheery trinkets and knickknacks and gaudy souvenirs until every inch of available shelf, tabletop, and cabinet were covered and her home was overstuffed with clutter.

My father also kept busy by making things for the home. While Mom tried to evoke a sophisticated Victorian age, Dad was going for a rustic early Canadiana look. He hammered cedar shingles around the tops of the living room walls. He built matching cedar shelves for his books and a wall unit to house the television and stereo. His masculine cottage in-the-woods look competed with Diane's feminine romantic look. The more wooden ducks and vintage glass bottles and beer steins my father laid out, the more plush brocades and deep fringes and lacey doilies my mother added. They were dueling decorators and the combination of both themes in the same rooms killed any chance of either achieving some measure of interior design success or harmony.

Mom said she always loved Mondays best. After the weekend, she couldn't wait until everyone went back to either school or work, so she could claim her house back again. She loved the feel of Monday mornings as the house settled back into a peaceful silence, washing away the noisy demands of a family that more often now left her ragged and exhausted. The silence restored her so she could make it through another week.

She found peace by surrounding herself with the things she loved, like music and singing. She was always singing. She often sang as she went about her work in her house or garden. Even her dramatic sneezes sounded like high-pitched opera notes. When we lived in the city, Mom surprised us one day when she brought home a new banjo. She said she'd always wanted to play the banjo and had scraped and saved a little money each week from the meager budget Dad gave her to purchase one. She took some lessons and persevered until she was able to play the chords of "You Are My Sunshine", which she played over and over while singing along. When we moved to Orangeville, her determination to play the banjo waned and eventually she left the instrument forgotten in its case to collect dust in the bottom of her bedroom closet.

Her love for singing and music could be attributed to her love of birds. Birdsong and birds made her happy. One day she arranged for guinea hens to be delivered to our hobby farm to complete the pastoral setting. The day the hens arrived was also the day of the séance.

It was a Friday evening and I had just pulled up into the driveway at the farmhouse, having caught a ride from a friend at university. I had finished exams that day and was looking forward to catching up on some sleep. Unfortunately, any thoughts of going to bed early were quickly extinguished. Several cars were parked at our house. It looked like we were having a party. As I walked to the back door, I noticed some strange plump, grey speckled birds wandering about the driveway.

I entered the mudroom and was immediately greeted with gales of women's laughter coming from the kitchen. I pushed open the kitchen door, and walked into a party of seven or eight highly excited and slightly intoxicated women.

My mother spotted me and yelled over the din, "Cindy! Cindy's home! How's my beautiful daughter?" Raising her vodka and orange juice to me in salute, she asked, "Do you want a drink?"

"Not right now," I said, giving her a kiss on the cheek.

"Are you sure she's *your* daughter," quipped a woman sitting at the table.

"I didn't know you were coming home," Mom said. It was not unusual for my mom not to know my plans. We never communicated when I was away at university. In the four years I was at school, my parents did not call me once to see how I was doing. It never occurred to me that our relationship might suffer from poor communication until I overheard Geoff's mom speaking on the phone one evening at length to her daughter who was also away at school. I found it curious that they would schedule weekly phone calls to catch up with each other. I was also envious that they cared enough.

"You look tired, Cindy," Mom said. "Do you want some coffee? Oh, wait. I can't make you some. The coffee grinder is broken." She pulled me aside. "Paul used it to grind weed in," she said, lowering her voice so no one else could hear her. "The little monkey. He had a bunch of friends over last weekend while your father and I were away curling."

"My little brother is growing up," I said.

"He's alone too much, that poor child. I worry about him."

"Mom did you see those odd pigeons outside on the driveway?" I asked.

"Pigeons? Oh, you mean the guinea hens. Aren't they funny? I just love them. Have you met Carol, Cindy? Carol's my psychic friend I told you about."

"She's amazing," said a woman leaning against the fridge smoking, an ashtray dangling from her hand.

I had heard about Carol. According to my mother, she was incredible at reading fortunes and, even more intriguing, she read past lives. I was curious to meet her. Carol was a quiet woman whose every word was carefully measured and every action carried out with a certain deliberation. Tall and big-boned, she was a woman of my mother's vintage who looked, at first glance, a modest housewife, not a person with mystical psychic powers. On first impression I was disappointed; however, I resolved to scrutinize her to see if I could detect any signs that might indicate her clairvoyant abilities.

I noticed she was the only one not drinking. The more I watched her, the more I realized Carol's strength was her power of observation. I didn't have to wait long before I would experience her other gifts.

"Bring your chairs into the living room girls," said my mother. "The séance is about to start."

"Séance? Here? You're kidding," I said astonished.

"Isn't it exciting! Carol has offered to hold a séance for us. Bring a chair in."

"Who are you hoping to conjure up?" I asked skeptically.

"My father," she said with a mixture of fear and awe.

Mom ushered her friends into the living room. The coffee table had been pushed back to make space in the middle of the room for a ring of chairs. Everyone took a seat, including me, and someone turned off the lights. The diminishing daylight from the window dimly illuminated the room, leaving the rest in semi-darkness. Carol sat at the front of the room at the break in the circle. Placed in front of her was one of our small TV tables on top of which balanced a white candle, and a small jade stone.

Carol said, "We are going to begin now. Whatever happens, don't get up. That will interfere with the spirit's path and may be dangerous for me."

Then she lit the candle and told us to hold hands and focus on the flame. After a minute, she said we needed to create more energy in the room and asked us to sing along with her. She started singing the chorus to *Knock Three Times on the Ceiling if You Want Me*. I couldn't believe it. But everyone was willing and, after a false start, each of us was belting out the lyrics until finally Carol said it was good enough and we could stop.

Carol, who was transforming into a medium before my eyes, was concentrating at a point just above the flame, her face thrown into grotesque shadow by the flickering candlelight. We sat still in hushed expectation waiting for something to happen. I looked over at my mother across from me, and silently mouthed, "What's happening?" She answered with stern squinty eyes and one hard don't-dare-interrupt shake of her head, which meant just be quiet and watch.

All of a sudden, the medium inhaled loudly and bolted straight up in her chair. Her focus was glued to an invisible object hovering over the candle. The women beside me squirmed in their chairs and squeezed my hands in anticipation. I felt a cold draft waft over my shoulders.

The medium said, "There is a spirit in the room." Someone gasped.

"It is a child. What is your name, child?" asked the clairvoyant.

After a moment, a small high voice said: "Susan." A chill ran along my spine. This was not Carol's voice. This was the voice of a young girl.

"I used to live here," said the girl spirit. I heard my mother draw in her breath.

"In the barn," the girl said.

The voice was now directly in front of me. I smelled smoke.

"I used to live in the barn," said the spirit. "There was a fire," she cried. The medium began to shake. The room grew warm. Carole began to thrash and moan as if in great pain.

"Help. I'm on fire," she screamed. "Help me!"

The room was now scorching hot. Someone stood up and quickly sat down again.

"Someone do something," a woman yelled. We didn't know what to do. Then, abruptly another voice appeared.

"June 29, 1932," he said. This time, the voice was unmistakably male. The psychic turned in her chair to face my mother. Carol's features had altered into a hard jaw and clenched teeth. "They wouldn't let me see you," the man cried.

My mother screamed. "Something touched my cheek," she cried. I trembled with fear.

"Tell Ellen I loved her," said the man. "Ask her about your baby bracelet."

Suddenly, the medium slunk down in her chair in a deep sleep her chin falling into her chest.

We waited for her to stir. Someone said in a whisper: "Is she OK?"

Then, as quickly as she had passed out, Carol woke up. She announced matter-of-factly, "That is all. They are gone."

The women slowly came back to life, releasing their hands and wiggling blood back into their fingers. The temperature returned to normal. The smell of fire and smoke had disappeared. Someone turned on a lamp. We sat back in our chairs and peered around the room to gauge the reaction of the others.

"No one will believe me," said a woman as she pushed her chair back. "I'm shaking."

"Wow! That was fantastic," said someone else. As we became re-energized we started talking all at once.

"I've never seen anything like that in my life."

"That was spooooky."

"Diane, why did you scream? What touched you?"

My mother hadn't moved from her chair. She was gently feeling her cheek. "His hand," she said softly staring into space. A tingle ran up and down my arms and across my shoulders.

"Does anyone know who Susan is?" asked someone else. "Diane, do you know?"

"What? Oh, I have no idea," she said distracted.

"Do you know, Mrs. Rose?" I asked our white-haired neighbour behind her. Everyone now turned their attention to Mrs. Rose.

"As a matter of fact, I did hear there was a young girl killed in a fire on this property. Susan must've been part of the O'Learys. The O'Learys would've lived on this farm in the late 1800's. The farmhouse burnt down in the fire."

"But why did the ... the spirit say she used to live in the barn?" I asked.

"I think I can explain that," said Mrs. Rose. "The farmhouse used to stand where the barn is now. The barn must've been burnt in the fire too. Later, they built the barn where the house once stood and rebuilt the house on this site. As far as I recall, my granny told me the girl was fourteen years old when she was killed in the fire."

"Well, I think we could all use a drink after that," said my mother jumping up abruptly and heading into the kitchen. I followed her, not trusting her sudden change of mood and bravado. I knew she was fragile and was having trouble holding it together. I helped her fix vodka and orange drinks for her and her friends. This time I poured myself one too. I was too wired to go to bed now.

"Mom, that voice? Who was that talking to you?" I asked remembering his voice with a shudder.

She took a gulp of her drink. "My father," she said choking on the words.

"How do you know? I mean, you never met him," I said.

"It was as if I had heard that voice before somewhere."

Carol came up to the counter to join us. She looked drawn and pale. I remembered my mother telling me that it took a lot out of Carol to communicate with the spirit world. She put her hand on Diane's back. "Are you all right?" she asked my mother.

"Uh-huh," Mom said and uttered a sob.

"Mom, did you hear what he said?" I asked in awe as the meaning of his words sank in.

"I know," she said blowing her nose. "He said, 'They wouldn't let me see you.' Those were the same words Aunt Eva used about my father before she died".

"He was trying to tell you something that was very important to him," said Carol. "What is June 29, 1932?" she asked.

"My birthday," said my mother.

"That makes sense," said Carol. "Spirits often announce a name or a date that will readily identify who they are and who they wish to reach. Your father was trying to tell you something that took place around the time of your birth." Carol paused as something occurred to her. "Didn't your father say something about your baby bracelet?" she asked, trying to remember what had taken place when she was connected to the spirit world.

"Yes, but I don't have one. I don't even have a baby book," my mother said looking forlorn and starting to cry again.

"Maybe you can ask your mother about it," suggested Carol.

"Huh! You don't know my mother. She won't talk to me."

"The important thing to remember is the spirits who have left us want to be at peace and want us to be at peace," said the psychic. "What else did your father say?" asked Carol softly.

"He said he loved my mother," my mother said wistfully. "I knew they loved each other," she said with conviction. She sighed as calm washed over her.

At last, she could lay to rest a part of her past that had tormented her until now. My mother had finally found some answers about her origin and derived some comfort from her parents.

It was then I noticed Carol's jade necklace. "Why do you keep a piece of jade on the table, and around your neck?" I asked her.

"To protect me from danger. Like the fire. And evil spirits that might show up." To reassure me she added, "But tonight there was no evil, just loss and grief."

Shortly after midnight, after the last guest had left, I was helping my mother with the dishes when I realized she was crying again. My mother always cried easily, whether she was sad or happy. One Thanksgiving, sitting at the dining room table after supper, she laughed so hard she cried and peed her pants, literally, and I had to fetch a big pot to put under her chair to catch the flow. But these days she cried more sad tears than happy ones. Several times I swear I saw her eyes wet and teary behind her glasses. I was frequently checking her eyes, saying, "Mom, why are you crying?" and she would always say she wasn't.

This time there was no denying it. A big tear slid along the concave curve of her nose, until it reached the upturned tip, where it balanced in mid-air like an aerial freestyler.

"What's wrong?" I asked her.

She couldn't look at me. She just continued to wash the glasses in the sink and said, "Nothing."

I hated to see her upset. I hated that she wouldn't tell me what was wrong.

She picked up a knife from the dish rack to dry it and it slipped out of her fingers and fell to the floor. "A man," she proclaimed with wide eyes. I bent over to pick it up.

"I haven't even cleared your bed off yet," my mother said with a yawn turning off the kitchen light. "I've been using your room to sew in," she told me as I followed her upstairs.

We pushed open the door to my bedroom. My mother's sewing machine was on my old desk along with cut-out pieces of a halter top pantsuit in progress. Sewing patterns poked out from a box underneath the desk. Along the wall, samples and scraps of fabric spilled out of plastic and paper bags piled high on top of each other. My bed was heaped with bolts and bags of material. "You've been busy," I said.

My mother cleared off the bed while I used the washroom. I climbed into my old bed and, before she left, she caressed my forehead and cheeks with her finger like she did when I was a little girl. I was tired, but I couldn't fall asleep. I turned on the bedside lamp. The light circled the corner of the ceiling where I noticed the wallpaper was coming off even more. A big piece flopped over so that I could see more of the old covered-up wall behind. There was another piece coming loose at the seam near my bed. If I just leaned over I could peel it right off.

It bothered me that my mother shut me out. I thought maybe I should have pressed her in the kitchen to tell me what was wrong. I knew she was trying to protect me by not talking to me, but I felt scared and alone. If I had persisted more, my mother may have broken down and talked to me. I pulled a piece of the wallpaper back, careful not to rip it. I was afraid of what I didn't know. I was afraid my mother would never reconcile with her mother. I was afraid she would never reunite with her own daughter. She wouldn't talk about Natalie. No one at home did. It was as though Natalie no longer existed. She had become another ghost in our house.

CHAPTER FORTY TWO

Rendezvous

 Natalie

It was a typical weeknight at the Ranbergs. We were sitting in the living room after supper with the television on. Fred was on my lap and I absentmindedly stroked her soft fur. I was restless and I felt like I was going to scream if I had to watch one more car chase. I picked up my book trying to concentrate over the noise of the television. I looked at John's profile beside me to gauge his reaction, but he didn't seem to notice. Usually, he didn't like it if I didn't watch the television with him. Gus was sitting in his Lazy-boy chair. Barbara was out at a decoupage class.

"What are you readin'?" Gus asked.

"*The Thorn Birds*. It's a story about a priest who falls in love with a young girl."

"Really? So you like romance?"

"Sure. I guess."

"Shhh!" interrupted John. "I'm trying to hear this."

I went back to my book. A commercial came on. Although the book was good, I couldn't focus. "John, let's go to the movies tomorrow night," I said.

"Can't. No way to get there," he said.

"Maybe I can drop you off," offered Gus.

"What are you goin' to do, Dad, wait and pick us up too? I don't think so," grumbled John.

"I wish I had my license," I said frustrated.

"You an' me both," said John.

"I really want to learn. Maybe I can take some lessons."

"I'll teach you," said Gus.

"You will?" I said uncertain.

John looked at me and then at his father. Then he slumped further down into the couch and glowered at the television.

I got up and went into the kitchen. I picked up the phone and before I realized what I was doing, I had dialed my old number. My mother answered. I didn't know what to say and almost hung up.

"Natalie? Is that you?"

"Uh-huh."

"Are you allright?"

I heard the sound of laughter in the background over the line. I poked my head around the corner into the living room to see if anyone was listening. John and his father were still immersed in their show. "Yep," I said.

"Listen, I'm going to be at Nana's on Friday evening. Why don't you meet me there?" she said.

I suddenly longed to hear the sounds of my own family. The Ranbergs were polite and good to me, but I missed the vitality of my family. Compared to my boisterous family, they were subdued and lackluster. I missed the passionate cacophony of sounds, the unmistakable symphony my family created when we were together.

"OK," I said.

It was a brave step for each of us. The inherent risks were understood between us; it was assumed both Harry and John were not to know about our rendezvous.

The day had been sticky hot without a drop of wind. Even though the sun was setting by the time I left work to walk to my grandparents' house, I was sweating by the time I reached Zina Street. The black tar was soft and squishy on my new white soft-soled shoes. A lonely cicada penetrated the heavy air with his high shrill.

August in Orangeville was quiet, stone dead, boring quiet. The streets were empty - everyone had either abandoned town for their cottage, or were hiding behind doors in their air-conditioned rooms should they be so lucky, or luckier still, in their own built-in swimming pools. The backyard swimming pool we had as children seemed like an eternity ago.

I had quit McDonalds and had a job in the deli department at the new Dominion supermarket in town (when I was little I used to think it was pronounced Gominion as I sang along with the radio jingle: "Gominion!...Mainly because of the Meat!").

By the time I got to my grandparents', my heartburn was acting up. I was going to see my mother soon.

Despite my grandmother's uneasy and usually tense relationship with her oldest daughter, she was willing to be part of the secret meeting. My grandparents were sitting on lawn chairs on their small porch outside their front door. This way, they could watch the action go by on Zina Street (good luck!) and catch the evening breeze (not today). I went up the two porch steps, and planted a kiss on my grandmother's upturned cheek.

My grandfather was reading the newspaper. "What's new in the world, Grampa?" I asked taking the lawn chair beside him.

"Oh, I was just reading about Joe Clark. Our new Prime Minister has his hands full trying to correct all the mess left behind after twelve years of Trudeau running the show."

"You mean Joe Who? At least Trudeau had some personality," I said. "People either loved him or hated him, but they knew who he was."

"I think we need to give Clark a chance. I think it was time for a change," said my grandfather. "Anyway, I should really be going," he said rising from his chair.

"Where are you going?"

"Your Nana has some errands for me to run in town."

How convenient, I thought wryly. Nana and I watched him get into his car and drive away. It was just like my grandfather not to want to stick around for the fireworks.

The sun was low on the horizon and its bright rays shot straight into our eyes so that we had to make a visor with our hands to see the car pulling into the driveway. My mother parked her car and walked over to us.

"Hello Mom. Hello Natalie," she said from the walkway below us.

Nana stood up. "Do you want some lemonade?" she asked her daughter.

"Lemonade?" my mother said lightly teasing, which somehow managed to come across as critical instead. "Since when do you have lemonade?"

"Since I bought it at the supermarket yesterday."

Mom tried again, "Is that a new dress, Mom?

"No."

"It looks nice on you Nana," I said.

"Do you want some lemonade, Natalie?"

My mother looked directly at me for the first time. "OK Nana," I said.

Nana went inside leaving me alone with my mother. I hadn't seen her since the day she had come into McDonalds. I was suddenly conscious of my appearance. I hadn't brought a change of clothes and I was still in my deli uniform. Splotches of tomato paste from a spill that morning streaked the white bib of my dress.

My arm was getting sore from holding it over my eyes. I let it drop and the sun prevented me from looking at her straight on. She became a wavering silhouette of shadow and light coming in and out of my focus.

"So how have you been, Natalie?" she asked as she moved to block the sun from me.

"Fine."

"I brought you some things I thought you might like." She held out a package in her hand. "I made you a suit."

"Thanks."

"Here let me show you." She came up the porch steps and sat down with a sigh like she was exhausted. She was always so dramatic like that. She removed the tissue paper and held up a wine red double-breasted jacket with shoulder pads and pleats in the back. Then she held up a matching skirt, the kind you just knew would swing gaily on your legs as you walked. It was a suit made for the office, a business woman's suit.

"It's beautiful," I said admiring the professional tailoring. And totally impractical. Just like my mother to make me something I would never wear.

"I know you probably don't have much use for it now. But I thought, down the road...when you get an office job."

"An office job? What type of office job did you have in mind for me, mother?"

She didn't hesitate. "Well, I can see you working in an office as a receptionist."

"A receptionist?"

"You would also be a good typist or some-one's secretary."

"How do you know? I would be a terrible secretary."

"No, you wouldn't, dear."

"Ma, you don't know. You don't know anything about me."

That stopped her. "Well," she huffed.

What my mother didn't know was that I had made the honour role when I graduated from grade twelve. What she didn't know was that on the afternoon of my graduation ceremony I had looked out from the stage of the high school auditorium to find, not my mother's face, but Barbara 's face, beaming up at me from the front row. Barbara had been so excited for me. She said I was the second one in the family to graduate. "Well, you're almost family, after all," she had said. She had taken a whole roll of pictures of me. Me on stage shaking the principal's hand, me standing outside the school afterward dressed in cap and gown and clutching my diploma. "I'm so proud of you, Natalie," she had said hugging me to her.

At the moment, my mother was still trying to come up with suitable employment for me. "Or, you could always get a job in a bank. I used to do that."

The guidance councilor at school had suggested I do grade thirteen and go on to university. But this was out of the question. I saw that now.

"Who would have ever thought I would have been any good at counting money. I was always hopeless at math at school."

Then my mother started to cry. I could never stand her crying. I felt my own eyes stinging. She searched for a Kleenex in her purse and blew her nose loudly.

We were interrupted by my grandmother bringing out a tray with a jiggling jug of lemonade and three plastic tumblers.

"Well, I see you two are getting reacquainted. Now, Diane, did you want some lemonade or not?"

My mother stayed for a while longer and then she said she had to get back to Paul. I walked her to her car. She opened the car door and started to climb in, then changed her mind and turned to me. "You silly girl," she scolded, squeezing me tight, half rebuking, half crying.

CHAPTER FORTY THREE

Fate

 Cindy

My father dropped the used mattress on the floor stirring up a handful of dustballs that had gathered in the corner. He looked around the room as it dawned on him this was my new bedroom. The bedroom I would be sharing with Geoff. Suddenly feeling uncomfortable, he hummed: "Ho, Hum and a bottle of rum."

In September of 1979, I started a co-op work term in downtown Toronto. At the time, Geoff was living in Mississauga. I needed a place to live and, even though the commute was horrible - bus, Go Train, and finally subway - I decided to move in with him. My father helped me move my things into Geoff's apartment. Geoff's parents had bought a new bed, a water bed, and given us their old mattress and box spring. My father and I loaded the bed into the company van, drove it to the apartment, carried it through the lobby, up the elevator and into the bedroom. Now that we had reached our destination, he was hit by the realization of what he had been accomplice to.

"So, daughter of mine, my little Cindy-Lou. So, you are moving in with Geoffrey, are you?" he said, not expecting an answer. I waited for him to say what was on his mind.

"Do you think this is the right thing to be doing, living together?" he asked.

"Why?" I was agitated. It was a little late to be having this conversation.

"Well, I guess the good thing is you two will certainly find out quick enough all the little things that bug you about the other person."

"You mean, like if he doesn't put the lid back on the toothpaste? Listen Dad, I'll be fine. I'm not going to come crying back home to you."

"That's good. I don't want to have to worry about you."

For the first time, I realized I was fully on my own. My father was no longer willing to accept responsibility for me. And he wasn't offering any reassurance that I could always come back home if things didn't work out. He did not want to offer promises he did not intend to keep.

My father began to fit the bed frame together. As he worked, he told me that before he married my mother, he fell in love. With someone else. Overnight on a northbound train heading across the United States. He said he met a woman, an American, and they hit it off right away. It was a four night journey. On the fifth day, he came very close to getting off at her stop and going home with her. But he didn't.

"Why not?" I asked.

"Because your mother was at home, waiting for me to return. I never saw this woman again. Sometimes I used to wonder what would have happened if I had gotten off the train."

His story both fascinated and frightened me. To think my father had a love life before my mother was too bizarre. It was also very romantic - he spoke like he had never quite gotten over this woman. I felt honoured to be taken into his confidence, and I treasured his secret carrying it around with me delicately, like the dead bird I found on the street as a child and brought home to bury. But it was strange to think of him as anything but my father. It was hard to imagine that by some fling with a stranger on a train, some chance happenstance, I wouldn't be here.

I was struck again how little I knew my dad. The older I got, the more mysterious his behavior seemed. I thought of the time a few months ago when I'd run into him on Broadway Street in downtown Orangeville. It was in the middle of the day and I'd been running errands. I was surprised to see my father walking briskly toward me on the sidewalk.

"Dad?" I said stopping him.

"Cindy? What are you doing here?" he said in a way that made me feel he wasn't happy to run into me, which was strange as I hadn't seen him for several weeks.

"I'm home for a few days."

He was anxious to get away and took a step to get past me.

"What are you doing in town?" I asked.

"Nothing much. See you at home."

As I watched him walk away I couldn't shake the feeling that he looked like he'd been caught doing something he shouldn't.

Now watching him put my new bed together, I wondered why he chose to tell me about his fling on the train. I asked him why he told me this now and he said, shrugging his shoulders, "I just wanted you to know."

As it turned out, my father had already begun the mental process of clearing house. He wanted to make a fresh start unencumbered and uncluttered. He was secretly preparing to leave.

I believed it was destiny that brought my father back home to the woman he'd known since he was seventeen years old. As it was his fate he should marry her and eventually leave her.

CHAPTER FORTY FOUR

Yearning

———— Natalie ————

I never did take a driving lesson with Gus. After he offered, he went on the road for several days at a time making it difficult to find the time for a lesson. Then, the weather turned and winter set in. The roads became slick with freezing rain and snow. The long sloping driveway grew slippery with ice making it a risky downhill ride that neither one of us wanted to tackle with me in the driver's seat. So my lessons were put on hold until we had a thaw.

Gus would regularly be gone for days at a time, and soon I began to grow accustomed to the family's routine when he was away. There were subtle changes that took place at home when he was absent. The way Barbara deferred to John, treating him as the man of the house; the way she refused to cook, serving only frozen TV dinners instead; and the way Michelle lipped her mother, knowing that without her father around, she could get away with it. Gus' work took him on long journeys all over the continent. When he returned home from one of these trips, instead of looking tired and in need of a break, he was surprisingly refreshed and relaxed. His days behind the wheel were like a vacation for him.

By January of 1980, John had his driver's license reinstated and he was able to drive again. This meant he could go back to work. It was great to have wheels again and the freedom that brought us. I looked forward to John being able to drive me into work on the weekends and pick me up after my shift. Once he got his license back, John was on a mission to make up for lost time. He began spending more and more time away from home, so that he went from being home all the time, to always being out. After work, he would head into town or elsewhere to have a few beers with his buddies in one of the local drinking holes. I didn't always know what he was up to; often I was in bed long before he came home so that we sometimes went for several days without seeing each other.

One Friday night in early spring I waited for John to pick me up after work. It was nine thirty and I had just finished my shift at the deli. I waited outside the mall doors, but after half an hour I knew he wasn't going to show. I walked to my grandparents' house. They gave me a warm reception and ushered me into their little den where I joined them to watch the hockey game.

We sat together until the game was over and I could see they wanted to go to bed. John had not called and I was angry at him, but I didn't mention it and my grandparents didn't ask. "You are welcome to stay overnight, Natalie," they said, and offered me the couch in the basement, which had been recently transferred from the living room. I was reluctant to spend a night in the fearful basement, but was grateful for their generosity and support. I spent a restless night, afraid to fall asleep in the cold, dark underground with the specter of the hole in the floor close at hand.

The next day, as my shift was closing, John showed up at the store to take me home. He apologized for not getting me the night before and said he had passed out at his buddy's house where he spent the night. I wasn't impressed. I got in his car and gave him the silent treatment.

"What's your problem? I said I was sorry."

I didn't answer him.

He put the car in reverse, floored the gas pedal and squealed out of the parking lot. We reached the highway and left the town behind us. I kept my face turned away from him and stared out my window.

"Natalie, don't do this. I have a God damn headache as it is."

"Well, maybe if you didn't drink so much last night you wouldn't have a headache. And you wouldn't have forgotten to pick me up."

"Oh, here we go. So now I drink too much is that it?"

I didn't say anything.

"Answer me, you bitch!" He said hitting the steering wheel with his hand.

"Yeah, you drink too much. You talk about your father drinking too much, well you're no different."

"Don't ever say that to me! I am not like him."

"Yeah, right."

His fist slammed into my upper arm. I was shocked. I hadn't seen it coming. Slowly I raised my right hand and rubbed my aching arm. I couldn't believe John had hit me.

"Damn it Natalie! Look what you made me do!"

We drove along in silence. I turned my numb face to the window and let the tears spill over the fading fields and watery, hollow driveways. Cows stared back at me with vacant, blank faces. A lonely horse in a dull paddock popped its head up. We pulled into the Ranberg's driveway and John turned off the car.

"I'm sorry, Natalie."

"How could you, John?"

"I don't know what got into me. You just made me so damn mad! I'm not a bad person, Natalie. Don't you give up on me. I made a mistake. It won't happen again."

A few days later, John went into town without me, leaving me home alone on a Saturday night. The next morning, I woke up to a quiet house. I poked my head into John's bedroom and found his bed hadn't been slept in. Barbara and Michelle were at church. Gus was probably at work.

The sun was streaming into the living room from the bay window illuminating the air with microscopic dancers of dust. I stood in a rainbow of sunlight on the carpet watching the colours collide over my slippers. It was the first time I had been alone in this house and it felt strange and liberating. I hadn't realized how much I craved being alone. Being alone here made me feel more at home than I had ever felt. I was able to forget that I was only a temporary member of this family, that I wasn't just someone passing through.

I went to the front door and opened it lifting my face to the sun. I stepped onto the verandah and leaned on the rusty wrought iron railing. The sun stroked the golden drooping heads of Barbara's daffodils just starting to peak out from graceful stems planted underneath the bay window. The gay chirping of robins sang over the constant din of highway traffic below. I was still dressed in my housecoat and nightgown, but there was no one around. The house was set on a hill well back from the busy highway; I would be but a slight blur to the cars and trucks whizzing by.

I thought of all the people going by in their vehicles on their way to places and lives I would never know and

I felt with a pang that I was being left behind. The world was rushing by and I was missing out. I yearned for far off places and adventures. I searched the blue horizon beyond the neighbouring forests and gently rolling fields and experienced a restless longing to explore.

The forlorn barking of a dog down the highway interrupted me. The wonderment of being alone shifted to loneliness. I bent over the railing and saw a disoriented face staring up at me. I was looking into the murky waters of a little pond that lay partially hidden under the verandah. I remembered that Michelle had stocked the pond with goldfish last year. I wondered if they had made it through the winter. I descended the stairs and went to the circle of rocks in the grass that encased the pool of water. I was leaning over the pond when I heard a voice behind me. "What do you see?"

"Gus!" I stepped back startled. "I didn't know you were home," I said.

"I've been cleanin' my truck." He looked at me with his sad smile.

"I was just seeing if I could see any goldfish."

He moved beside me and we peered into the dark pool of water. "There's one! And another!" I said delighted, crouching down to see the fish in the shadows. I looked up and saw he was watching me. I stood up. A shiver ran through me. It was cold down here in the shadow of the verandah, out of the sun. "Well," I said crossing my arms over my chest to keep warm, "I better get back inside."

"There's somethin' I've been meanin' to show you," he said.

I hesitated. I was still in my housecoat.

"Come on. It will just take a minute," he said.

I followed him to the driveway where he gestured to his shiny red and chrome Peterbilt. Living in a trucker's home, I had learned not only the manufacturer of Gus' truck but could distinguish between a Mack and the top serial numbers of Peterbilts as they flew by me on the highway. The tractor was missing its trailer. It struck me as grotesque without it, a gigantic head imbalanced on a stunted body. Gus opened the driver's door.

"Have you ever seen inside one of these?" he asked. He climbed inside the cab. "Come on up, Natalie. I'll show you my home away from home," he said, offering me his hand.

I looked into his face and saw his eagerness. I wavered. At that moment we heard a car turn into the driveway. It was John. He pulled up beside me and got out of his car. "What are you doin' out here in yer nightie?" he asked me suspiciously.

I stared at him not yet ready to forgive him for abandoning me last night. His clothes and hair were ruffled and unkempt and his face puffy from lack of sleep.

"I was just goin' to show Natalie the truck yer goin' to have one day, Son," called Gus from above us.

John looked hard at his father. "I'll show her," he said and brushed past me and swung himself up onto the running board.

"Suit yourself," said Gus moving back into the sleeper compartment behind the front bucket seats.

John looked down at me from his place behind the wheel as though he was making up his mind. He reached down to offer his hand. I took it and let him pull me up. John moved over to the leather passenger seat and I sat in the driver's seat.

I was surrounded by an amazing assortment of aerodynamic controls, aluminum levers, chrome switches, and a sea of buttons and dials and knobs. I couldn't believe how high off the road we were. "I feel like I'm a pilot in a cockpit," I said. "You must see a lot from up here."

"I do," said Gus from behind me. "I'm lucky. I get to see the world go by from up here. You see things differently when you are always lookin' down from above."

"What do you mean?" I asked.

"Well, the way I see it, thar are three kinds of people in this world. Thar are people who never look up; they may be aware someone or somethin' is thar, but they are too afraid to take thar eyes off the road in front of them, so they just stay put. Then, thar are people who feel that somethin' is creepin' up on them and sneak peeks over thar shoulder to gauge how best to stay out of the way."

"My father, the philosopher," said John, pleased despite his mocking tone.

"What is the third kind?" I asked.

"The third kind are those who aren't afraid to look around them. They aren't afraid of what's behind them, or what's in front of them they can't yet see."

John looked at his father with admiration. He loved it when his father spoke like this. He smiled proudly at him, a rare and beautiful present for his father.

"They are also the same ones who smile up at me," Gus said, moved by his son's affection.

I looked away and bit my lip nonplused by the outward show of emotion.

"You want to drive her?" Gus asked.

"You mean now?"

"Why not?"

I opened the door. "I'll leave you two alone," I said and jumped out of the truck. I thought of my own father. I felt a longing to share just such a closeness with him.

CHAPTER FORTY FIVE

Christmas '80

———————————— Natalie ————————————

It was a third storey walkup and from the living room window I could look into the top branches of a maple tree. It reminded me of the view from my old bedroom in the attic. I rented the apartment on the first of July. It was time for me to move on. I had lived with the Ranbergs for over a year, long enough. I needed to be on my own again. I had been working full-time for several months and could now afford to cover the rent by myself.

I had been reluctant to tell John I was moving out. I didn't want to upset him. When I finally told him I had rented a place in town, he flew into a rage and accused me of doing things behind his back. He didn't mean to hit me, he was just so upset, he snapped. Afterward, he left and went into town. He came back home with a new dress for me. Red with a black zipper down the front.

Once he calmed down and had a chance to think, he began to see it wasn't such a bad idea after all. He realized we would have more privacy and more opportunity to be alone if I had my own place. He said maybe he would move in with me.

That was a few months ago. He hasn't mentioned it since.

Bev lay across my bed reading the December issue of *Cosmopolitan* magazine. "Listen to this," she called to me in the bathroom where I was shaving my legs. "It's a questionnaire entitled: "How to Rate Your Orgasm". Choose the answer that comes closest to describing what it felt like the first time you experienced an orgasm: A/. a sneeze B/. a flood or C/. better than chocolate. Which one do you pick, Nat?"

I paused with the razor at my ankle and thought about it. "None of the above comes close."

"What do you mean?"

Bringing my leg down from the rim of the bathtub, I stood in the doorway. "I'd had sex for quite a while before I figured out what it was all about. You know, had my first orgasm. We were making love and I was on top. All of a sudden something happened down there like I had never felt before."

"Like what?"

"Like a volcano erupting, all fire and heat and hot lava spilling out of me."

Bev sat up. "Wow."

"Yeah, it was amazing."

"Were you with John?"

"Of course."

The phone rang from the front room. John wanted to know if I was coming for Christmas. I hesitated; I hadn't made my mind up yet. I scrambled to find a good excuse to buy more time. I knew Bev was listening from the bedroom.

"I think I am getting together with Bev. She is going to be in town for the holidays." As soon as I said it, I wished I hadn't. John didn't know I still kept in touch with Bev. He certainly didn't know she was over right now. I knew he wouldn't be pleased.

"Bev? Really? You still hear from that dyke?"

I ignored him, hoping he would drop it. After a pause, he said, "Well, what should I tell Mom? Are you comin'?"

"Tell her..." I looked around my apartment uncertain. I saw the black and white photo displayed on my new wall unit of me standing with my siblings by the poolside in our bathing suits squinting into the bright sunshine. I hadn't been home for Christmas for two years. "Tell her, yes, I'll come."

Cindy

Christmas 1980 brought the regular family members to the farmhouse: Nana Darwen, Grampa Russ, Aunt Heather, Uncle Alex and Christopher. The last time we had all been together was for my parents' 25th wedding anniversary party the previous October. Christine had planned it all, right down to the guest list. She invited old friends and neighbours from the city, including, to my surprise, Mrs. Kristin Murray and her husband. Mrs. Murray, or Kristin as she told us to call her when we were kids, was a vivacious blonde with an intriguing German accent who was married to an Englishman. She was a talented seamstress and shared my mom's passion for sewing. They were inseparable for a few years. Whenever Kristin was around, she had a way of making the ordinary new and exciting. We hadn't seen her since we moved to Orangeville and Mom never spoke about her anymore.

Everyone had gathered around my father in the living room while he made a speech. He said, "I'm a lucky man. I'm blessed to be married to a wonderful woman for twenty five years. We've had our ups and downs, but Diane has always been good to me." He paused and glanced at Mrs. Murray. "I've been faithful," he said, "except once when I strayed. To Diane," he said and raised his glass.

Later in the evening, my sister, Christine, pulled me aside in the kitchen and said, "I can't believe he said that in front of everyone with Mom standing there. How could he be so insensitive? He's ruined everything!"

Now here we were a couple of months later together again to mark another celebration. This Christmas we also had Christine's new fiancé, Bruce, and Michael's new girl-friend, Victoria, join us. Victoria was the daughter of the former mayor of Peace River, Alberta, something she liked to point out when given the chance. Victoria, never Vicki or Vic as she was quick to correct, was poised, sophisti-cated and wore all the latest fashions. She arrived at the farm house with purple wool legwarmers wrapped around her long legs and dainty open-toed leather sandals on her pretty, polished feet.

Christmas at our house was my favourite time of year. It was fun, exciting and, even when we were old enough to know better, still a little magical. When we were children, my parents made each Christmas special for us and, as we got older, we kids contributed more each year to the family traditions. Hoping to keep the childhood memories alive, while creating new ones, we took on some of our parents' responsibilities. My father still handed out the presents (to be opened one at a time only while everyone watched) and my mother still stuffed the turkey, but as young adults we spiced the customary Christmas events with unique, new flavours.

Michael had moved on from cooking to assume the role of head bartender introducing daiquiris as the new Christmas cocktail of choice. Christine, home for the holidays from Trent University, coordinated the menu and organized the meal preparations. She had always been adept in the kitchen (and consequently always vied for elbow space with our mother) and this year she added an element of gourmet dining with her contribution of fancy little appetizers discovered while she was working as a hostess at the nearby Millcroft Inn. Christine had earned the nickname Lou from her time spent working in the kitchen. As a young girl, one of her specialties was home-made pizza. We dubbed it, Louisio's Pizza, after her middle name, Louise, which in turn got shortened over the years to "Lou".

Paul and I organized the before and after-dinner games. We tried to come up with charades that would stump the players and checked the Bingo game for numbers, adding raw macaroni noodles for extra markers.

This year my mother took on a new job for Christmas. She was to lead us in Christmas carols around the piano. She was a novice player and had only taken a few lessons, but playing the piano was the fulfillment of a childhood dream for her. She realized that learning to play at her age was no easy task. She knew a few carols, which she valiantly struggled through, but the more significant challenge, other than a general lack of proficiency, was my mother's overall distressing reaction to Christmas carols. She hated listening to them because they always made her cry. Not happy tears, but melancholy tears of some undisclosed childhood grief.

Natalie had been missing from our last two Christmases. I had come to accept her absence as our reality. The hole her disappearance had rent in our family had begun to feel part of the fabric of our everyday life, like the missing foot of my mother's favourite Royal Doulton figurine.

But today she was coming for a visit! My mother had tried to sound casual about it, telling each of her children individually over the past couple of days that Natalie may drop in on Christmas afternoon. She didn't sound too certain, not fully believing Natalie would show up, or not wanting to expect it too much, in case she didn't. She told me in hushed clipped sentences leading me to believe it was our little secret, but when I discovered everyone else seemed to know already, I wondered why she felt compelled to keep it a secret. Surely, my father must know? Perhaps she just didn't want him to hear her talking about it, didn't want to ruffle him unnecessarily. Natalie's expected arrival added to our already heightened excitement. She would be the biggest present of the day.

Now that she was due to be in our house again, I thought how remarkable it was that she had been gone for two and a half years and we had barely missed a beat, as if she had never been there. I didn't understand how we did that. Whenever I stopped to think about how we had carried on without her, I eventually ended up in the same place - seeing her smirk at us in the courtroom. The sting that her smirk still left on me made it easier to tell myself that she wasn't with us because she had wanted it that way. The memory of that one little cutting grimace was still enough to justify turning our back on her. It had allowed me to fool myself into believing she had left us on her own volition rather than we had abandoned her.

We had reached that inevitable mid-afternoon lull on Christmas day where the first-round of presents have all been opened, the big brunch clean-up completed, the novelty gadgets and toys assembled, and we had exchanged our Christmas pajamas for our new Christmas outfits. With the excitement of the hectic Christmas morning behind us, we took a moment to pause and re-gather as a group. Appetizer trays of mini cocktail wieners (my mother's recipe) were brought in from the kitchen alongside scallops wrapped in bacon (Christine's recipe). Feeling giddy and slightly guilty by the evident surplus of gifts and general overindulgence, we turned our attention to the next item of utter satiation on the agenda - our first cocktail of the day.

We were making an inaugural toast and the volume was starting to heat up, when an unfamiliar car pulled off the highway onto our driveway. It had been snowing heavily all day covering the car tracks made earlier by family members. From our living room window we heard the car crunch and squeal as it rolled over new snow and watched it dig new grooves into our property. Natalie's profile came into view from behind a steamy passenger window like a glimpse through a porthole on a ship. The driver was a man I didn't recognize, but knew must be John's father.

The room grew quiet as each of us watched in silent expectation. Natalie got out of the car and headed to the back door. No one moved. Did we need to let her in? Would she knock or just show herself in? Finally, it was Michael who went to greet her at the back door, reprimanding us under his breath for making her wait. From the mudroom, he announced her arrival with an enthusiasm meant to be heard from where we sat in the living room, "Natalie! Come on in, sister." I waited for her in my chair beside the Christmas tree amidst stray scraps of wrapping paper and ribbons and piles of opened presents stacked proprietarily about the room.

She didn't know where to look. Her eyes flitted about the room like it was too bright for her to take in all at once. Michael announced her arrival again, "Natalie's here!" as if we didn't see her standing in the living room doorway. He stood rubbing the palms of his hands together, as he does when he is excited, and grinned from ear to ear. For Michael, everything was all right now that Natalie was home to celebrate Christmas with us.

Natalie remained at the doorway with her coat still on. Nana was the first to greet her from her chair.

"Hello Natalie, come and give your Nana a kiss," she said in a tremulous voice that was slurred as much by the glasses of wine she had consumed as by any admission of emotion. If Natalie saw that Nana was "tipsy" (it wasn't polite for us to call her drunk) she didn't seem to notice, but bent down and hugged her. Then she hugged Grampa. Next, she embraced Aunt Heather who sniffed and wiped at her eyes.

Christine said, "Hello, Nat," in the affected demure tone she puts on when she is being sensitive or wants to attract attention to herself. Paul shyly waited his turn in the corner of the room. Natalie acknowledged him next and he blushed, smiling back at her.

I said in a big, happy voice, "Hi, Nat!" as if I had just seen her yesterday, wanting to sound like we were still friends. She gave me a strained uncertain smile, not ready yet to trust.

She looked hesitantly around the room and found who she was looking for. My father was watching from under the hall doorway, not fully committed to being in the room. Everyone grew quiet. This was the first time they had been in the same room since court.

"Hello, Natalie," he said at last in a low voice filled with emotion. "I think we have more presents to open."

CHAPTER FORTY SIX

Compassion

 Cindy

Natalie spent the next hour politely opening presents and watching others do the same. I noticed she had put on weight and kept smoothing the front of her skirt across her puffy tummy. Her face was pale and she had purple streaks under her eyes. Maybe she wasn't used to our noise and hyperactive energy that overcomes us when we are altogether, or perhaps she was made uncomfortable by our generosity, and embarrassed she didn't have any gifts for us. In any case, she looked overwhelmed.

I wondered what she was thinking, a guest at her own family Christmas. She had lost her confidence. She sat stiff and straight on her chair like someone at a formal function on their best behaviour. She bore little resemblance to the funny, spontaneous sister I remembered. She had lost her spark. She joined us in gales of laughter as we watched Michael open what had become a traditional family joke - a re-gifted, tacky plastic fish. This year it was Uncle Alex who gifted it back to Michael, breaking it into several pieces before wrapping it. Her laughter came then in loud, brassy tones tooted over the volume of everyone else. It sounded jovial and joyous at first, but if you really listened you could hear underlying sadness in the notes that were belted out.

"What did you get for Christmas Natalie?" I asked.

"A necklace," she said twisting it around her neck.

"It's lovely."

"How's Geoff?"

"We're engaged."

"Congratulations. Your ring is beautiful."

"We're thinking of a wedding date either this August or the following spring after I graduate."

"Is Geoff coming today?"

"He'll be here after dinner. He's spending the day with his family."

Lowering my voice, I asked her about John. I tried to sound politely casual, but as I said his name it stuck in my throat and stumbled on my lips. When had it happened that the mention of his name could evoke such dread in me? It struck me how fearful I had become of my sister's boyfriend.

"He's fine."

"Mom, tells me you're not living with his family any more."

"No, I moved out months ago."

"But you are spending Christmas with them."

"Uh-huh."

I had a lot of questions, but she was clearly uncomfortable talking right now. I decided I needed to get her alone to talk to her.

Natalie didn't stay long. She suffered through the gift exchange and small talk and then brought her glass into the kitchen and asked if she could use the phone.

Mom said, "You're not leaving yet are you?"

"I'm expected back now," Natalie said.

"Oh, fiddle-dee-dee!" said my mother. "Surely they won't mind if you stay a little longer."

But Natalie wouldn't be budged. I wondered again how it was possible that she had left us. I didn't understand how she could just leave like that, could just walk away from us. How could she claim membership to another family knowing her own family was still here?

After Natalie made her phone call, my mother seemed preoccupied with something on her mind. "What is John's mother like?" she finally managed to ask Natalie.

In the five years Natalie had known John, my parents had never met his parents.

"Oh, she's lovely. *Very* kind. *Very* generous," she said. "She took me shopping for my Christmas present. I got to pick out my own clothes."

My mother was not expecting this. The hurt crept into her face.

"And the father. What's he like?" she asked, needing to know, even if it meant inflicting more pain.

This time Natalie stopped to consider, reminding me of my father in the way she slowly gathered her thoughts before answering. "His father is wonderful, really. The salt of the earth. As a matter of fact, he's the one who convinced me to come today. I wasn't sure about it and he told me not to worry, to go and have a good time."

My mother glared at Natalie with her hands on her hips.

Before I had a chance to get her aside and talk to her, she was putting on her coat again and heading out. When Mom saw Natalie was leaving already, she threw her a curt "Goodbye" that sounded more like "Good riddance". Natalie pushed open the screen door when my mother reached out and placed her hand on her shoulder. Natalie stopped and turned toward her. My mother folded her into her arms and rocked her back and forth. When they finally let go, they both had mascara running down their cheeks.

Right on cue, the car arrived to pick Natalie up and take her away again. I stood at the back door window straining to catch a glimpse of the driver. All I could see was a hat with earflaps, its brim pulled down low over a man's brow. The snow had finally stopped falling as I watched the car pull away from our house in the dull gray light of an encroaching winter evening.

I walked back into the kitchen and the choppy refrain of "Joy ToThe World!" hit me as my mother banged clumsily away on the piano.

I thought of seeing Natalie sneer at us in court that day. Hunched down on the court bench, her little pinched face poking out from a coat two sizes too big for her, she now seemed to me so utterly fragile and vulnerable that day. I wondered how I could have seen her any other way. She was just a young girl, lost and afraid. Any remaining anger toward her dissolved and I was suddenly filled only with compassion. My heart ached for her.

———————————— Natalie ————————————

I was glad when Gus came to pick me up. I couldn't have stayed much longer. I climbed in beside Gus and we drove away, but not before he saw my red eyes.

"Are you all right?" he asked.

I twisted the chain of the new necklace that hung at my throat. It was a ruby stone encased with small diamonds. My Christmas present from John. It was beautiful, but I couldn't get used to the weight of it around my neck.

"I told my mother I could only stay for an hour."

I replayed the visit in my head. I had not been prepared for the hard lump in my throat when I saw Michael at the back door. I didn't trust his girlfriend. She thinks she's too good for us. Paul nearly brought me to tears. It hurt to see how much he's grown since I last saw him. Cindy seemed happy to be getting married. I got the impression she had something more she wanted to say to me. Christine was irritating the way she kept bossing her fiancé, Bruce, around. Poor guy, he couldn't do anything right. I heard that she had broken up with Rob when she found out he was screwing her best friend. That must have been tough. All the same, I hope Bruce doesn't marry her.

"So what did you do?" Gus asked.

My heartburn was acting up. "Not much. Opened presents."

My father was uncharacteristically quiet and stayed at the other side of the room from me. The creases in his forehead have deepened since I last saw him. He has more grey in his hair. But it suits him. We didn't talk. I know he doesn't know about my new relationship with Mom. I know she doesn't tell Harry about our conversations on the phone. Or about the times we have met at Nana's.

"So, how did it go?" Gus tried again once we were several miles from the farmhouse.

It had felt strange to be home again. Everything looked the same, but foreign. I felt on display and hadn't known what to say or how to act. I'd forgotten how chaotic Christmas was at our house. Had forgotten how loud they could be when altogether. Like a percussion band, their high pitched squeals and peals of laughter resonated around the room. I had missed that sound.

"It went fine," I said, resting my hands on my stomach to ease my indigestion. Everyone is happy and having a good time." I thought they were carrying on just fine without me. A tear slid down my cheek and I turned my face away.

CHAPTER FORTY SEVEN

Confession

 Cindy

One morning in early January while I was still home for the Christmas holidays, we woke to a fresh blanket of snow. My father was pulling on his ski pants in the mudroom.

"Can I come?" I asked.

"If you want," he said.

I squirmed into my ski suit and laced up my boots in the mudroom by the warmth of the pot belly stove. My father already had the long wooden skis lined up outside on the snow. He had acquired the skis second-hand. They were "practical" which meant they could strap onto any of our bulky, everyday snow boots. They were never waxed ("Cripes, what do I need wax for!").

The high blue sky glistened with eye-watering brightness over the sparkling new snow. Sparrows chirped and flitted amongst the branches of the evergreen trees whose snow laden branches swung softly like the heavy white sleeves of a visiting Bishop's splendid gown. We fastened our skis and pushed off, heading for the forest behind the house. The cold stung my nostrils and made my forehead ache. Soon, clouds of condensation froze around our mouths as we exhaled heavily. The air was still and clear and filled our ears with a rush of silence like being under-water. The silence was measured only by our breathing and the mesmerizing rhythm of the "swoosh-swoosh" as our skis cut fresh tracks through the snow. Ahead of us, Toby and Duke bounced and leapt with excitement over the mounds of new-fallen snow.

We poled past the spot where the earth dipped, and hidden in a recess in the earth was the pond, now frozen solid with ice. I remembered the almost mystical feeling when I first discovered that secret place. How I was deter-mined to keep it to ourselves, to reserve the knowledge of it for our family only. I remembered our first winter at the farm, when the pond froze over, and my father shoveled off the snow so we could skate on it. Christine, Natalie and I slung our skates over our shoulders and trudged the long trek through heavy snow until we reached the pond. We found our father's shovel sticking up in the snow beside the natural rink where he'd left it, and we took turns clearing off the new snow.

We sat down on the ice and changed into our skates. I watched Christine glide gracefully across the surface in a perfect spiral, one leg stretched out behind her in ara-besque. She was always the best figure skater in our family. She had taken the most lessons and could even do some jumps and spins. I, on the other hand, was never any good. The skates always hurt my ankles.

At the time, I had wanted to keep that secret place to ourselves and not share it with the world. I wanted it to be our family secret. Since then, I'd learned to fully appreci-ate the power of secrets. I knew the secrets we kept could cost us dearly. No one ever went to the pond anymore. We hadn't visited it in years.

The dogs' barking brought me back to the present. They had the scent of something, a rabbit or a deer, and raced toward the woods. We followed them and soon reached the edge of the forest bordering on the last field. We ducked under the fringe of the poplar trees. Here, the snow was several feet deep and tough going. Duke and Toby disappeared into the dense snow-covered forest of maple, aspen and ash. I was warm now and sweating in my toque and long underwear. We reached the place where the forest opened up into a large clearing and my father stopped to wipe his dripping forehead on a hankie he pulled from his pocket.

Then we noticed the deer standing in a grove of birch trees in the middle of the clearing. Snowflakes fell softly on the doe like the centre of a giant glass snow globe slightly shaken.

"Dad, look," I whispered.

"Pretty isn't she?" he said. The deer lifted her head and looked directly at us, motionless.

We dared not move. "For the life of me," my father said, "I can't imagine why anyone would want to shoot one of those beautiful creatures."

"Dad," I said softly, "whatever happened to your gun?"

"My gun?" he said, startled by the question. "Oh, the police confiscated it."

He was quiet so long he surprised me when he said, "Funny you should ask though. A few weeks ago a policeman came to the door and brought it back. Just like that. Said the confiscation period was over and I could have it back. "

We stood silently watching the deer nuzzle the tree bark for something to eat. I wondered how much longer she would stay there before she caught our scent and bolted.

"Why do you ask?" he said.

"I just wondered if you still had it. I hate guns."

We continued to watch the doe, and then my father said, "You know what I'm whizzed off about is that some people might still think I knew who was in the car when I shot at it. It bothers me that I can't be sure the truth will ever be made clear. To think that anyone might believe I fired at the car knowing Natalie's boyfriend was inside. That upsets me. I hate to think I would be perceived as taking revenge on John."

Suddenly the deer ran off into the woods. From where we stood it was as if she had never been there.

"It was the saddest day of my life when she left," my father said. He had tears in his eyes.

I had no idea. "Dad, I don't think she has a clue you feel that way."

He nodded his head up and down slowly digesting this. He sighed and said, "Maybe you're right," and dug his poles into the snow. He gave a high whistle for the dogs and heaved himself forward. Catching momentum, he made large strides toward home. I pushed on close behind him.

CHAPTER FORTY EIGHT

Trust

---— Cindy ——---

On February 24, 1981 Prince Charles announced his search for a bride was over and he was officially engaged to a nineteen year old Kindergarten teacher, Lady Diana Spencer. As the world tuned into the preparations for the biggest wedding of the twentieth century, I made my own wedding plans. I signed Geoff and me up for ballroom dance lessons so we could waltz like royalty around the ballroom floor at our wedding. While Diana hired a Vogue team of fashion designers, my mother and I drove to Spadina Street in Toronto to pick out patterns and material. This time the wedding was a sure thing, and my mother was free to unleash her creative energies on the whole wedding collection including my bridal gown, the maid-of-honour's dress and four bridesmaids' dresses. For the bride's gown we chose a cream satin brocade in an off-the-shoulder neckline trimmed in antique lace (my mother died the lace in tea to match the satin) narrowing to a slim-fitting bodice and v-waist. The maid-of-honour's dress was a floral print while the bridesmaid's dresses were in complementary autumn shades of chiffon. I wanted Natalie to wear the chocolate brown shade.

I was in the final stretch of finishing my degree and home for the weekend when I visited Natalie at the Dominion in town. I had never been to see her at work before and she was startled to see me standing across from her at the deli counter. She was self-conscious and quickly masked her initial pleasure at seeing me behind a cool reception. I took my cue from her and tried to be casual, as if I dropped in on her regularly. Nevertheless, it was strange for me to see her behind the cold cuts in her deli apron and white hat, mechanically running the industrial slicer back and forth. We were both wary about seeing each other again and held our emotions in check.

She had cut her hair very short, deliberately unfeminine and unflattering. She wore no makeup and her face was bloated. She had put on more weight since Christmas. She seemed uncomfortable with me watching her work so I moved away from the counter pretending to be interested in making a purchase. I found out her day was almost over and I offered her a lift somewhere. She accepted and I drove her home.

Natalie had moved to a top floor apartment of a three floor house. It was a dark brown house with matching brown stairs that ran along the outside of the house. Large maple trees surrounded the side of the house shutting out the sunlight and casting long shadows over the house. Natalie asked me if I wanted to come up. She led the way, climbing the stairs like she was bearing a heavy load.

The door opened into the main sitting room. Heavy dark drapes had been drawn across the window overlooking the stairs. Natalie removed her shoes and pulled the drapes back to let in the late afternoon light. A large grey and white cat jumped off the back of the couch and weaved across Natalie's legs purring.

"Fred!" I cried and bent down to pat the cat that had once belonged to our family. "She's huge."

"I know. Isn't she? She's a glutton."

"Remember the time she got her tail caught in the screen door?"

"Poor Fred. Snapped the tip right off."

The unexpected horror of it now seemed funny. We laughed together at the memory.

I stood up and looked around. The room was long and narrow and extended into a dining room area with table and chairs. The sitting room was well-furnished with a large plum-coloured couch, two upholstered arm chairs, and a modern wall unit supporting a new television set. There was also a heavy dark end table and matching coffee table which looked familiar. Everything was neat and tidy and spotless.

"You've got a great place," I said.

"Not bad," she said. Her response reminded me of our father.

Most remarkable was the number of various framed photographs that decorated the apartment. The wall beside the window was hung with photographs. The wall unit was filled with them, as were the end and coffee tables. Looking down the hall into her bedroom I noticed more photos crowded on her dresser. I took a closer look at the prints in the living room and found that these were all family photos, our family photos. There was a variety of old black and white snapshots mixed in with more recent coloured prints. There was one I had never seen before of my mother as a child taken with my grandmother. There were some I had grown up with and always loved the best. There were photos in expensive frames, tasteful frames of my sisters and brothers and me, others of my mother and father. Our family dogs, Toby and Duke, had their own places of honour, as did Fred the cat. Here in Natalie's apartment lay our family enshrined in photographs.

I didn't want to embarrass her by mentioning the photographs and her obvious need to surround herself by her family. But she surprised me; she wanted to talk about them. She enjoyed showing the photos off and some of her old energy returned as she pointed out some photographs that our mother had given her. She put on a record and turned on the kettle for tea. I followed her into the kitchen. A large bottle of Rolaids sat on her counter. She shook two into her hand and downed them with a glass of water.

"Do you ever talk to Mom?" I asked.

"Sometimes."

I wanted to tell her that our mother really missed her, but something held me back. She seemed so distant I didn't know how to reach her. The kettle boiled and screamed at us and Natalie busied herself with making tea and putting out the milk and sugar. I told her I just took it black now. She nodded her head and said, "I see".

We brought our tea into the main sitting room and Natalie turned up the stereo.

"I just love this song," she said settling down into one of the armchairs. It was Pat Benatar's, *Don't Let It Show*. She listened to the music lost in her head for the moment. Fred jumped on her lap almost spilling her tea. "Dufuss!" she cried at the cat pushing it off her lap, reminding me again of something my father would say.

"Those pieces," I said, breaking the silence and pointing to the end and coffee tables. Were they Nana's?"

"Yes. She gave them to me when I moved in here. Along with some photos."

I gulped. I had never received anything like this from her. My grandmother gave me homemade acrylic wool slippers. "Have you seen her lately?" I asked.

"I see her at least once or twice a week."

It came as a shock to discover that Natalie had been seeing my grandmother regularly. I never imagined the two of them would have developed a friendship. I felt I had been usurped as our grandmother's favourite. "I haven't been to see her for a while. I think I'll drop by later on today," I said.

She just looked at me listlessly, slightly nodding her head. "Mom really misses you, you know," I said.

"Mmm." She appeared to be sizing me up, deciding how much she could trust me.

It was then I noticed the men's work boots on the mat beside the door. I felt the blood drain from my face. I don't know when John had become such an acute threat. Since the shooting, the thought of him filled me with dread. I had grown afraid of running into him, afraid that I might see him when I turned a corner in town. Once, I thought I saw him across Broadway Street in his black leather coat and averted my face so he wouldn't recognize me. The anxiety I associated with him had developed over time into a need to avoid him at all cost. Now I could feel his presence in this apartment like a cold draft and knew he'd been here recently and was likely to return.

"And, John, how is he?" I forced myself to ask. For years my family had tried not to speak his name at home, circumnavigating around it if possible. If one of us dared to mention it out loud we lowered our voice and looked over our shoulder, like we were afraid to resurrect an evil spirit.

She looked out the front window, her face concealing her thoughts. "Fine. He's fine."

"So, he lives here with you?" I asked.

She turned to me quickly. "No. He lives with his parents still."

I stared at the couch. In my mind I could see John stretched out on the long couch watching television with a beer in his hand. It was like he was in the room.

"Anyway, he's working today," she said, sounding relieved. "So when are you going to be finished school?" she asked, changing the subject.

"I have one more school term after this one. I'm doing a double work term at the Ombudsman's Office in Toronto starting in May."

"Oh." Then, "What are you taking again?"

"Mostly English. A lot of dance. Natalie, you could go back to school."

"I don't know." She stood up and gathered Fred into her arms from her perch on the back of the couch. "Well, to be honest I've been thinking about going to college in Brampton and getting some secretarial training."

"That's a good plan. Will you continue to live here then?"

"What? Oh, I guess so, yes." She said looking around. I noticed there were no photos of her and John. No photos of John anywhere. "I need to keep my job here," she said.

I stood up and returned my cup to the kitchen. I was washing it out at the sink when I heard her chuckling behind me.

"What's so funny?"

"Nothing. It's just the way you still stand."

I looked down at my feet and saw I was unconsciously standing turned out. After all the years of ballet training, the position had become natural.

"Natalie, there's something I need to ask you," I said. "I want you to be in my wedding party. I want you to be my bridesmaid."

It was her turn to be startled. "Me?" she asked.

"Of course, you. You're my sister. Lou is going to be a bridesmaid too. Erin, my friend from school, is going to be the Maid-of-Honour. I couldn't choose between my sisters for that role. That wouldn't be fair."

She smiled gratefully. We were interrupted by heavy footsteps climbing the stairs. Someone tried the locked door. Natalie glanced anxiously at me and stayed glued to the spot. A key turned the lock and John pushed open the door.

CHAPTER FORTY NINE

Fear

 Cindy

He saw me and came to an abrupt halt in the doorway his hand still on the doorknob as if he'd entered the wrong house.

My blood was pounding in my ears. Now that I was face to face with him, I was more afraid than ever. As he entered the apartment, I felt the room shrink around us squeezing out space so that the three of us had no room to move, no air to breathe. John looked at us as though he had caught us conspiring against him. I felt trapped and wanted to leave but didn't dare.

"What's she doin' here?" he asked Natalie, throwing her a dark and suspicious look. Without waiting for an answer, he crossed the room and plunked down on the sofa, shooting out his long legs on the coffee table so that his black cowboy boots landed with a thud on the table. He sat back folding his hands behind his head and studied Natalie who was frowning at his boots.

"She don't like it when I put my boots on her furniture," he said, grinning snidely at Natalie.

I compared this older version of John against the picture I had stored in my memory. He was wearing a black t-shirt tucked into jeans fastened with a wide metal belt. I could still see traces of the insecure, shy youth who rarely looked at anyone full on, but John had grown more comfortable in his own skin. His face had lost its boyish softness and had been carved into tough, angular lines. His jaw and cheekbones drew sharp curves under a bold sweep of bangs that graced his forehead like a signature. He had always been handsome, but now he carried his good looks with a menacing confidence. I could not detect any evidence of the tender, sweet youth that had glittered intermittently from behind a rough exterior like little pieces of quartz blinking in the sunlight.

He saw me watching him and threw me a hard look, fully acknowledging my presence for the first time.

"Why are you here?" he asked again, this time addressing me directly. With a shock I realized he had never spoken to me before. For all the times I'd thought of him, imagined him with my sister, his presence growing more dark and sinister in my recollection as the years wore on, I'd never actually spoken with him until now.

"Cindy is just in town for the weekend," Natalie said before I could respond. "She's going back to Waterloo tomorrow."

"She's never been around to see you before," he said, staring at me. "University, eh? Did yer little sister here tell you she's been thinkin' of school too? Of course she's smart and all, like the rest of yous, but she'll never do it. She's too lazy."

Natalie's face was like a window blind snapping shut, cutting off the light within. I wanted to reach out to her, to shake her and wake her up. I wanted to pull her away from this place. She didn't belong here.

"I think she can do it."

He gave me a long, measured look.

"How was work today?" Natalie asked, changing the topic.

"Cocksuckers! They laid me off. They still owe me from last time."

"What will you do?" Natalie asked, chewing on her nails.

John took a pack of Player's Plain from the rolled up sleeve of his shirt. "John, you know I don't allow anyone to smoke in here," she said firmly.

"Oh, yeah, I forgot. Just because you don't smoke now, no one else can."

"You can go out on the balcony if you want to smoke," she said.

John hesitated for a moment, then pulled a metal lighter from the pocket of his jeans. He flipped it open and looked defiantly at her. "I'll work fer Dad again," he said lighting his cigarette. "I can always count on him havin' somethin' for me."

"Well, I should really be going," I said standing up.

Natalie showed me to the door. "Here's my phone number," I said, writing it on a piece of paper I pulled from my purse.

I glanced at John, who was boxing Fred's ears. Dread wash over me. I felt it in the way Natalie looked anxiously over her shoulder at John. Tension and fear lurked in the room like an ominous shadow. I wanted to warn her, but I didn't know against what.

"Call me," I said and left.

Natalie

"What were you and your sister schemin' up?"

"Nothing. She's getting married in August."

"Huh." John took a slow drag on his cigarette. "Maybe we should get married."

I busied myself cleaning up in the kitchen. John got up from the couch and stood in the kitchen doorway watching me. I rinsed my cup.

"Well, do you ever think of that?" he asked.

"I don't know. Sometimes."

He stepped into the room. "Who knows what you and yer sister were up to. I'll bet she was fillin' yer head with all kinds of garbage like how come yer still with a guy like me."

I sighed and leaned my back against the sink crossing my arms over my chest. "Why shouldn't my sister and I be able to have a conversation without you getting all weird on me?"

"Weird?"

"You're always thinking I'm talking about you behind your back. I'm sick of your paranoia."

"Paranoia! Now I'm paranoid?" he cried, crossing to the sink in large strides. He towered over me, pressing me into the sink.

"Go away!" I said annoyed, turning my back on him.

He shoved his finger at my face. "I saw you, you know. I saw you with him."

"What are you talking about?"

He leaned into me angrily. "On Friday night, when I came to pick you up. I saw you come on to that slimeball behind the counter."

"Who?" I threw him a look over my shoulder like he was crazy, while I quickly searched my memory for who he could be talking about. "Do you mean Ted from grocery? Yeah, he's a real threat," I said sardonically. "All five feet of him."

"I saw you kiss that puke. Don't lie to me!" His face loomed over me twisted and ugly.

"John, please."

"I've seen the way you carry on with other guys. Yer always flirtin' an' teasin' an' comin' on to guys. Yer nothin' but a little slut!"

I was shaking. I forced myself to sound calm. "It was Ted's birthday. What you saw was me giving him a friendly birthday hug."

"Liar!"

I didn't see it coming in time. I swerved to avoid contact but his right fist managed to slam into my cheekbone with a force that sent me to the ground.

He stood over me breathing hard. "Now look what you've made me do!"

I lay there stunned and sprawled against the kitchen floor. He bent down to help me up. "I'm so sorry Natalie. I didn't mean to hurt you. You just make me so Goddam mad!"

His face over mine was blurry and unrecognizable. The words driveling out of his mouth were gibberish. I pushed him away with what little strength I still possessed.

He sat on the floor with me and held my limp hand while I turned my cheek away and cried.

"Don't ever leave me Natalie," he said over and over. "I don't know what I would do if you left me."

CHAPTER FIFTY

Change

 Natalie

A couple of weeks later, Michael came by the house. He took me for lunch in The Café in town. He wanted to know what my plans were. He told me I needed to think about getting away from Orangeville. By then, my black eye had almost healed completely and I had used makeup to conceal the rest. Still, we both knew he meant I needed to get away from John.

I told him I liked working at the deli and that I made good money there. I told him I liked my life and I was happy. He didn't look convinced.

"You need to make some changes, Natalie," he said.

When did you become a father? I thought. But I didn't get mad at him. I let him talk. I liked sitting with my handsome older brother in The Café by the sunny window eating creamy Caesar salad and grilled garlic bread. I was kind of hoping someone I knew would see us together and wonder who I was with.

"I'm going to go to college," I said.

"That's a good start." I sipped my Coke pleased. "Listen, if you need some money, if it will help, I can help you."

"I'm OK thanks."

"Well, think about it. I'm here if you need me."

Then Michael told me he had already begun organizing the next barn party. CareyOn'81 was to be held at the end of July this year. He said it was going to be the best one yet.

"You should come," he said.

My stomach churned and sharp pangs of heartburn traveled up my chest. I should have known the garlic would upset my stomach. "I'll think about it."

"Don't give up on yourself," he said.

Michael stirred me to do things with my life. He was part of the world I had learned to live without, but maybe he was right. Maybe it was possible yet to make changes to my life. I wanted to go to our party.

When I got home I phoned Bev and asked her to come with me. She asked if John was coming too.

"He doesn't know about it. And he's not going to know."

"Natalie," Bev said kindly. "You deserve to be happy. You deserve to be with someone who makes you feel good about yourself."

I heard my father's words in my head: "You can never stop loving someone."

"But I love him."

"Love doesn't look like what you have with John. You deserve love to be better to you."

Cindy

Michael took CareyOn '81 over from our father who said he was done with hosting barn parties. He said four was enough and that my summer wedding was all the party he wanted to hold this year. He made this declaration in the spring when Michael was home visiting. Michael, who had been looking forward to the annual event, said he was happy to organize it. Our father said as long as he held it a few weeks before the wedding, he was happy to step aside and watch his oldest son take up the lead.

Michael enlisted a crew of friends and family to help with the preparations. As we had done the previous year, Michael had admission tickets printed for the barn party. We now charged $5.00 per person to pay for the band and other expenses. No one without a pre-paid ticket would be allowed in. We started this after we found the party was getting unruly with people showing up who we didn't know. (The year before, unbeknownst to our parents, Paul had invited his whole grade at school.) Michael had black t-shirts made up with "CareyOn' 81" in red letters that he handed out to his crew, storing the rest for the first one hundred guests. He rented outhouses and delivered bales of hay, auditioned bands and invited everyone he knew. This was to be our biggest barn party ever. It was also to be our last.

July 25, 1981 dawned grey and overcast, a character-istically muggy Ontario summer day. The air settled in damp and heavy pulling the sky down to meet the steaming waves of humidity rising from the earth. Rain threatened the horizon and late afternoon lightening flashed over the fields in the distance. The fields that summer were not ripe with tall cornstalks; the farmer had planted a rotat-ing crop of young, green canola plants instead. As evening approached, the precipitation held off and patches of clear skies opened up over the fields behind the barn pushing ominous black clouds further east.

I was excited about seeing both old and new friends again. One of these was a ski-instructor buddy of Geoff's. He had lost the fingers of his right hand in an accident several years earlier and since then went by the name of

Shorthand. Upon meeting my father, he held out his hand to greet him.

"Hi. My name is Shorthand."

My father looked down at the hand clasped in his and said, "You sure are. And my name is Shotgun Harry."

"Nice to meet you Shotgun Harry," smiled Shorthand.

I was dancing in the barn with Geoff when I saw Natalie arrive with her friend, Bev. Natalie looked nervous and hugged the back wall near the door. I thought how difficult it must be for her to show up here again in front of everyone. Geoff and I greeted her with big hugs to reassure her we were very pleased she had come.

"Nice T-shirt," she said sarcastically pointing to Geoff's CareyOn' 81 shirt.

"I could probably get you one if you played your cards right," Geoff said grinning. Then he said something in her ear that made her laugh out loud. I was grateful to him for making her feel welcome.

A piercing whine interrupted us. The chilling sound of bagpipes filled the barn. We turned, startled to see a man dressed in kilt and full Scottish regalia march into the barn playing the bagpipes. Natalie looked perplexed.

"Mom's idea," I yelled over the deafening noise. "She's into anything Scottish right now. Have you seen her yet?"

"I saw her at the house. She said she'd be down in a minute."

She searched the barn. It was quickly filling up with people. We moved further inside away from the din of the piper. I knew who she was looking for. "Dad must be minding the corn," I said into her ear. "Still his favourite job."

We watched the piper circle the barn and waited for him to leave before we continued talking.

"What a party!" said Bev.

"I'm glad you came," I said.

"Me too. Although I didn't have a choice. Natalie said I had to come with her or she would never speak to me again."

It occurred to me what a good friend Bev was to Natalie.

Suddenly thunder boomed and the rain that had held off all day poured out of the sky. People who had been mingling and eating and drinking outside ran for the cover of the barn. The dirt path leading up the slope to the barn door soon became a slippery muddy slide.

Before long, the barn was crammed with guests, the air steamy with little clouds of humidity spouting from two hundred warm, wet bodies. I spotted my father who had joined the guests inside, rain running off his forehead and shoulders. He was talking to Michael pointing toward the back southwest corner of the barn and gesturing at the crowd with a worried expression. I excused myself from Bev and headed over to see what was up. I reached my father as something behind me caught his eye. I saw he had spotted Natalie amongst the dense throng. A loud clap of thunder burst just outside the barn door. A terrifying crack ripped through the air followed by a heart-stopping bang.

CHAPTER FIFTY ONE

Crash

—————————————— Cindy ——————————————

People screamed and ran toward the barn door. Others remained in their places watching the panic, uncertain what to do. The band stopped playing. Dad and Michael pushed their way against the flow of the retreating swarm toward the back recesses of the barn. I followed in their path. All of a sudden Dad stopped and threw his arms out wide and yelled, "Stop!" Michael and I pulled up short behind him. This part of the barn was unlit and in the dark we hadn't seen the huge gap in the floorboards. One more step and we would have fallen in.

"Oh my God! What happened?" I cried.

"The floor gave way. Is everyone OK?"

"Is there anyone down there? Helloooo," we yelled into the dark gaping hole.

"You kids better get away from there. The boards are rotten. It's not safe," said Dad. He pulled a flashlight from his overalls pocket and aimed it over the edge.

"Anyone down there?" he yelled again. Then he turned around and started for the barn door. Had he heard something? We followed him. The downpour had ceased as quickly as it had come and the rain had subsided to a light sprinkling. Dad went around to the front of the barn and entered the crumbling stalls pointing his flashlight into the decrepit pit.

"What are you doing, Dad?"

"I thought I heard something down here. Where's Paul?" he asked.

"I'll go find him," I said, alarmed.

I ran toward the house looking for Paul. Many of the guests had started to leave and were heading for their parked cars on the highway. I searched the house and checked his bedroom. He wasn't there. I heard raised voices outside and looked out the hall window.

In the dark, I could make out the shapes of vehicles parked along the shoulder of the highway. I saw clusters of people at the side of the road. It was then I noticed two cars side-by-side in the middle of the highway. Their engines idled, their headlights pointed away from town. I heard one of the drivers blare his horn and yell. I heard Duke barking from the mudroom below where he had been shut in for the party. Dread washed over me and I ran downstairs and out the door.

At first my view was blocked by the mob of people and vehicles on the road. I reached the highway and saw Natalie get out of the car across the highway and slam the passenger door. I recognized the drivers. John gunned his engine. Grant reciprocated flooring his gas pedal. A mixture of fear and excitement flooded through me as I realized what was happening. Grant and John were lined up behind the white quarter mile line drawn across the highway. Just then Duke ran barking toward the cars. Someone had let him out. I ran toward the cars, shouting "No!" and waving my arms above my head to get them to stop. "Go home Duke!" I screamed.

The cars roared loudly, someone yelled, "Go!" and the cars shot forward.

I jumped back onto the shoulder. The vehicles raced down the highway with a wild shriek. Duke ran after them. All that was left behind was the burning smell of rubber in the air. Mrs. Rose' words echoed in my head, "Brian was such a nice kid". I ran after the cars. Grant's car was in the lead. Suddenly, the other car swerved at a sharp angle and a long high screech rose in the air as the driver slammed on the brakes. The car twisted and spun before it ran out of control toward the ditch. It nosedived over the side of the road and came to a halt, its tail lights thrust up to the branches of an overhanging tree.

I was running full out. I tripped on something on the road and fell into slippery wetness. I landed on my knees and slid on a warm wet puddle of blood. My hands grabbed some fur. Duke was trembling uncontrollably. I pulled off my jean jacket and draped it over him. It was then I saw Natalie running along the highway past me. She reached John's car and disappeared into the ditch. Her cry pierced the air.

I stayed with Duke. An unnatural silence filled the air broken only by the distressed panting of the dog. The blood oozed out and saturated my jacket. I patted Duke's face and tried to soothe him with my voice. A minute later we were encircled by a hysterical group of bystanders from the race. I was still kneeling over Duke when I heard the siren coming from down the highway.

CHAPTER FIFTY TWO

Purge

— Natalie —

It took me a minute to realize where I was. I was in my old bedroom in the attic. It had been very late when my mother and I finally left the hospital last night. It was my mother who suggested I come back to the farmhouse. She said it wouldn't do to be alone in my apartment. She led me up the attic steps and turned down the covers in my old bed. I climbed in and she softly traced my forehead with the tip of her finger until I fell asleep.

Now it was morning and the details of last night flooded back to me. When I found John slouched behind the wheel of his car, blood spilling out of his forehead, I thought he was dead. By the time I heard the sirens, I realized he was breathing. My mother drove me to the hospital behind the ambulance. She was waiting with me in the emergency room when Dad arrived with Paul covered in dirt and hobbling on one foot.

"Oh my God, what happened to you?" cried Mom, rushing to Paul.

"I think I've buthted my ankle," said Paul.

"Lord help us," she said, collapsing into the waiting room chair. "How?"

"I fell through the barn."

"He was covered in muck and manure," said Dad.

Paul had fallen through the old rotten floorboards in the corner of the barn where he'd been drinking in the dark with his buddies. When the floor gave way it created a huge boom and triggered a stampede of people trying to flee to safety.

The four of us waited in emergency - Paul for a doctor to examine his ankle, me to find out if John had woken up, and my parents waited for both of us. Paul's x-ray's confirmed a broken ankle. "He was lucky," said Dad. "It could have been a lot worse. His fall was broken by the muck in the stalls."

When the doctor came to take Paul to get his cast made, Dad told him he'd join him in a minute. He turned to Mom and me. "I didn't want to say anything in front of Paul," he said. "Duke was hit on the road. He didn't make it."

The nurse told us John had suffered a serious concussion, but the doctors were confident he would recover.

***

It was still early. I got out of bed and quickly got dressed careful not to disturb Christine who was sleeping in her old bed beside mine. I crept past the closed bedroom doors of my parents and Paul and went downstairs. In the kitchen I paused and felt a familiar comfort wash over me like opening the long lost pages of a favourite bedtime storybook.

Something caught my attention over by the window. I went closer for a better look and saw a snug black shape tucked up beside the red and white gingham window dressing. I jumped and quickly backed away. I fled outside to escape the bat.

I walked out of the driveway and headed south along the highway turning my back to town. I deliberately didn't want to have a plan or destination. I just needed to keep going.

It started raining. I pulled the hood of my jacket farther across my forehead and walked with my head down. I tried not to think as I watched one running shoe plant itself down after the other, sponging up puddles along the shoulder of the road. The wind picked up and whipped around me. I pushed on. The teeming rain clouds melted into the earth forming one borderless, solid gray horizon. The sky turned black and hurled stones at me. Hard pellets pricked my skin like bullets. I lifted my face to the cruel white hail pelting me, relishing their harsh bite. I closed my eyes and opened my mouth to soak in their sting, to swallow them and the pain they caused.

The wind and hail battered and blew me about until I felt weak and giddy. I started laughing. I couldn't stop. I shrieked into the wind and listened to it carry me away. I stopped and stood beside the road feeling empty and purged.

I resumed walking, barely aware of approaching vehicles behind or ahead of me. The hail stopped and the rain ceased and still I walked. I walked until my feet were blistered and I had reached the village of Alton, more than five miles away. I was spent and my body was aching, but it was clear now what I had to do next.

I found my mother in her sewing room. Once Cindy's bedroom, the room had been transformed over the years. The only thing that remained from when it was my sister's bedroom was her old bed. My mother had stuffed this room to the rafters with bags upon bags of fabric. Crinkled viscose rayon peeked out behind fine crepe de chine, supported by a pile of polyester zigzagged knits, courtelle jersey, satinized jacquards, and romantic cotton voilles and chiffons. There were prints and solids, florals and stripes. Bolts and scraps, remnants and swaths. Inside the bags were patterns pinned to dresses ready to be cut, pieces of pantsuits cut and waiting to be sewn, slacks waiting to be hemmed, zippers to be torn out, buttons to be replaced, and other projects so long ago abandoned they were now forgotten and out-of-style.

A half-finished housecoat cascaded over onto fox fur trims, spools of ribbon, and colourful zippers of various lengths. Along the wall across from the foot of the bed, the former vanity-turned-desk had been replaced by a table that now held a new Pfaff sewing machine. Wire shelves held an assortment of supplies: measuring tapes, cards of buttons and needles, two pincushions - one small for the wrist and one shaped like a large tomato, a box of pins, pinking shears, scissors and a half-used bag of sequins. In front of the window stood a female bare-chested mannequin wearing a pair of orange stretch knit pants. The bedroom closet door was open and revealed an even wider assortment of fabrics and supplies. Cindy's wedding dress hung on a hook on the inside of the closet door. On the back of the bedroom door hung my half-finished bridesmaid dress.

Through this clutter, my mother had cleared a path to her sewing machine. She was settled at her machine absorbed in her sewing. The gentle hum of the sewing machine was soothing and familiar. It was my mother's sound, the sound of creation, of diligence and devotion. I had missed that sound. I knocked lightly on the open door.

She jumped. "Oh, Natalie, you scared me!"

"Can I come in?"

"Of course."

While she worked quietly, I cleared a spot on the edge of the bed. I was happy to just sit and watch her. It felt right to be here in my old home again. It seemed impossible that I could have ever left. I could not remember what could have been so important before to make me leave.

With her back to me while she pinned, my mother said, her voice garbled, "Your father is waiting to talk to you." She swiveled around in her chair and looked at me sternly. She removed the pin from between her lips. "He has missed you so much," she said, her voice catching. She looked down at the fabric in her hands and her shoulders shook.

I took a deep breath. "I love you, Mom," I said.

She looked up. "What did you say?"

"I said I love you."

"No. Not that part."

"Mom."

She smiled at me through her tears. "I hated Ma."

CHAPTER FIFTY THREE

Home

 Natalie

That evening I stood by the window in the attic. The setting sun enveloped me in a warm pool of light, dappled shadows from the branches of the maple tree outside the window danced against the wall. Across the highway, I watched the wind gently rustle the long field grass. A peaceful breeze blew in from the open window and with it the sweet smell of freshly cut grass. My father's smell.

He entered the room timidly, hesitating at the top of the stairs. "Natalie," he said. I turned around. His blue eyes searched my face intently. "Natalie, I have something I need to tell you. It's very important to me. I want you to know that I never knew it was John in that car. I never knew who anyone was until the police told me later. You believe me don't you Natalie?"

I realized the enormity of what he was saying. I saw how important it was that I believed him. I was standing on the edge of the diving board again, ready to dive to him.

"I believe you, Dad."

He reached for my hand. "We almost lost you." He squeezed my hand. "You know," he said, swallowing hard, "You are welcome to stay here. There's no sense in rushing back home to your empty apartment. Your mother would feel better if you stayed."

I see him tucking me into bed. I have the covers pulled up tight under my chin, a big excited grin on my face. He is perched on the edge of my bed and leans over me as he whispers in my ear,

"Down in the Lee Hi Valley." My eyes grow wide in expectation and I giggle.

"There lived a little Hindu." My eyes grow even bigger. I laugh into my belly.

"He didn't have no clothes." I pull the covers even tighter under my chin and scream for mercy.

"So he had to make his skin do!" My father's voice rises into a deep crescendo as he reaches under the covers and tickles me to death. By now I am writhing in hysterics on the bed.

I shout, "No more." He stops.

But it's not over. He dive bombs and tickles me under my armpits. "Please stop! Please stop!" I choke, trying to get my breath.

Finally, he stops and says, "That's enough," and kisses me on the forehead.

I have tears in my eyes from laughing. I don't want him to leave. From outside my bedroom door he calls, "Sleep tight, Pepper. Make sure the bugs don't bite".

Later that night my parents were reading in bed when Mom felt something move close to her. She looked over and saw a bat hanging on her bedside lamp. She screamed and jumped out of bed.

"Go get a broom," Harry said.

She ran downstairs and outside to the garage. She found her curling broom leaning against the wall. Returning to her bedroom, she swept the bat into a paper bag with her curling broom.

"What should I do with it now?" she asked Harry, holding the bag firmly closed.

"Put it in the garbage can."

"I'll do no such thing!" She carried the bat downstairs and took it outside into the night taking a flashlight with her. She went as far as the old carriage house before stopping to shake the bag open. The tiny creature plopped out onto the wet grass. It lay stunned for a few seconds before it opened its wings and took flight. The beam of the flashlight caught it before it flew into the shadow of the barn and out of sight.

The next morning I went downstairs and lingered on the second floor, remembering what it felt like to be in the farmhouse again. I walked to the end of the hall and looked out the window. The sun had broken through the clouds. Overnight, the farmer's field had turned into a sea of golden bright canola.

I turned my head and saw the portrait of Christina straining toward her farmhouse across the dry field of grass. I felt the invisible but inextricable strings that endured between her and her world in the farmhouse. I knew her strength and courage, her fierce will that propelled her to drag her damaged body back home. I realized my return had always been up to me. I just hadn't been ready before. I was ready now. I belonged here.

A few days later I gave notice to my landlord. I told John I was breaking up with him. I told him I was moving on. I didn't tell him where I was going.

CHAPTER FIFTY FOUR

Beginnings

Cindy

At three o'clock in the afternoon on the twenty second of August, 1981, I walked down the aisle of St. Mark's Anglican Church of Orangeville. It was the same church my parents were married in twenty six years earlier. The reception was held at the Chinguacousy Golf and Country Club. My father had tried to persuade me to hold the party in the banquet room above the Orangeville Curling Club. "I've seen it done up really nice for functions. You'd hardly recognize it," he said. I knew no matter how nicely decorated, the room was always going to be the dull, smoky hall over the rink where I had once entertained club members on stage in a hula skirt swaying my hips Hawaiian-style. Once I saw the elegant room at Chinguacousy with its sliding glass doors opening onto tiered balconies, overlooking rolling lawns, I wasn't to be swayed. Even after he generously threw in $5000.00 in cash if we would take the Curling Club, I wouldn't change my mind.

After we returned from our honeymoon, we invited my parents over for dinner to see our new apartment. Sitting around the dining table after dinner, my father had a story to tell. He said he was working at the golf course as a starter, when he noticed two couples lining up to tee off. He said one of the men seemed to recognize him but my father couldn't place him. The couples teed-off and started off down the fairway when the man changed his mind and came over to my father.

"You're Harry Carey aren't you?"

"That's right."

"I'm Bob McNenemy. I'm your distant cousin. Our grandmothers were sisters."

"Is that so? Small world. Nice to meet you, Bob," my father said shaking his hand.

"That fellow over there is my brother. We are here with our wives." Bob paused and lowered his voice. "You don't know this, but I'm the one who returned your gun to you. I'm on the Caledon police squad."

"You don't say. Well, now don't be going telling your brother and your wife about me. I wouldn't want them to think badly of me."

"Oh, no. As a matter of fact, everybody on the force thought you got a raw deal anyway."

"I appreciate that, Bob."

Natalie moved back home. She and Fred had the attic to themselves as Christine was away at school. Natalie started Sheridan College in Brampton. By now she had her driver's license and commuted to school in our mother's new Ford Escort (the Mustang had finally been put down). When Natalie graduated and got a job at Wardair, she bought mom's car from her. She didn't see John anymore. She didn't say, and we didn't ask. We all breathed a little fuller.

While it was wonderful to have her back, it was but another beginning as much as an ending. It was part of another older story that had been building for a long time, a process that had been set in place before Natalie was born, that could no more be prevented than trying to stop a child from growing. Eventually, no matter how our family might once more be threatened, the truth had to come out.

My father was beginning the last passage of a long journey that would eventually lead him away from us. In 1988 my parents were legally separated. At first their separation was amicable; they walked through the farmhouse together dividing up the furniture fairly taking note of who got what, what they would keep and what they'd give away or discard. It seemed like they were getting along better than ever. But soon after they sold the farmhouse, Mom found out that Dad had a girlfriend and everything changed. Mom became bitter. When she learned that Dad had been having an affair for a few years with a woman in South Carolina and that his golfing buddies and their wives had known long before she did, she was furious and ashamed. She moved away from Orangeville. She said she was never so glad to leave a place. I never knew how much she hated it until she left.

Dad sold the business and built a small retirement home overlooking the Orangeville Reservoir. He got another German shepherd, Misty, a darker version of Duke, and he spent his days hiking through the bush with his dog when he wasn't golfing or curling. He spent the winters in South Carolina where he lived with his girlfriend, Iris.

Michael didn't marry Victoria, but Victoria married Natalie's new boyfriend from Toronto, Tom. Tom and Victoria went away on vacation to Florida one November as friends and came back as lovers. Christine didn't marry Bruce, but she did marry David, three weeks before Natalie was married. I was in both wedding parties, pregnant with my third child. Toby, our first family dog, lived for a record eighteen years before she finally didn't wake up from her bed in the mudroom one day.

Single again, my mother was free to explore and create a new life for herself. She bought a condominium in Oakville and covered it in Renoir and Monet reproductions, satin bows, lacey tablecloths, and chintzy souvenirs from her travels. Thanks to Grampa Russ who surprised her with lavish gifts, she got the mink coat she longed for, a full-length black fur with a matching hat. She took advantage of Natalie's new job at Wardair, which offered her greatly reduced airfare rates, and travelled the globe. She made it to Dubrovnik after all and came back with a new diamond bracelet. She was in New Zealand with her Sweet Adelines chorus when she received the news her mother had died.

Mom was torn about cutting her trip short and returning home for the funeral. In the end, she stayed and missed it. She said her mother would not have cared if she was there or not.

While she was alive, my grandmother never recuperated from the consequences of having to deal with the public scandal and shame of being pregnant out-of-wedlock. When she died, she took the secret of her lover, William Fretwell, and the mystery surrounding that time in her life, with her to the grave.

After the funeral and my mother's arrival back home, she was packing up her mother's clothes and personal belongings from her house when she came across an old sealed envelope stuffed in the back of her mother's bedroom dresser drawer. The envelope was unmarked. Turning it over in her hands, my mother felt a small, circular object inside. Opening the envelope, she found a sterling silver baby bracelet. She collapsed on the edge of her mother's bed. She knew she was holding something from her father. She stroked the dainty bracelet and something rough brushed against the tip of her finger. She examined it closer and discovered an inscription on the inner rim. The inscription read: 'To Diane Love Bill'.

"I knew he loved me," she said.

Mom told me about a dream she had. She was sitting at a large boardroom table and at the head of the table sat her stepdad, Russell. He wore devil's horns. When I asked her what she thought that meant, she started crying. She told me then that Russell used to come into her bed. It started after he returned from the Navy. She was thirteen years old. She never told her mother, but she thought she knew. She told me she was convinced her mother hated her.

Several months later my dad took me out for dinner. We were on dessert before he told me he wanted to explain why he left my mom.

"It was all to do with the sex," he said.

I choked on my coffee.

He didn't seem to notice. "We tried, but your mom was not very..." he paused, searching for the right word, "adventurous."

"Huh," I said, remembering the morning when I was a little girl and my parents had barred their bedroom door shut with Dad's dresser. I could hear Mom giggling from their bed. My sisters and I banged on the door for our parents to let us in and they told us to go away.

"All those years I thought I was the one who wasn't good at sex. But once I met Iris all that changed. I knew it wasn't me," he said.

I did not want to hear about my father's sex life with his girlfriend. There was something I needed to ask him though.

"Dad, did Mom ever tell you Grampa Russ used to come into her bed?"

"She told you?"

I nodded my head.

He paused. "When we were first dating, she told me Russ used to come to her bed at night."

"What did you do?"

"I didn't know what to do. I didn't know how to help her. I never told anyone."

He studied his hands on the table. "A few years ago I thought I would ask Russ about it," he said. "But I changed my mind. I just couldn't believe that he could do that. That's not the man I know."

I needed more. "When you had sex the first time, was Mom a virgin?"

"I'm not sure. I had nothing to compare it to."

Dad reached for my hand across the table. "I will always love your mother," he said.

***

Last year I drove by the old farmhouse. It looks pretty much the same except the maple trees beside the driveway are a lot bigger. They managed to thrive despite being uprooted. The old barn isn't there anymore. The roof finally fell in. Someone, perhaps the farmer, set fire to the remains. All that is left now is a large charcoal stain on the landscape. The property looked empty and deserted without the old barn. My eyes kept returning to where it had once stood behind the farmhouse, refusing to believe it was gone. I could still feel the presence of its walls and roof like a force around me. The old barn would always remain a part of this place.

I pulled the car over to the shoulder of the highway and paused at the top of the driveway. There were people home. I saw a car in the driveway, wash hanging outside on the line, a child's bicycle lying on the lawn. Inside, lives carried on just as ours had. I saw the white rock under the maple tree where several years earlier we had buried Duke. As I turned the car around to head into town, I noticed a faint white line across the highway.

EPILOGUE

Reunion

———————————— Cindy ————————————

My son polled the room and announced with chagrin, "It's official, Mom, you are definitely the loudest."

I begged to differ. "I am not. Aunt Natalie is by far the loudest of us all."

Geoff raised his eyebrow at me in silent disagreement. He had never fully gotten used to our noise. When he first started coming by the farmhouse, it didn't take long before our high hoots and shrills forced him to lie down on the living room couch and nurse his headache. He doesn't get headaches from us anymore, but he still shakes his head baffled at how instantly we crank up the volume when we get together.

My family has always been exceptionally loud. Now my children can't stand the noise. They're not used to their mother shrieking with laughter. The shrieking is a phenomenon that's developed over the years. My voice rises an octave when I see my siblings now. I can't help it; I get so excited. Today we were celebrating my mother's seventieth birthday.

A big part of my excitement is because I don't get to see my family very often. No one could remember the last

348

time we were all reunited. We all live so far apart. Harry lives in Florence, South Carolina (where he still hosts REBOS breakfast for the neighbours each New Years day). Diane married Robert, a Scott, and settled in Burlington, Ontario. Michael lived in Minneapolis for a few years before he exchanged wives and cities and moved to San Fransisco. Christine moved overseas to Cambridge, England with her husband, David, eventually settling in a small, French village in Switzerland with her second husband, Mark. I moved to Edmonton shortly after Geoff and I were married before settling in Vancouver. Paul moved to Toronto.

Natalie was the only one of us who chose to stay in Orangeville after the family moved away. The first to move out, she was also the sibling who clung to home the longest. She settled with her husband in a house in town for ten years before she finally moved away from Orangeville. On April 16, 2004, when she was forty two years old, she gave birth to a daughter, Rachel.

We certainly aren't close in proximity to each other. But the thrill of being together surpasses the distance and long periods of separation. Close is a relative thing. People can live with each other and not be close. Or, they can rarely see each other and still feel a close connection. There have been periods of time when we were not close; once we shifted so far our foundation of trust became weak and fragile, our mutual support on the verge of collapse. We were lucky, we managed to mend the cracks and rein-force the bond.

My mother blew out the candles on her cake. "I am lucky that my children enjoy each other so much," she said with happy tears.

We may be over-the-top happy to be together because we know from past experience how fleeting our time together can be. We know first-hand how easy it can be for a family to be torn apart.

ACKNOWLEDGEMENTS

I am deeply grateful to: Maggie Jansen, Ed and Leanne Metcalfe, Lou Greene, JoAn Maurer, Marlyn Glover, Sally Ratcliffe and Carol Thorbes for their encouragement and valuable feedback on the manuscript.

I would like to thank Justice Douglas Maund for providing background and information pertaining to the legal proceedings, Michael Sanders for general information regarding criminal legal proceedings, as well as staff at the Archives of Ontario for providing court records and transcripts, excerpts of which have been included in CareyOn.

I am deeply grateful to my parents, Harold Carey and Diane McLaren, and my siblings: Michael, Christine, Natalie and Paul for their contributions and support, without which this story would have never been told.

I would also like to thank my husband, Geoff, and my children Cleo, Blake, and Erica for their patience and understanding for countless hours focused on my *other* family.

CPSIA information can be obtained at www.ICGtesting.com
Printed in the USA
LVOW11*0723120815

449727LV00004B/4/P